AF588317

FROM D-DAY TO A DEFEATED GERMANY

FROM D-DAY TO A DEFEATED GERMANY

ONE SOLDIER'S ACCOUNT OF THE FIGHTING FROM NORMANDY TO THE HEART OF HITLER'S THIRD REICH

Serjeant Pete Morris with Matt Morris

FRONTLINE
BOOKS

FROM D-DAY TO A DEFEATED GERMANY
One Soldier's Account of the Fighting from Normandy to the Heart of Hitler's Third Reich

First published in Great Britain in 2026
by Frontline Books
An imprint of
Pen & Sword Books Ltd
Yorkshire - Philadelphia

ISBN 9781036191917

A CIP catalogue record for this book is available from the British Library

Typeset by Lapiz Digital
Printed and bound in the UK by CPI Group (UK) Ltd,
Croydon, CR0 4YY.

Printed on paper from a sustainable source by
CPI Group (UK) Ltd, Croydon, CR0 4YY

The Publisher's authorised representative in the EU for product safety is
Authorised Rep Compliance Ltd., Ground Floor, 71 Lower Baggot Street,
Dublin D02 P593, Ireland.
www.arccompliance.com

For a complete list of Pen & Sword titles please contact
PEN & SWORD BOOKS LTD
47 Church Street, Barnsley, South Yorkshire, S70 2AS, England
E-mail: enquiries@pen-and-sword.co.uk
Website: www.pen-and-sword.co.uk
or
PEN & SWORD BOOKS
1950 Lawrence Rd, Havertown, PA 19083, USA
E-mail: uspen-and-sword@casematepublishers.com

CONTENTS

A Brief Introduction vii

Chapter 1 Squad Drill and a Freezing Stag 1
Chapter 2 Morse Code and a Move South 18
Chapter 3 Cider, Nettles and Artillery 28
Chapter 4 Clock Mending and Aquatic Sports 39
Chapter 5 8th Armoured Brigade 55
Chapter 6 D-Day and the Battle of Normandy 73
Chapter 7 Arnhem and Beyond. Into Germany 99
Chapter 8 VE Day, Displaced Persons and the Dive Inn 130

Afterword 156
Index 158

A BRIEF INTRODUCTION

My father, Douglas Charles Morris, was universally known as Pete. It was never clear why, though his mother did tell me a story that when she was pregnant with him the local doctor would visit to check on her and enquire, on examining her, "How's little Pete doing?" She claimed the name stuck with her, and later with him. I've used that nickname to refer to him in this edition of his memoir because to those who knew him any other name would sound odd. Pete was born in Ontario at the end of 1918. His parents had emigrated to Canada about five years earlier. They returned to the UK in 1922, when Pete was aged three, and settled near Caerwys, a small town in Flintshire, where Pete lived for most of the rest of his life. He joined the army in 1939 at the age of twenty, having trained as a marine radio operator and worked as an aircraft engineer.

Pete wrote his war memoir in the early 1980s, when he was in his sixties, so there is a question about how accurate his memories were. I remarked to him when I'd read the document that I was surprised by how well he remembered the war years. At the time of that conversation he would have been in his early seventies; I, in my late thirties. I said that I could barely remember my years at university, only a decade or so before. "Ah," he reflected, "it'll come back to you, you know." He turned out to be right about that but it doesn't do anything to prove how accurate such recovered memories are. The crucial thing is the truthfulness of his account. I have no doubt that these pages contain the truth as he remembered it. He was not a man given to any sort of falsehood. In some parts of the memoir, especially in some pages after D-Day, Pete must have been working from a diary. Sometimes he writes in the present tense and sometimes some of the detail is too specific to be recalled without notes. A diary is the only explanation. But it's obvious that most of the document is written from memory.

On the 80th anniversary of D-Day, in 2024, I posted a page of his memoir on Instagram. The extract described what was happening around Pete at about six o'clock on the morning of that day. A few of my small number of followers on Instagram commented on the extract, mentioning how powerful it was. One of the comments came from one of Pete's grandsons, my nephew, who said he would like to read the whole thing. I decided then that the document should be made available to Pete's grand- and great-grandchildren. I would make a digital copy and – at the same time – try to edit it. This is the result. The original document is about twice as long as this book and it was a sad task deciding what to leave out – for example, a description of Pete's marriage to my mother, Rose Gurney, in 1942. But within the original document, when describing the marriage, Pete writes: "Hitherto I have avoided reference to any domestic or romantic matters. This is intended to be about soldiering as I saw it and not an autobiography." So when it came to making cuts the soldiering stuff survived while much of the personal stuff had to go.

For a man who had few literary aspirations – he read little fiction, and less poetry – Pete's writing is highly literate. I've tried to change as little as possible because if the merit of the memoir is authenticity, over-enthusiastic editing would only detract from it. It's Pete's voice and if occasionally it makes you wince, well – none of us is perfect. Sometimes he seems a little pleased with himself but that is not unusual among memoirists. I have changed some things. Pete spelled accurately but had one or two blind spots: "preceeded"; "civillian"; I have corrected these. He was keen on use of the comma; almost every time he uses the word "but" he brackets it with commas. I have deleted these. In a few places I have changed the order of words – for example, to move an adverbial phrase if it made the sentence easier to read and understand. Pete was taught the old rules of grammar and I was tempted to iron out some of the formalities that derive from that. I would also have liked to simplify some of the more forced sentences, where the style overcomes the content. It would have been easy to change "he seemed to have sustained no injuries" to "he didn't seem to be hurt." I would also have liked to tinker with some of the cliches he was fond of, such as "roared with laughter" which occurs more than once. But I resisted these temptations because, remarkably enough for a man more educated in science and engineering than in the humanities, and writing largely from memory of events at a distance of several decades, Pete produces lucid, accurate prose.

There is one bit of tinkering which seemed necessary. The original manuscript contains only three chapter headings: The Civilian Army; Chronological Hiatus; and Bonjour Normandie. Most of the material relating to the civilian army and the chronological hiatus has been cut, so Pete's headings don't work. To get round this, and to make the narrative more digestible, I have divided it into eight chapters and invented chapter headings. I have placed the phrase Bonjour Normandie at the start of Chapter Six: D-Day and The Battle of Normandy.

Most of the notes are about trying to explain things which are obscure. Pete was a highly skilled electrical, electronic and mechanical engineer and often in the pages that follow he makes reference to equipment and techniques that need a bit of explaining. I've also tried to add useful notes about the military context and weaponry and the places in which Pete found himself. Thank heavens for the internet. I've learned a lot from reading these pages and tracking down and understanding the obscurities. I'm sure I've made many mistakes. My father died a generation ago, in 2000, but I still regret that I missed the opportunity to go through his manuscript in detail with him while he was still alive.

The novelist Robert Harris, roughly the same age as me, once said that our parents and grandparents were tested in a way that our own generation never was. These pages make clear that Pete passed the test. It would be inapposite for me to offer dedications for a bit of editing and research. It's my father's story and he wrote it down. But on his behalf this book might be dedicated to his daughters and his grandchildren and great-grandchildren, with a special mention for his grandson Steffan, whose comment on social media prompted me to the task of editing.

Matt Morris 2025.

Chapter 1

SQUAD DRILL AND A FREEZING STAG

Early in October 1939 I received my call up papers. I was told to report to The Second Signals Training Centre at Prestatyn in Flintshire on the 29th of November at ten o'clock in the forenoon.[1] When the day arrived I collected the documents that I had been told to take with me together with gas mask, razor and personal toilet articles. This only left time for a lecture from my mother telling me not to have anything to do with 'any bad women'. My father took me to Prestatyn, a matter of nine miles, and dropped me off by the camp gates. With mounting apprehension I walked the last fifty yards to where a soldier was standing with a rifle outside a small building. As I approached he called out 'Corporal, here's another one for you'. Whereupon another soldier, this one with two stripes, came out of the building and greeted me with 'Got yer docs?' I gave him my papers, which he studied as though he was endeavouring to translate from Greek. As he was thus engaged another two people who were obviously in the same boat as myself arrived, followed closely by three more. The corporal perused all the papers produced by the recruits and told us to 'wait here'. When there were ten of us assembled the corporal instructed one of his men to 'take them away'. It was only ten o'clock and I was already a lifetime away from things familiar. We walked, or rather shambled compared to the smart arm-swinging gait of the trained soldier who escorted us. He advised us to 'Move it along there or you'll get bloody lost!' We arrived at an open compound where there were what seemed like

1 Local Government reorganisation has since moved Prestatyn into Denbighshire.

hundreds of recruits all carrying small cases and gas masks, all looking bewildered and self-conscious. Several of the soldiers were smoking cigarettes, so I filled and lit my pipe and, as no one seemed to mind, most of the other recruits lit up cigarettes. It started to rain.

After what seemed an age someone shouted 'cigarettes out' and there approached what we took to be an officer, very smart in service dress and Sam Browne belt. He addressed one of the soldiers beyond our earshot and on his coming closer we heard him tell the soldier to 'get them sorted into squads'. We were formed into single file and walked down a narrow passage between two huts. At the end of the passage was a corporal who counted us into batches of thirty-six. As each batch was counted, a man with three stripes shepherded us away from the main throng to a section of the camp that we were come to know as A Block, a double row of huts built back to back. We were allotted three to a hut and were told to dump our suitcases et cetera on the bunks and reassemble outside. The man with three stripes stood outside smoking a cigarette when we joined him. He beckoned us around him and addressed us thus: 'My name is Morphew. You will address me as Serjeant Morphew or just Serjeant. You have been sent to me to be turned into soldiers and this I intend to do. This gentleman on my right is Serjeant Reardon and he is my assistant. You will address him as Serjeant Reardon or just Serjeant.[2] The gentleman on my left is Signalman Wilson. You will address him as 'Trained Soldier'. He is here to help you settle in to army life and answer any queries that you might have. He will escort you to the mess hall at meal times and you will not, repeat not, go to the mess hall other than as a complete squad. Any questions so far?'

'Yes Serjeant Morphew sir, where do we get a pee, we're busting.' To this reasonable request the serjeant replied 'You don't call me sir and the latrines are the buildings in the centre of each block which from now on you will call the barrack block. Now fall out and report back here in ten minutes.' We wandered away to the latrine block and found that they were well appointed and almost brand new with six shower cubicles in each block. On reporting back to Serjeant Morphew we were told the programme for the rest of the day and the following morning. We would be taken by the Trained Soldier to the Quartermaster's Stores to draw our blankets. We would then be taken

2 Both spellings serjeant and sergeant were in use in the Army from the 1920s onward; some regiments, such as the Rifles, retained the Serjeant spelling. Pete was adamant that the Signals used a J rather than a G.

to the mess hall for dinner. After dinner we would visit the regimental barber. This would be followed by a talk on the formation of the Army and the ranks and appointments that made up the succession of seniority. This would bring us up to tea time, after which the Trained Soldier would instruct us as to the making up of a box bed, during which time he would answer any questions that might arise. After this our time would be on our own until reveille at 0630 the next morning.

One recruit named Hawkins asked if he could visit his aunt who lived in the town of Prestatyn. The reply he received from Serjeant Morphew left us rather flabbergasted. 'You won't be leaving the confines of the camp for at least a month. You will be in uniform tomorrow and we cannot have people slouching about the town until you have been taught to straighten your shoulders and walk in a military manner. You will not even be allowed to visit the NAAFI until you are in uniform. Any questions?' 'Yes serjeant, what please is the NAAFI?' This from Hawkins. 'The NAAFI is the services canteen. The initials stand for Navy, Army and Air Force Institute and it is a civilian organisation run in conjunction with the War Department to cater for the comforts of service personnel. In the NAAFI you will be able to buy all that you require for your immediate needs that are not catered for by army issue. It is now ten minutes to dinner time. The Trained Soldier will take you to the mess hall. Carry on, Wilson.'

The Trained Soldier assumed command. 'I want twelve of you to stand with your heels on the edge of that flower bed. I want another twelve of you to stand in front of them and the last twelve to stand in front of the second rank. Got it? Now move!' After much shuffling and barging about we got ourselves in three lines of twelve. The Trained Soldier went to one end of the squad and stood for a moment with an odd expression on his face. The two serjeants turned their backs and tried not to laugh. Trained Soldier straightened his shoulders and shouted 'Stand still now. All right now, face me and when I move you will follow me to the mess hall. When we come out of the mess hall you will form up exactly as you are now and follow me back here. Got it?' We lurched into some form of left turn and followed the Trained Soldier like an untidy flock of sheep. The two sergeants stood watching with their faces wreathed in smiles.

Without stopping to perform any further drill movements, we filed straight into the mess hall. There were rows of wooden tables at which sat hundreds of troops all eating heartily. Our squad filed past a servery where we picked up a plate and knife, fork and spoon. A line of servers doled out meat, potatoes, carrots and cabbage. We filed to the tables, where we sat and ate the not too unpalatable meal. During the time we ate a very young officer walked up and down between the tables shouting 'Any complaints?' We were all too bewildered by the strangeness to complain about anything and were only too pleased to have the meal over and be outside away from the overwhelming din of the mess hall.

Back at 'A' block we entered our huts to find that on each bed were three blankets, some of which were grey and some blue. We sat around and talked until the Trained Soldier shouted 'All right, let's have you.' We assembled outside where Serjeant Morphew told us to fall in in three ranks of twelve after the style of the pre-dinner formation. He addressed us again.

'You now collectively rejoice in the name of 36 Squad of the Depot Battalion of 2nd STC (Signal Training Centre). It is our job to teach you the basic drill movements in order that the squad can be moved about as a tidy unit. You are now a 'shower', but in a week from now you will be a manageable body of men. After the first week you will draw rifles and we will begin to teach you arms drill and musketry. You will also be given instruction on the Bren gun and Boys anti tank rifle.[3] On your beds you will find blankets. Serjeant Reardon arranged for the Quartermaster's staff to bring them for you in order to save time. The twelve people in the front rank will now follow Serjeant Reardon to the regimental barber. The Trained Soldier will show the rest of you how to make a bed. I advise you to pay attention to him because if you don't do it properly you will probably freeze during the night. Take them away Serjeant Reardon, carry on Wilson.'

Wilson went to each of the huts in turn and demonstrated how to make up a bed. A boy named Harrington asked where the sheets and pillows were, more in sarcasm than as a serious question. The huts were ten feet by eight and had a two-tier bunk on one side and a single bunk on the other. The front wall was entirely filled up with the door, and a window at either side. The door faced due east. Since the prevailing wind was from the west it was fairly well protected from the weather. God help us if the wind veered to the east.

---

3 The Boys rifle was often called the elephant gun. It was manufactured by BSA and later in Canada. It was in use in the early part of the war but improvements in Panzer armour rendered it largely ineffective. The Bren gun was a light machine gun. There was a series of versions from the 1930s through to the 1990s. It was based on a Czech version made at Brno; the name Bren derived from the first two letters of Brno and the first two letters of Enfield, where it was made in the UK.

The first batch of twelve returned from the barber with their short back and sides to the tender mercies of the Trained Soldier. As I was a member of the second rank I was in the next batch to follow Serjeant Reardon to the barbers. It was rather like shearing sheep and the two barbers seemed to be in competition for the shortest time taken. Clippers, hand operated and not electric, were run from the back of the head right over to the front to leave a tuft over the forehead. Three runs of the clippers and the job was done. Those clippers pulled most of the hair out instead of cutting. The barber informed us that this haircut was 'on the King' and all subsequent haircuts would have to be paid for at 3d a time.[4]

I don't think that many of us slept a great deal that night. The rough blankets and lack of a pillow together with the excitement and strangeness of our new life all contributed to wakefulness and we were glad when half past six came with the Trained Soldier shouting at each door 'Come on, let's have you!' In the ablutions we stood with an exploratory finger under the tap, waiting for the water to run warm, until the Trained Soldier came in and told us that there was no warm water and that it was cold from now on and the sooner we got used to it the better. After breakfast we formed up in our rough squad and were escorted to the Quartermaster's stores by both the serjeants and the Trained Soldier. The stores consisted of a whole row of huts full of all the paraphernalia of army requirements for the day to day needs of the average Tommy. At the door of each hut stood a member of the Quartermaster's staff ready to hand out our kit. Before the issue started our names were called and we went forward one by one to a table at the side of the first hut, where we received a pair of identity discs, one red and the other, with two holes in, green. On the ones I received it was stamped 'Morris D. C. 2361401 C of E.' So the issue of kit started. 'Blouses, Battledress. Trousers, Battledress. Shirts, Angola drab, 3. Socks worsted, grey, pairs, 4. Drawers cellular, short pairs 3. Drawers woollen, long, pairs, 2. Boots, GS pattern, pairs, 1. Laces leather 3. (The odd one was to hang the identity discs around the neck.) So it went on and on. I never did understand why the kit bag was not issued at the first hut so that all the rest of the gear could be placed in it at the outset. As it was we tried vainly to clutch all

4 3d was three pence. After the UK currency was decimalised in the early 1970s, there were 100 new pence to the pound. Before that, there were 240 old pence to the pound. Thus 3d was worth a bit more than one new penny.

the articles at once. After the issue of the kit bag it was plain sailing. I remember thinking at the time that you could come into the army as naked as the day you were born and be completely catered for in every respect in a matter of minutes.

Our second night in camp was passed in more relaxed conditions, occasioned by several pints of Simmonds Nut Brown Ale available at the NAAFI, where we had all been to buy the polishes necessary for kit cleaning. Before lights out we all made sure that cap badges and the two small buttons on the front of the forage caps were gleaming. The fact that there were no pillows was no real hardship now that we had our 'drawers, woollen, long' and other kit to roll up under our heads.

After breakfast on our third day we were lined up in our 'three by twelve' formation and told to stand still and pay attention. Serjeant Reardon and Trained Soldier stood out in front of the squad in the 'at ease' position. From Serjeant Morphew came, 'Properly at ease, now, ATTEN – pause – NOW!'. At this command the two came smartly to attention, heels together, feet at an angle of thirty degrees, thumbs in line with seams of the trousers, heads up, chins in, and looking their own height. It looked so easy. The demonstration was repeated about ten times with the demonstrators facing us and with their backs turned to us so that we might see how the hands were held in the 'at ease' position. 'Right,' said Serjeant Morphew. 'You will now do it yourselves. Properly at ease everyone ... ATTEN ... NOW!' At once there were three casualties, one of which was myself. In our enthusiasm to do well we had lifted our right feet too high and brought them down on our left ankle bones. After much grumbling and groaning the exercise was resumed and after fifteen minutes we were able to come to attention and stand at ease on command with reasonable presentability.

The next exercise was turning left and right. These exercises were more difficult because they involved the inclusion of balance. Serjeant Morphew told us that the important thing at the moment was to remember how the movements were made and that perfection would come with practice during squad drill later in the training. By break time we had learned how the 'about turn' manoeuvre was carried out. The break lasted just long enough for Serjeant Morphew to fill his pipe, light it, and enjoy a few puffs. I did the same and during the operation the serjeant came up and asked 'What do you smoke, Morris?' I replied that I was happy with Three Nuns curly cut. He had smoked the same tobacco for years. We discussed the relative merits of the various brands and agreed that at 10d per ounce our Three Nuns was better than Bruno at 8d.[5]

Serjeant Reardon and the Trained Soldier now showed us how to march with the arms swinging up to shoulder height with the right arm forward when the right leg was back. We tried it. It was awful and Serjeant Morphew told us so. Before we did it again Serjeant Reardon gave us a talk on the commands that we would be hearing from now on. When the squad was fallen in, the man on the right of the front rank was 'marker' or 'right-hand man' and up to now this position was always taken by a man named Chappell who had been briefly in the Army before. He seemed considerably older than the rest of us and was of taciturn disposition and always stood by himself. Nevertheless he knew more about drill than the rest of the squad and seemed very anxious to please the NCOs. With the 'marker' position made clear to us, Serjeant Reardon continued by telling us that if he wanted the squad to move forward after falling in he would give the command: 'The squad will advance – by the right – quick MARCH.' The first part of the order told the squad what was to be done. The second part indicated that 'dressing', or keeping level, was to be taken from the man on one's immediate right and the final or executive part of the order told the squad when to actually start moving. Conversely if the squad was to move away from the instructor the command given would be: 'The squad will retire – about turn – by the left – quick MARCH.' After giving a few moments for the information to sink in, it was demonstrated to us practically by having us carry out the movements up to the stage before actually marching. This was followed by moving to the right and left in threes and dressing by the right or left as the case might be. By lunchtime most of us had got hold of the basic principles theoretically. We found that putting it into practice was quite a different matter.

Towards the close of our first week we were reasonably competent at simple drill and it was possible for the NCOs to move us about as a squad and not as a complete shambles. With infinite patience the two serjeants and the trained soldier taught us the rudiments of saluting on

---

5 Before decimalisation of the currency, money in the UK was divided into pounds, shillings and pence: LSD – from Latin: Libri, Solidi and Denarii. There were twelve pennies to the shilling and twenty shillings to the pound. Thus 8d was a little more than three post-decimalisation pence, so it can be deduced that, even allowing for inflation, tobacco in 1939 was very cheap.

the march, wheeling, right and left forming, and even slow marching. Generally speaking the impression we got was that the instructors were well pleased with the progress we were making. At the beginning of the second week we were marched to the armoury to draw our rifles. They were covered with grease. We were told to open the butt traps and make sure that the oil bottle and pullthrough were present. Each man was issued with two sections of regulation 'flannelette' or more commonly four by two. This material came in a roll four inches wide. It was white and graduated off every linear two inches by a red line woven into it. One of the armoury staff cut off two sections for each man with a pair of scissors. It seemed to be more precious than pearls. We also received a piece of rag with which to remove the grease from the rifles. The piece of old woolly jumper that I was given wasn't big enough to remove the grease even from the bolt.

On our return to our lines we were instructed to memorise the number which was stamped on our rifles. Mine was W32780. Then we retired to our huts to endeavour to remove the filth not only from the rifles but from our hands as well. I realised that the cleaning of our weapons was not going to be easy with the materials provided. Since we still had our civilian clothes I decided to sacrifice my civvy shirt. I ripped it up and very soon had a presentable rifle. Having been used to dealing with firearms all my life, I was probably better equipped with gun lore than most of the others. Getting the pullthrough weight down the barrel through the thick grease was a nightmare but I finally managed it with the aid of a thin twig cut from the privet hedge near our billet. Not daring to use the precious flannelette, I tore a strip off the shirt and finally got my barrel reasonably clean. An hour before tea we were paraded with our new rifles when the instructors, one to each rank, gave a them a cursory inspection. Said Serjeant Reardon: 'Gather round. If you can't see me, get where you can see what I'm doing. This,' he went on, hefting a rifle by its point of balance, 'is a mark three, star, short magazine, Lee-Enfield and you will treat it with more respect than you would your sister.[6] Look after it and it will never let you down. You have removed the worst of the grease from your rifles but they are still filthy.' He then showed us how to remove the magazines and bolts. I had already worked this out for myself so I had a head start in cleaning inside the magazine prior to the lecture. He showed us how

---

6 'The Short Magazine Lee Enfield – SMLE – was adopted for British service in 1902. Variants of the design subsequently saw service in both World Wars.' – Imperial War Museum.

to unscrew the head of the bolt and clean around the firing pin. 'Do not,' he went on with heavy emphasis, 'take any more bits off the rifle. Also make sure that you never get your bolt mixed up with someone else's.'

We were told that before we left Depot Battalion we would have the honour of doing a main gate guard and flying picquet[7] for the whole camp. This news was received with some trepidation as we had been told that at least once during the twenty-four hour tour of duty the Brigadier came out and inspected the turnout. To make matters worse the guard commander would not be either of our NCOs. A serjeant and corporal from another squad would be in charge of us. There would be a whole day of practice before the guard was mounted. This didn't make us feel much more confident.

Ten days before Christmas we were due to mount the guard at four o'clock in the afternoon, and by three o'clock both our squad serjeants and the NCOs of the guard were fussing around like a gaggle of old hens, checking this, adjusting that, correcting the angle of a steel helmet there, until finally they seemed to be satisfied. Then it started to snow. Or rather, it was sleet driven by a very strong wind from the east, with the temperature dropping rapidly. As the sleet arrived, it froze instantly and long before we reached the area of the guard room we and our equipment became coated with a layer of ice up to a quarter of an inch thick. The actual guard mounting, which was supposed to be the daily ceremonial of the camp, was a shambles. The orderly officer did his best but the wind blew the sound of his voice away and neither the old guard nor we, the new guard, could hear the commands. Finally we caught the words: 'New guard – to the guardroom – DISMISS.' When we had all filed in, we were able to take stock of our condition. Our greatcoats were a sheet of ice with cracks where we had been bending our arms during rifle movements. Every piece of equipment was coated with sheets of the stuff. It was in every nook and cranny of our webbing, rifles, steel helmets and even our new gaiters. The guard commander sent us out three at a time to shake the worst of it off on the verandah, which was fortunately facing west and sheltered from the howling easterly gale. The sentry was by this time in a terrible state, taking into account the fact that he had only been on stag about twenty minutes. Every bit of him was covered in ice which was getting thicker by the minute. The orderly officer instructed the guard commander to change the sentry every half hour instead of

7 A small body of troops sent out from a base to look out for the enemy.

every two hours. I was pleased to be detailed for flying picquet as I imagined it would be easier than standing about by the main gate. The flying picquet was a two-hour stag and I quickly worked out that since I was on from 1600 to 1800, I would be on from 2200 to 0001 and 0400 to 0600. The flying picquet did not patrol during the daytime and stayed in the guardroom on call. My fellow picquet was a hefty fellow named Dan Johnson. Dan was, or had been, a sorting clerk for the Post Office. He lived in the Crewe area and his job was to travel on the Irish Mail train from Crewe to Holyhead sorting letters in the mail van all the way there and all the way back. He had a very keen sense of humour and we enjoyed each other's company. Dan and I seized our pick helves[8] and sallied forth to patrol the eastern end of the camp. This end of the camp was the Depot battalion and contained our own A block lines. As soon as we got to the roadway running east and west we got into trouble. We had to lean forward against the gale but found that when we did so our steel-shod boots would not grip on the ice and we landed flat on our faces. For several minutes we tried to make progress but were being blown westwards instead of our intended direction to the east. 'We'll have to wrap something around our boots,' yelled Dan in my ear. 'Let's go back to the guardroom and find something.'

When we entered the guardroom the guard commander wanted to know what the hell we were doing back so soon. He just didn't believe that conditions were so bad and on going outside himself into the roadway was flat on his face and being blown along in a matter of seconds. He crawled back to the guardroom on his hands and knees. We asked for a couple of sandbags apiece. These were readily forthcoming and Dan and I tied them around our feet. This idea proved fairly satisfactory and we managed to patrol our area at an unbelievably slow pace. When we reached our own huts we decided to nip in and have a quick smoke. This was, of course, strictly forbidden and probably a court martial offence. Our plan was frustrated by an enormous coating of ice on the doors of the easterly-facing huts. We just couldn't get the door open so bang went our smoke. Instead of patrolling the area every fifteen minutes we only got around twice in the two hours and returned to the comfort of the guardroom covered in ice. The next two on flying picquet went out with sandbags already wrapped around their feet.

The two picquets who had been patrolling the west end of the camp had fared much worse than Dan and me. It had been all too

---

8 Pickaxe handles.

easy to go westwards to the limit of their patrol but when they had turned to come back they had found it almost impossible to make any headway. They had a tale of disaster to tell. Due to a shortage of hutted accommodation at the time, the operators' battalion were training in large marquees and the sheer weight of ice on the large area of canvas had brought them all down on top of the equipment inside. In the darkness it had been impossible to tell the full extent of the damage but there were fatigue parties crawling about under the canvas in an attempt to salvage the training equipment. Shouted orders were blown away by the wind and generally the whole place was a disaster. The flying picquet had eventually made their way back to the guardroom by gripping any projection that was available on huts, fences or railings. During their two hours of duty they had only been to the western end of the camp and back to the guardroom. Conditions were quite shocking but patrolling was not relaxed and the sentry was still required to patrol his short beat. Grumbling among ourselves, we contended that if we couldn't get about as legitimate inmates of the camp, then neither could saboteurs/thieves/spies et cetera. How naïve we were about military discipline.

When Dan and I went out again at 2200 the freezing sleet had stopped but the wind was worse than ever, blowing with tremendous gusts which if they caught us unaware would throw us against buildings or railings with frightening force. Keeping our feet was if anything more difficult than during our previous stag. It seemed that the temperature was slightly higher than freezing and as a result the surface of the ice had a coating of water which made it more slippery than ever. On our second tour of the area we called in at the boilerhouse on the pretext of checking if the civilian boilerman was safe and sound. Dan nipped in and had a quick smoke while I kept an eye open for anyone in the vicinity. When it was my turn I was delighted to find that the boilerman had just made a brew of tea. As he only had two enamel mugs Dan and I stood outside sharing the spare one. It was a pretty dangerous place to play fast and loose with the rules since the boilerhouse was facing the serjeants' mess. When we reported back to the guardroom our supper was available. It had been brought to the guard just after we left to do our patrol and it was now nearly two hours old and the tea was awful. We ate bread and margarine with a slice of bully and washed it down with putrid tea. It all helped to pass the time.

I have always found that guardrooms generally are the most uncomfortable places imaginable. Out on stag it was either too cold or too hot, wet and windy or frosty and incredibly boring. In the guardroom it was invariably too crowded with some silly sod getting his great feet in the way. Trying to doze was out because of the card school, or if the serjeant of the guard forbade cards, then some idiot would be snoring his head off with his mouth wide open. It was always very stuffy due to the blackout restrictions keeping doors and windows shut. The place was also full of tobacco smoke and reeked of someone's sweaty feet. Such are army guardrooms! By 0400 Dan and I were glad to be outside again. This time we had been issued with a 'lamp, electric, hand' and a list of the early calls, mostly the cooks. The cooks were permanent cadre and had their billets at the far end of B block. The guard commander told us to make sure that each recipient of a call signed the early calls book and to tell each one that conditions outside were very bad. The first snag was at 0415 at a corporal cook's hut. It was facing east in the B block and the door was covered with ice, making it impossible to find a number on the door. As all the huts were identical, we were firmly on the horns of a dilemma. As our next call was at 0430 we had to do something pretty quickly. Dan got out his knife and hacked away the ice on a randomly chosen door and eventually found the number. We could only assume the numbers followed the same pattern as our own lines. We counted the number of doors until we thought we were in the right place and rapped hard on the door. Nothing happened for what seemed like ages and then there was a muffled voice calling something. We were getting desperate and Dan, using the end of his pick helve like a billiard cue, neatly potted the letterbox flap open. There must have been a cascade of ice inside for the inmate yelled 'What the bloody hell are you doing?' 'Are you Corporal Soandso, this is your early call and it's a quarter past four.' Dan was shouting through the letterbox. 'All right, all right, I'll open the door,' said the corporal. Dan was still trying to retrieve his pick helve from the letterbox which had been trapped by the spring-loaded flap. He gave a mighty heave and fell on his arse on the ice when it came free. 'I can't open the bloody door,' moaned the corporal. 'It's covered with ice,' I told him, holding up the flap with my thumb. 'You take the catch off the lock and stand back from the door.' 'Right,' said Dan to me and hurled himself at the door. It opened with a crash and ice flying everywhere. I proffered the book and pencil to the corporal. The poor man was standing in his shirt and drawers, cellular, short, surrounded by chips of ice. A terrible gust of wind entered and blew up his shirt front. 'Jesus! Look what you've done to me hut.' 'I'm sorry corporal but it's terrible out there and we're in an awful hurry,' I told him. 'Try to wrap something around your boots so that you don't slip over.' He signed the book and looked at me as though I was barmy.

'Don't try to take the piss out of me, son,' he said pulling on his trousers. 'And shut that bloody door!'

We arrived at our next call at exactly 0430. This hut was on the other side of the block and faced west with the number plainly visible. After knocking, Dan shouted through the letterbox: 'Early call serjeant it's four thirty.' After much mumbling and grunting the door opened and I shoved the book and pencil at him. He signed in the appropriate place. 'The guard commander asked us to tell you to wrap something around your boots to help you get a grip,' I told him politely. 'Piss off' said he and slammed the door. 'Surely' said Dan 'these buggers must have seen what it was like last night when they went to bed. It started just before four o'clock.' 'Probably still too dozy with sleep to remember but they'll damn soon find out as soon as they put a foot outside,' I shouted back at him. We went through our list of early calls, several of which were for 0430 hours. Since we couldn't be in several places at once we called them as soon as we could in sequence. Some of them were downright rude, some were polite, and some were even grateful for the information about the slippery conditions. It wouldn't be our fault if breakfast was late for the whole camp. We had a whole page of signatures in our book.

The last of our calls was at 0600 and having accomplished the final one we made our way towards the guardroom. On our way we met our relief, who told us that there was a brew going in the back door of the cookhouse. We decided to risk it, since we had finished our stag and our relief was out on patrol. When we sneaked into the cooks' domain the first person we met was the corporal of the icy door. 'I suppose you young buggers want tea,' was his greeting. He filled a couple of mugs and brought them over to us. 'I'm sorry if I was a bit short when you called me but I didn't realise how bad it was until I fell on my arse as soon as I stepped outside and I thought you were trying to be funny. I twisted my back, I think I'll have to go sick with it later on. Do you want more sugar?' Dan and I swelled with pride. Here was decency indeed for humble recruits from a corporal. NCOs were human after all. The wind had by this time dropped considerably and the ice was beginning to melt. It was, however, still dangerously slippery but we still had our sandbags round our feet so were able to proceed to the guardroom without problems. We had no further patrol duties to perform and we sat around until Dan and I with two other recruits were detailed to fetch breakfast for the guard. Donning our sandbags, we shuffled across to the mess hall to collect the insulated containers of food. The squads had not yet started arriving for breakfast and we discussed what it would be like marching as a squad on the ice. At that moment the shaded lights of a three-ton truck came down the road. As it passed we could see two chaps on the back busily shovelling out sand. The smell of breakfast made us realise how ravenous we had become and it was a great sight to see the bacon and beans, porridge, bread, margarine and tea being put into the various containers. It was just about the best meal I had tasted since my last breakfast at home on 29 November. A good pipe of Three Nuns afterwards tasted even better.

On 21 December part one orders stated that personnel in the following squads would proceed on ten days' privilege leave starting from 0600 on the 23rd. Squad 36 was one of those named and broad smiles abounded in every block in Depot Battalion. It was not difficult to see the wisdom of sending seventy per cent of the camp on leave for Christmas. The Army didn't have to feed us. The permanent cadre could have a well-earned rest. The officers would be spared the chore of carrying out the traditional Christmas gunfire routine of serving the other ranks at dinner and early tea.[9] The prospect of ten days at home after being cooped up in camp for almost a month without having put a foot outside was wonderful. It would also give me the opportunity to spend my twenty-first birthday with my family, this falling on 29 December. On the 22nd the list of postings was published and I was delighted to read that I had been posted to No. 13 Squad of Operators Battalion, or OS13 for short. Also posted to OS13 from our squad were Cook, Johnson, Harrington, Hawkins, Andrews and a couple more whose names elude me. We were delighted to be able to continue to be part of the same squad since we had formed a small group and had during the last weeks become firm friends. Serjeant Morphew informed us that we were to leave our kit in our present huts and report back to Depot Battalion on our return from leave. Rifles were to be labelled with our names and handed in to the armourers' stores.

My father gave me a lift home on 23 December and I was delighted when he told me that my old friend Tony Meade was arriving on leave in the evening at Holywell junction and that I was to meet him at 1935 off the Chester train. We called at the Black Lion for a couple of quickies before lunch. I was filled with chagrin to learn that William Youngers best Scotch Ale was no longer available due to transport

9 Gunfire is black tea with a splash of rum. It features in a number of different traditions in the British forces, including Commissioned Officers serving other ranks on Christmas Day.

trouble involved with wartime priorities. Hitherto it had come direct from Edinburgh by train. The local brew had to suffice but I was worried in case Tony turned round and went straight back to his squadron for being deprived of his favourite tipple. After lunch I was surprised to be growled at by our two Alsatians and it was several minutes before they became their old friendly selves and I could only assume that they objected to the smell of the army about me. During the afternoon I went with my father and another LDV commander to look for a suitable observation post on high ground covering the approaches from the sea to the Vale of Clwyd. I was impressed by their keenness and imagined that the same thing was going on throughout the length and breadth of the United Kingdom. I felt that any attempt at invasion would be turned away with great ease by men like these who knew the terrain and commanded the loyalty of thousands of countrymen. Had I an inkling of the utter ruthlessness of the Nazi war machine that was to be displayed a short five months later I would not have had such a happy Christmas.

I presented myself at Holywell junction station at 1930 and was told that the Crewe and Chester train was running thirty minutes late, so I took myself to the Queen's Head in Greenfield and had a pint to while away the time. Here I met several people that I knew and they all appeared surprised to find me in uniform. Full mobilisation was not yet under way. After all the war was as yet barely four months old and premises, camps and aerodromes were not yet constructed to cope with large-scale induction to the forces. The bulk of British regular and territorial troops were already in France together with a few squadrons of the RAF where they had been stationed since the outbreak of war. The news bulletins still only referred to 'patrolling activities' along the Western front. American commentators had coined the phrase 'phoney war'. Back at the station Tony's train arrived 45 minutes late and I was delighted to see that he was wearing the rings of a Flight Lieutenant. Secretly he informed me that this was his embarkation leave and that his squadron (77 Bomber) was due for overseas. I had been given strict instructions that we were to go straight home and not call anywhere on the way. After dinner we sat around and exchanged gossip. My mother could not decide whether we would have preferred turkey or goose for Christmas dinner so she had arranged turkey for Christmas Day and goose for Boxing Day. This was not reckless extravagance but good husbandry since feed for stock was getting scarce and expensive and the best way to cull stock was by eating them. At that time the census of stock had not been taken and only cattle and sheep and pigs were registered with the authorities and this only in a half-hearted way. It had been a very long day and the excitement had made us all very tired, so it was decided to stay in and leave visiting until tomorrow. Tony came up with the gladsome tidings that he had procured eight gallons worth of petrol coupons to cover his embarkation leave period. This meant we could more or less go where we liked.

During the evening of my twenty-first birthday we were drinking in the Black Lion. There were very few patrons, due to it being winter time and also to the shortage of fuel, but those who were present enjoyed the repartee from Mrs Roscoe, our favourite landlady. She was known as 'The Reluctant Dragon' because she ruled her pub with a rod of iron but was reluctant to stop serving after closing time. As the evening got more beery Tony produced a .38 Colt automatic, which he always carried for use in the event of being trapped in a burning aircraft. Mrs Roscoe bet Tony a round of drinks that he couldn't hit a cracked half-pint pot that hung on a hook from the bar shelf, the end one of a row of ten. 'You're on,' said Tony, and drew a bead on the pot and missed it by two inches. 'My turn now,' from Mrs Roscoe. She took the pistol and without even hefting it for balance let go at the pot and smashed it to smithereens. That was two rounds gone. 'Tony. I think you owe me a round of drinks,' said she. 'Nice gun, isn't it?' Without further comment she continued shooting and smashing pots all along the shelf until the firing pin clicked on an empty chamber. Six good pots and one cracked one in a welter of glass all over the cocktail bar. Two resident guests came roaring downstairs fully expecting to find the place littered with dead and dying. These guests were Turner Layton, the very popular singer, with his girl friend.[10] The girl friend had been installed at the Black Lion away from the expected bombing of London and he visited her almost every weekend. Altogether they were a charming couple but totally unused to our ways. The event did, however, help to break the ice for them and they joined in the merriment for the rest of the evening. One thing that did surprise us was Turner Layton saying that he sang only for money. Tony told him: 'I only fly for money but not a fiftieth of what you sing for!' Even Layton's girl friend could not persuade him to sing us a note. The trouble with having a birthday between Christmas and New Year is that the whole week becomes an

10 Turner Layton, born in Washington DC in 1894, was an African American singer, songwriter and pianist. He was successful on both sides of the Atlantic, working in the UK from 1924. He had a regular slot at the Cafe de Paris, a London club. He died in London in 1978.

all-in session of over-refreshment. The New Year came and went in the same fashion and by that time we were almost looking forward to getting back to camp for a rest. I decided to return to camp well before 2359 in order to avoid floundering around in the dark looking for my kit and making my bed by torchlight. I was all organised and having a jar in the NAAFI by 2100 on 2 January 1940.

Chapter 2

MORSE CODE AND A MOVE SOUTH

It was a sorry-looking 36 Squad that was paraded by Serjeant Morphew at 0730 hrs on 3 January. Most of the boys had been travelling for long hours the day before and looked weary. Only those who have made wartime train journeys can know how utterly frustrating and tiring they can be. Even a comparatively short run from London could be fraught with delays and cancellations. In 36 Squad we had people from as far north as Elgin and Aberdeen. The buffets and canteens on the stations were so crowded that it was not worth the effort of standing in a queue, only to hear one's train departure called just when one had reached the head of the line. After the first works parade we were separated into trades as per the orders published before we went on leave. Personnel from the other three depot squads were also being sorted into trades and we joined them to form OS 13 (Operators Squad Number 13) which was forty strong and full of strange faces. Of course all of them were as raw as ourselves. Shouldering our kitbags and with rifles at the trail, we were marched off to our new home in Operators Battalion at the extreme western end of the camp. Before handing us over to our new NCOs, Serjeant Morphew stood us at ease and thanked us for being a good squad and wished us all well in OS 13. The NCO i/c OS 13 was Serjeant Ratcliffe and his assistant was Corporal Smith (Smudger).

On the morning of 4 January we were taken to a training marquee and introduced to a Creed Morse training machine. Hitherto I had always listened to Morse with a pair of headphones which we had to supply ourselves. Here however a loudspeaker was used to avoid issuing large numbers of headphones. Upon a large blackboard at the front of the class had been chalked the alphabet with its Morse symbol opposite each letter. Serjeant Ratcliffe went over each letter intoning the Morse symbols as he did so.

'A. Dit dah.

B. Dah dit dit dit.

C. Dah dit dah dit.'

On and on it went until at 1000 he said: 'Right Corporal Smith, have 'em back here at twenty past.' To our amazement we gathered that we were to get a morning NAAFI break and to get there and back in time Corporal Smith doubled us all the way to the NAAFI and all the way back. What the hell, we got a precious cup of tea and no matter how pissy it tasted, it was a privilege. To cope with the vast and sudden influx of bodies at this time of the morning the NAAFI girls had to work very hard. By late afternoon the Creed machine was sending Morse at zero words per minute and the students were picking out the occasional letter. I was doodling on my message pad and didn't notice the Serjeant standing behind me. He called me to the back of the class and asked my name. 'Well Morris I hope I'm not going to have trouble with you. When you are learning Morse it is essential that you pay attention, otherwise you will get behind the rest of the class and will never be able to catch up.' Obviously the time had come to tell him I could already read Morse. 'I'm sorry to appear uninterested Serjeant but I took a second class PMG certificate a couple of years ago.' He shouted to Corporal Smith to carry on and beckoned me to follow him. We entered another empty training tent and he pushed a pad and pencil in front of me. The instrument he was sending on was a Fullerphone,[1] a line telegraphy device which had a rather pleasant ringing note. At fifteen words per minute I was able to copy his sending almost 100 per cent. After he had perused my copy he pushed the speed up to twenty and I was still able to get it down pretty accurately. After he'd looked at the higher speed copy the roles were reversed and I had to send to him. After a brief burst to get the feel of the key I went off at twenty per minute and gradually speeded up until I was almost at 25 per minute. I told the serjeant that I had not had any practice at all for over a year. At this he laughed and told me that the speed for Group E exam was eight words per minute and for B3 – or pass out – the speed was fifteen words per minute. We chatted for quite a time, not as serjeant to recruit but as man to man, and I was able to ask

1 A device used to send signals by direct current along a wire, making the communication almost impossible to overhear. It was developed by Captain Algernon Fuller during the First World War. Fuller was a Major General in the Second War.

him about the Fullerphone and what its use was. Finally he told me to accompany him to the Battalion office, into which he disappeared. After a few minutes he re-appeared and smartened me up, tunic done up, hat on straight and all buttons fastened. I was marched into the inner sanctum where I saluted a Major, no less. 'Let me see, your name is Morris, er, Serjeant er, er yes, tells me that you can read Morse.' He seemed like a very vague man. 'Yes sir, I have a Second Class PMG certificate in marine radio operation.' 'Very well, er, Signalman, off you go.' I saluted and turned about as smartly as I could and left the august presence. Outside Serjeant Ratcliffe was waiting for me. I told him what had taken place inside the office, whereupon he smiled and said: 'He only wanted to see if you could speak English.'

The following morning the squad was busy at Morse when Serjeant Ratcliffe again called me to the back of the class. 'Morris, did you read Battalion orders last night?' 'No Serjeant, only company orders,' I had to admit. 'Well go and read Battalion orders and bloody well go now,' he hissed at me. I took off in terror of being put on a charge. When I found Battalion orders I perused every line until I came to:

'Ranks and Appointments. Promotions.

The following have been promoted to A/U/L/Cpl.

2361401 Sigmn Morris DC

This promotion has been made within the establishment of the unit.'

I read every word of the orders in case I had missed something else and then, bewildered, I walked back to the training tent to find the two NCOs grinning like a pair of Cheshire cats. 'Serjeant,' I pleaded, 'What the hell does all this mean?' 'It means that I wanted another Morse instructor and you're it. You understand of course that the stripe carries no pay and you will lose it on posting. Otherwise you are a Lance Corporal and are entitled to the facilities of the corporals' mess. Now get over to the Q stores and draw a couple of tapes.' Before I left he grabbed my arm and chalked a stripe where I was to sew on my new tapes. I discovered later that sewing on a lance stripe was the very devil of a job. Sheepishly I asked the bod in the stores for two stripes and was amazed to hear him say 'Certainly, corporal.' I looked behind me, thinking he was addressing someone behind me. No, he meant me all right. I thanked him and he told me I was welcome. Straight back to the hut and out with the hussif[2] and I tacked on the stripes.

2 A hussif, huswif or housewife was a sewing kit with needles and thread etc in a rolled or folded piece of canvas.

I reported back to Serjeant Ratcliffe and Corporal Smith, who were standing at the back of the class talking. 'What do you want me to do now, Serjeant?' I asked him in all innocence. I was unprepared for what happened next. 'Fall in outside,' he yelled to the class. 'Corporal Morris will take you down to NAAFI. Corporal Smith whispered: 'I'll wait for you in the corporals' mess.' The squad fell in outside. Corporal Smith called them to attention and motioned me to take them away. My first command, 'Move to the right in threes,' came out in a reedy falsetto. Someone tittered and the serjeant barked: 'Quiet, you're at attention.' 'By the left, quick march.' More bass modulation this time. They moved off. On the way to the NAAFI I gained confidence and told them to pick up the step as someone had got out of step with the rest of the squad. 'Left, left, left right left,' I called out. They did exactly as I wanted. I was drunk with power. On arrival at the NAAFI I halted them. Told them to be outside in fifteen minutes. Dismissed the squad and went over to the corporals' mess where Smudger Smith, as I was now entitled to call him, was waiting for me. After a quick tea and a wad, Smudger said; 'You'd better go and get 'em.' Back at the NAAFI they were waiting for me outside. 'Right. Fall in.' This they did with surprising speed. The squad got under way without any trouble and the step was perfect. To my horror I saw an officer approaching. My mind went blank and I panicked. The nearer the officer came the more flustered I became. When he was five paces away I suddenly remembered. 'Squad, eyes right.' I saluted and the officer returned the salute smartly, after tucking his cane under his left arm in a very regimental manner. Corporal Smith caught up with me and we followed the squad back to the training area, where I fell them out and they filed into the tent. 'Not very difficult really, is it?' he asked quietly. 'It was Serjeant Ratcliffe's idea to throw you in at the deep end like that. Having done it once you won't have any more trouble.' It was true. I did not have any more nerves throughout the next six years. There and then I decided to grow a moustache. It would make me look more mature and give me more authority.[3] I soon realised that the crafty Serjeant Ratcliffe had played a blinder in getting me a stripe. He could swan off with the Corporal and leave me in charge of the squad. God alone knows where they used to go to but during the Morse periods I seemed to be in sole charge.

Most of the members of OS13 were looking forward to passing the Group E proficiency test, as this would bring another sixpence per day

---

3 Pete wore a moustache for the rest of his life.

in pay. As a recruit the pay was two shillings per day or fourteen bob a week.[4] Any recruit who was married or had dependent parents was immediately stopped seven shillings,[5] which left only one shilling a day for all cleaning materials, postage and entertainment including cigarettes or pipe tobacco. People like Dan Johnson, an ex-Post Office employee, and some other lucky devils, were in the happy position of 'having their pay made up'. This meant that their past employers continued to pay their civilian remuneration during their army service, on the understanding that they would return to their original employer after hostilities had ceased. The Group E, or Group Eddy as it was better known, was a test consisting of Morse at eight words per minute and an oral procedure test to a minimum standard at which an operator could be allowed to function under the direct supervision of an experienced soldier or an NCO. Since the squad were to sit the Group Eddy test, Serjeant Ratcliffe suggested that I had better take the B3 test. I had been able to devote considerably more time to the procedure contained in 'Signal Training. All Arms' while the rest of the squad had been doing early Morse training so he considered that I would pass with no trouble. All operators were to be posted to units with B3 qualifications and the good Serjeant was convinced that I would be able to leave with a B2 under my belt. Basically the main consideration was Morse speed. For B3 it was necessary to read 12 words per minute with 100 per cent accuracy; for B2 the requirement was 18 wpm for a three-minute duration period of reception. To be tested for B1 it was necessary to sit an examination at Command HQ and test facilities were not available at Signals Training Centres.

Every member of the squad passed the Group Eddy at the first attempt and I was also successful in obtaining a B3, which entitled me to an increase of a shilling a day, making a total of four shillings a day – one pound and eight shillings a week.[6] Here was military opulence on a grand scale. It was, however, soon spent in the snug of the Railway Inn. Mild beer cost 5d (about two pence) a pint, bitter was 6d and a bottle of Guinness was also 6d. No one ever drank spirits, as this was

4 An extra sixpence per day would raise the weekly pay from seventy new pence to eighty-seven and a half new pence. It's not easy to compare this to modern money but a hundred to a hundred and fifty pounds might be about right (in 2025). It seems a pittance, but of course the recruits were fed and clothed.

5 This was to ensure that they paid for their family's upkeep.

6 One pound and forty pence.

considered the privilege of elderly gentlemen in their mid-thirties. For those who did splash out on whisky the cost was 8d per tot of one quarter of a gill.[7] Cigarettes such as Players, Gold Flake and Craven A all cost a shilling for twenty but Woodbines, Star and Park Drive were 8d for twenty.

Training continued without interruption as April passed into May and the time came for the B3 tests to take place. The B3 was to include testing on all types of operating in which we had been trained and this included a large-scale wireless exercise over active service distances, and sending and receiving traffic while on the move in Humber wireless pick-ups. On a beautiful May morning we were told to report to the MT (Motor Transport) lines where a large number of Humber pick-ups waited with trainee Drivers MT in attendance at each one. There were to be several 'nets' in the exercise so as not to make the groups too unwieldy. The control stations were situated in camp and we were to keep in communication during our drive out to the sites given in our map references allotted to each station. There was an NCO in charge of each vehicle and while one of the other operators was netting the eleven sets to Control we found our map reference on the map. Our location was at the top of Halkyn mountain about four miles beyond my home. I was told to sit in the front of the Humber with the NCO i/c and driver to show the best route. I was able to call in very briefly on my parents. They invited us to call in on the way back to the camp for tea provided we could spare the time. The NCO i/c said that we would make the time! My mother was concerned at not being able to provide a full-scale meal on the rations available. I knew that there would be lots of eggs available and as we hadn't seen a fresh egg for months I knew that the boys would be delighted at the thought of boiled eggs and fresh bread and butter.

We arrived at Halkyn mountain before any of the other stations had reached their locations and had our fixed antenna erected and our arrival confirmed by the base station at camp. We could not get down to the serious business of traffic passing, upon which our proficiency would be assessed, until all the other stations had established their fixed aerials. When all had arrived, the sheaf of messages was opened and each operator sent six to base and received six in return. This all took a considerable time and it was after four in the afternoon when

7 The modern single measure is one sixth of a gill – thus the measure in 1939 was between a modern single and a modern double measure. A gill is one quarter of a pint.

we received the signal to pack up and return to camp. This was our chance to drive like the wind to my home, where we were fed on eggs and fried potatoes, washed down with lashings of tea. The NCO i/c, driver and three other operators all seemed grateful for the grub and short period of relaxation and were profuse in their thanks to my mother. My father gave me a ten shilling note to 'buy the boys a drink'. We were by no means the last truck to arrive back at camp and we assumed that some had either lost themselves or had swanned off on some other jaunt of their own. After all, we were almost trained soldiers and surely could be trusted.

The traffic that was passed to me on this exercise was at a speed upwards of 18 wpm and my return messages were over 20 because I knew that the operator on the base station was our own squad serjeant, having recognised his 'fist' on his preliminary call. All but three of OS13 passed the B3 test. The odd three were required to undergo further Morse practice. I was detailed to take the extra tuition class and they all were eventually cleared for B3. Serjeant Ratcliffe asked me for my pay book, which he took to Company Office and when he brought it back I found that my B2 qualification had been ratified by the signature of the Major i/c training. I now held the same rating as the squad serjeant but lacked about fifteen years of his experience in Army operating. I still maintained that my Morse was better than his.

As young soldiers under training we had very little opportunity to read newspapers or listen to the radio, so we did not know of the grave situation in Belgium and France. The first we knew of the catastrophe was the arrival during the first few days of June of large numbers of troops in a very dishevelled state and looking as though they had not slept in weeks. Some of them lacked complete uniforms and some even wore plimsolls. Most wore steel helmets or no hats at all and some had less animation than zombies. One or two of our squad made a point of buying newspapers and we realised that we had been kicked out of France via Dunkirk, bag and no baggage. Dan Johnson told us that all that bullshit about hanging out the washing on the Siegfried line had been a wee bit premature.

About the middle of June our postings were published in part two orders and the vast majority of OS13 found that they were being sent to 3rd Divisional Signals, whatever that meant. We were totally ignorant of the army outside the training camp and although we knew our own jobs as Operators Signals, we had not the slightest idea of what was in store for us in the world outside. We soon found out! We had been on small marches around the countryside near Prestatyn, wearing webbing with small pack, water bottle, rifle and a minimum of weight.

This we found irksome enough but when we were told to parade at 0700 hours in the complete outfit we were stunned. Greatcoats were to be worn over which we had webbing with small pack on the right side and water bottle on the left. Respirator at the alert (on the chest) and big pack on the back, rifle slung on the right shoulder and full kit bag on the left shoulder. With typical army efficiency we stood around with all this gear on while the powers decided that due to lack of transport we were to march to the station in Prestatyn to board a train for we knew not where. I have a mental picture of Dan Johnson returning from the messroom after breakfast and jeering at us and yelling that we looked like 'bloody Christmas trees'. I never saw Dan again.

That march to the station was a shambles. Since we were an armed party stronger than the guard, we were entitled to have the guard turned out and a present arms salute. Out came the guard very smartly and came to the present. The chubby Second Lieutenant in charge of our party gave us 'eyes right' when he meant 'eyes left' and as he quickly corrected himself some clown at the front dropped his kit bag from his shoulder and bent to pick it up. Needless to say the rest of the column tripped over those in front and whole squad became a whirling heap of arms, legs and kit. At this juncture the Brigadier came striding out of the Officers' Mess and addressed the chubby subaltern very quietly, pointing his cane into the camp. We all had to file back a full hundred yards inside the camp, form up, and do it all over again. This time we got it right and finally we were away. Bearing in mind that it was mid-June and that we were wearing greatcoats and full kit, it will be appreciated that we were somewhat warm. It was the last straw when Chubby looked at his watch and, realising that because of the fracas at the gate we were running late, gave the order to break into double time. When we eventually arrived at the station and were told to file away on the platform on the 'up' line, we were allowed to put down our kit bags and slacken our belts, a blessed relief. At this moment an Austin pick-up arrived with Chubby's kit, which the driver unloaded and piled on the platform near where we were standing.

By now the sun was really up and the temperature was rising and we sweltered in our greatcoats. No one knew what time the train was supposed to leave as it had not been disclosed on orders and we waited almost an hour for it to arrive. Finally it puffed into the station and the civilian passengers boarded first in the corridor coaches. The coach allotted to us was a non-corridor antique which had probably been brought out of retirement in some railway museum for the duration of the war. Harrington remarked that we couldn't be going very far as there was no corridor and consequently no toilet. This was a very astute observation on the part of Harrington, but a long way from the truth. Our detachment consisted of men from all trades comprising A personnel, Electricians Signals and Instrument Mechanics; B trades, Operators Signals; C trades, Linemen; and D trades, Drivers and Despatch Riders. Chubby did a quick sum and divided the number of compartments into the number of bodies. It worked out at six men per compartment. This sounded rather good but when we climbed aboard with all our kit we found that only a small part of it would fit on the luggage racks and the rest had to be strewn about as to leave as much room as possible for our comfort. Two men were detailed to carry the mound of Chubby's kit to the guards van while he retired to the first class section of the train. There were no NCOs with the detachment and we were left to our own devices. The day before we left Prestatyn orders decreed that 'all the following NCOs will revert to their permanent rank of Signalman, with effect from date.' I had to unpick the stripes from my blouse and greatcoat. I packed them away safely in case I ever made L/Cpl again.

By the time the train arrived in Chester most of us were busting for a pee and when we drew up on the platform there was a mad rush for the gents. Seeing the exodus from the train, Chubby must have thought he had a full-scale desertion on his hands and he started to run up and down like a portly Rhode Island hen looking for her chicks. It hadn't occurred to him that there no toilets in our section of the train. When all had returned to the coaches, a whistle blew and a flag was waved and away steamed the train, all except our coaches. They stayed by the platform like a stranded whale. Half an hour later more coaches and a locomotive reversed up to us and were coupled up. The front part of the newly-formed train was full of troops and we could not see any civilians at all. Eventually we chuffed away and after a few miles the sun shone on the left-hand side of the train, indicating that we were heading roughly south. Our next stop was at Shrewsbury, where there was again a stampede for the toilets.

The other troops were infantry of the East Lancs Regiment and they had the usual complement of NCOs together with a Lieutenant who as senior officer present assumed command of the train. This was probably a very good thing as Chubby would most likely have lost us all. The East Lancs NCOs came down the train telling all personnel that we were not to eat our haversack rations until four o'clock in the afternoon, when it was hoped that a brew up of tea would be meeting the train. This was more like organisation and at least we knew that someone was in charge. In retrospect it was all done for security reasons and later we realised that we were reinforcements and replacements for a very depleted fighting division newly returned from France. Just before four that afternoon we steamed into Gloucester, where we de-trained and filed into the station yard where a temporary cookhouse had been erected. Only tea was available but at least it was hot and very, very acceptable. Thirty minutes later we had rejoined our kit in the coaches and were waiting to resume our journey. The East Lancs had even posted sentries to guard the train during the tea break. Very commendable. Our haversack rations had dried up and were not very appetising and most of us were still eating them when we resumed our seats in the train. At half past six we arrived at Temple Meads station in Bristol. We were told by Chubby, who had it seemed found his voice, to don our complete kit and fall in on the platform. He called the roll and found everyone present. We followed him out to the station yard. It was impossible to march. We formed up again near a motley collection of impressed vehicles. Laundry vans, removal vehicles and very occasionally an army three-tonner.[8] Standing by an Austin pick-up was an RSM of Signals, who saluted Chubby and then ignored him. He took command of the situation and had us aboard the trucks in a matter of minutes.

---

8 On 4 June 1940 the Secretary of State for War, Anthony Eden, told the Commons that 35,000 motor vehicles had been impressed for the War Department since the outbreak of war.

Chapter 3

CIDER, NETTLES AND ARTILLERY

After what seemed an endless drive through Bath, the convoy eventually arrived at Frome and pulled up in a field behind a public house called the White Swan. The field was on a gentle slope and was practically covered with large marquees with concrete floors. The concrete had been rolled when wet with an anti-slip spiked roller and was in consequence as rough as a bear's back. The RSM fell us in and had the roll called. Again all were present. He told us to listen carefully. 'You are now members of 3rd Div Sigs and will be here for any time from a day to a week, at which time you will be posted to your permanent units in the Division. You will now deposit your kit in the marquees behind you. They are your billets and you will find two blankets per man on each bedspace. Leave your kit and report back here in five minutes with your mess tins and eating irons. Right now fall out. MOVE.' We did exactly that because the thought of food was a spur, having had only a dry haversack ration since six in the morning. The meal was delicious and was our first taste of Maconochie's stew.[1] This, together with slices of bread, filled us to capacity. A mug of hot sweet tea finished it off perfectly. The serjeant cook apologised for it being a scratch meal and promised to do better for breakfast. He was of, course, taking the pee out of us.

---

1 Maconochie's stew was a tinned ration originally produced by an Aberdeen-based company for the troops in the Boer War. It was still part of rations in the First World War but it had a dubious reputation, not least for causing flatulence. It may be that by the Second War the name had become attached to any generic meat and vegetable stew that the cooks could produce.

After the meal I looked around for somewhere to wash my mess tins but could find nothing and had to settle for wiping them out with grass. I eventually found the ablutions, which consisted of two six-foot tables, GS (general service) and several bowls, galvanised, ablution. A good strip-off wash and shave was very necessary after the extreme heat of the day. Our group consisted of OS13 members Hawkins, Harrington, Cook, Andrews, Stevens and myself. Andrews suggested that a pint would go down very well, so we walked down the field to the White Swan, which we expected to be full to the doors with troops. We were very surprised to find the place almost empty of soldiers and only a handful of civilians. 'Sorry boys no beer, only cider,' said the landlord. So we settled for cider. Sweet was two and half pence and rough one and a half. We became reckless spenders and started on the sweet. The first two pints went down without touching the sides and we were halfway down the third when one of the old chaps asked where we came from. All except myself came from London and the South East and, seeing no breach of security, we told the old boy where our homes were. 'You bain't used to drinking cider then?' We agreed that we were not but hastened to assure him that we liked the taste and that we were enjoying it very much. 'Take care with 'un me dears, it plays merry hell with the legs,' the old chap rumbled.

Andy said 'Silly old sod, this stuff is like gnat pee,' and we all agreed that it hadn't the horsepower to pull the skin off a rice pudding. At ten fifteen the landlord called time and we rose, or tried to rise, to leave. Our knees had turned to rubber. Our heads were as clear as crystal and our speech unslurred. We staggered out of the door, while the old boy in the corner roared with laughter. The entrance gate to our field was only a few yards from the pub door, which was just as well since locomotion on rubber legs was extremely hazardous. On the way up to our marquee Hawkins suddenly gripped hold of a fence post and said 'Hell I'm busting for a crap, I'll never make it to the latrines.' There was no doubt this was true because the latrines were right at the top of the field away from the sight of civilians. Andy suggested that Hawkins jump over a low fence bordering the camp to drop his slacks. This Hawkins did with alacrity and presently we heard 'Anybody got any message pad on them?' All operators carried a few sheets in their inside battledress pockets and Stevens threw some over to Hawkins. After a few seconds, perhaps half a minute, there was the most bloodcurdling yell, long drawn out and spine-chilling. When we got to him Hawkins was rolling about in agony on the ground. We half dragged half carried him to our side of the fence and tried to calm him down. It seems that as he was pulling up his pants he staggered backwards on his rubber legs and fell over and as he did so a fresh bunch of strong young June nettles had gone up between his shirt and his back right from top to bottom. We lifted his shirt from his back and in the light of a match inspected the damage. It was very severe indeed and there was no doubt that the poor devil was in awful pain. Andy commented that he would have to go to hospital to get treatment of some sort. We knew that Hawkins was a haemophiliac and wondered if he would be all right. We eventually got him to the tent that was doing duty as an orderly room and finally someone rousted out the orderly officer, who called in the MO. In the end Hawkins was whisked off to Frome hospital, shirtless and kneeling on the passenger seat of a pick-up truck. It was now close to midnight and we felt it was time to get to bed provided that we could find our bedspaces in the dark.

We had certainly been ruined at Prestatyn Training Centre with its spring mattresses and numerous blankets. Here we had two blankets and a greatcoat laid on roughened concrete. When the sun peeped over the horizon we were up and about long before reveille, stiff and cold and miserable, and to get warm we ran up and down to the ablutions and back three times. Stevens announced that he was going for a walk in the town but we decided against it on the grounds that we didn't know when we were going to get breakfast or be called for a parade. After what seemed an interminable wait the cooks shouted that grub was ready. Needless to say, we were first in the queue, washed, shaved and properly dressed, much to the surprise of the Orderly Officer and the Serjeant Cook. The latter murmured something about bullshitting recruits. The Orderly Officer remonstrated with him gently, saying it was refreshing to see people properly dressed so early in the day and not to discourage us. We remembered that these men had newly returned from France, where it must have been very rough. After breakfast we, the new intake, were paraded by a serjeant who we came to know as 'Tashy' Ward, due no doubt to his wearing a large black moustache. He was what was called 'dead regimental' and went exactly by the book. Some of the old Signalmen told us that he came from one of the gunner regiments and we should avoid getting posted to his section. He called us to attention and kept us standing without making any attempt to stand us at ease during his pep talk. His preamble was: 'All those idiots among you who were involved in the nettlebed incident last night will report to me immediately after this parade. The front rank will report to the cookhouse. The centre rank will tidy up the area. The rear rank will wait here pending instructions from the RSM. Got it?'

We were fallen out and our small group stood on one side and waited for 'Tashy' to descend on us. After keeping us waiting as long as possible, just to let us know who was boss, he fell all five of us in and marched us to the Orderly Room tent. He moved inside while we stood at attention outside. Up came the RSM and demanded: 'What are you men doing here?' Andy told him that we didn't know why we were standing there and that the Serjeant had paraded us there. The RSM grunted and went inside the tent, whence there presently came raised voices. We heard the RSM say to whoever was inside with Ward; 'You bloody well won't, you know. They're only a bunch of kids and you don't know the real truth of the matter yet.' More murmuring, which we were unable to hear. Andy said out of the side of his mouth: 'Tell the absolute truth, it sounds as though we're in the shit over something.' We all agreed.

We were called into the tent one at a time and as each man came out he was sent to a point out of earshot of the others. When my turn came the RSM stood me at ease and asked me to give my version of the incident of the nettles. I told him (Ward and the Orderly Room Serjeant were present) exactly what had happened as I remembered it, omitting nothing and putting nothing in. When I had finished the RSM told me that it was being considered whether to put us all on a 252 (charge sheet) for disorderly conduct prejudicial to military discipline. It seemed that Serjeant Ward was under the impression that we had beaten up Jack Hawkins and thrown him in the nettles. I ventured to suggest that it would be a simple matter to ask Hawkins what had actually happened. He told me that Hawkins had not yet regained consciousness. He was still on the danger list due to his being haemophiliac, a point that the MO had omitted to tell the hospital staff when Hawkins was admitted, in spite of the fact that several of us had told the Orderly Officer and the MO at the time of the incident. When I rejoined the others we all agreed that Andy was a genius in suggesting that we tell the strict truth. When all the group had been interviewed in the tent we were called in and told that pending Hawkins's evidence we would not be charged and that if our story was true, Hawkins would probably be charged on the grounds that nettle stings could be construed as a self-inflicted wound. As though the poor sod hadn't been through enough pain and strain. What the hell sort of army had we come to? Wait and see what the outcome would be was all we could say. In the meantime we asked if we could visit Hawkins when he was conscious. We were warned that under no circumstances were we to try to contact him in any way. Weeks later I spoke to Hawkins on the phone at the section to which he had been posted, 7th Guards Brigade. He told me he had been charged and had been admonished by the CSO (Chief Signals Officer) at Divisional HQ.

At works parade next morning lists of names were called out and those called were assembled with their kit and driven away to their new units. Stevens, Andrews and myself together with about ten other chaps of different trades were called and we, with our gear, were loaded into a 30 cwt truck and driven off.[2] About a mile down the road the truck stopped at a cafe and the Serjeant came round to the back of the vehicle and asked if anyone wanted a cup of tea and a wad (bun). When we had all got our tea we stood around outside the cafe while the Serjeant introduced himself as Andy Young, a native of Stirling. Serjeant Young told us that the 3rd Division was a regular unit consisting of three infantry brigades, three field artillery regiments, a medium artillery regiment, a light anti-aircraft regiment and all the usual support units, which we would find out about later. He told us that we were going to a small town called Glastonbury, not many miles away. On our arrival we were taken to our billet, which was a newish empty house standing in its own grounds a few hundred yards from the town proper and in the shadow of the famous Glastonbury Tor. After we had dumped our kit in the rooms allocated to us, we assembled outside and automatically fell in ready to be inspected by another serjeant. He told us to gather round, which we thought was a very odd command but we obeyed and pressed round him to hear the pearls of wisdom. 'My name is Peebles, Freddie Peebles, and I come from Stirling, the gateway to the highlands. You have already met Serjeant Young. This regiment is a territorial unit[3] and its home is in and around Dundee. We are the only territorial unit in the 3rd Division. We have three Field Artillery regiments in the Division; the 7th Field, the 33rd Field and ourselves the 76th Field. We were very badly cut up in France and lost almost half the signal section at Dunkirk and at sea when the Gracie Fields was hit by a bomb.[4] You are their replacements.

2 In Imperial measures thirty hundredweights amounted to about one and a half tons, so a 30 cwt truck was a small lorry. In this case it would probably have had canvas covering the bed of the truck.

3 The Territorial Army, originally a volunteer reserve force, was mobilised and expanded as part of the Second World War effort. Many TA units were deployed to France as part of the British Expeditionary Force.

4 The *Gracie Fields* was a paddle steamer of the Red Funnel Line, built in 1936 and requisitioned for war service in 1939. She received a direct bomb hit when making her second run to Dunkirk on 29 May 1940.

They were all gallant men and good friends and I hope you will be able to take their places and be happy in this section. The section is officially known as F Section Signals 3rd Div Sigs. The other two Field Regiment sections are E and G. The light Ack Ack regiment is H. The three infantry brigades are J, K and L sections. You will soon learn the formation of all the units. Our full section strength is 39 other ranks and one officer. Our officer is 2nd Lieutenant Smith and at the moment he is on leave. We also have twelve of the section other ranks on leave as well. They will be returning at the end of the week. I think I have told you enough for the moment. Grab your mess tins and get down to the cookhouse for dinner.'

The new intake automatically fell into three ranks to proceed to the cookhouse. This caused hoots of mirth among the old hands and gunners that we passed. After dinner we thought it better to slouch back like the others. We were gradually getting the impression that our new unit was 'a right shower'. After a few days we were quite sure that they were a shower. All the Signalmen called the section serjeant by his Christian name. The other NCOs seemed to have no control over the Signalmen. Dress was sloppy with ORs walking about with tunics undone and no gaiters. No equipment was blancoed and arms and equipment were filthy. After making allowances for the fact that they had been in France and had lost all their equipment, they were still sloppy compared with the Div Sigs troops who had also been in France. At Div HQ brasses were polished and webbing freshly blancoed. Saluting was punctilious and the rapport between NCOs and men strictly military. The result of this difference in outlook between the old members of the section and us newcomers was a rift forming and dividing the two halves of the signals community. When the OC Section 2nd Lieutenant Smith returned from leave, proper morning works parades were resumed and an attempt to smarten up the section was made. It was obvious that the NCOs had let everything slip while the OC was on leave.

New equipment began to arrive in large quantities and vehicle allotments began; three Humber wireless pick-ups, and one gin palace – this vehicle was a box-like truck for use as a wireless vehicle and signal office combined; three Ford 30 cwt trucks; and an Austin pick-up for the OC. Three 500 cc side-valve BSA motorcycles for the despatch riders and one 500 cc OHV Norton for the section serjeant. A whole host of wireless and line equipment arrived and had to be fitted into the vehicles while the drivers were busy painting divisional and regimental signs on the front and rear of each vehicle. The divisional sign was a red circle with three black triangles, apex downward, in the circle.[5] The regimental sign, for Signals only and on the other mudguard of the truck, was a square divided horizontally, the upper half white and the lower half blue. Superimposed on this was a red 44 to indicate the junior artillery regiment of the division. The other two field regiments were 42 for the 7th Field Regiment and 43 for the 33rd Field Regiment. All our gunners' vehicles had the red and blue square of artillery with the 44 superimposed.

The 76 H Field Regiment Royal Artillery consisted in mid-1940 of two batteries, 302 Bty and 303 Bty. Each battery was divided into three troops of four guns. The Regimental Headquarters, to which the signal section was attached, was the administration and command centre. Royal Signals personnel were never permanently attached to the batteries. RA signallers were responsible for their own communications, working forward to their own gun troops and rearwards to a Signals control operator at RHQ. Royal Signals operators maintained a wireless link forward to the batteries, rearwards to Division and laterally to Brigade. As soon as lines were laid and telephone communication established, the radio links were closed down to preserve security.

An indication of how pathetically short of equipment the army had become after Dunkirk was the guns that were issued to the regiment pending the arrival of proper 25 pounder gun/howitzers. The sight of 1914–18 French 75 mm guns on wooden wheels would have been laughable if we had not realised how serious the situation had become. Here we had a very senior infantry division of the British Army so lacking in artillery that it had to make do with antique guns from a foreign nation. The cart-type wheels on which they were mounted made it impossible to tow the guns and limbers at more than a few miles an hour. Gradually the other equipment came in and was distributed to the various sections and departments of the regiment. The Light Aid Detachment (LAD) was issued with its recovery vehicle, gas and electric welding equipment and a host of other necessities. The LAD were Royal Army Ordnance Corps troops and were responsible for gun repairs as well as vehicles. The regimental survey party who were responsible for cartography and gunlaying were also kitted out afresh. The medical officer, Captain A.T. Blair, received new surgical equipment. All ranks were issued with a second battledress and spare boots. Kit inspections were held and replacements issued to all the

5 During the Second World War the insignia of the 3rd (United Kingdom) Division became a 'pattern of three'; a black triangle trisected by an inverted red triangle.

personnel who had returned from France. Reinforcement troops like ourselves already had full kit. Looking through the G1098 scale of equipment for a Field Artillery Regiment with the thousands of items of bits and pieces is an awesome procedure.[6] It is doubtful if a unit is ever fully equipped and is probably always short of some item or other.

In early August the regiment moved to the Weston-super-Mare area and the RHQ was established in buildings at the north end of the sea front. The Signal Section was billeted in an empty house opposite a swimming pool about five minutes' walk from the signal office. This was the first time a proper signal office had been established. In Glastonbury the exchange was in the orderly room, which was most inconvenient both for the gunners and the signals staff. With a separate signal office we were able to have a stretcher (borrowed from the MI room) to sleep on during night duty as the alarm bells on the exchanges were loud enough to wake all but the most unconscious of sleepers. Better still, we could chat up the girls on the GPO exchange without any interference from the gunners.

The cookhouse was in an underground car park, which was conveniently situated between the billet and signal office. The billet had been a boarding house, three storeys high and in rather bad condition. Andy, Cook, Stevens, myself and a couple of the original operators occupied a first-floor back room. We had two-tier bunk beds and straw palliasses. Here indeed was luxury after sleeping on the floor at the Glastonbury billet. Next door was an ice cream-cum-milkbar, which never seemed to do much business but was always open until it went dark each evening. Across the road was a sweets and cigarette kiosk run by Maisie and her sister Mitzi, who took it in turns to run the kiosk and drive the lads wild with sexual frustration. One beautiful evening Andy and I were sitting with the two sisters on a seat outside the kiosk looking out over the Bristol Channel when we saw an aircraft coming straight towards us about fifty feet above the water. I said it was a Spitfire but no, Andy said it was a Hurricane. When it opened fire on the buildings behind us we knew it was neither. Instantly Andy and I both leapt up and ran for the billets, upstairs and under our beds. When the sound of the aircraft engines died away we both came out very shamefacedly. 'What the hell do we say now?' Andy was as ashamed as I was. 'Let's tell them we are on fire picket,' was all I could think of. This was unanimously decided upon and we swaggered back to the two girls, who were still sitting on the seat. As we approached

---

6 The G1098 is a list of a unit's war equipment.

them I said in a loud voice: 'If there had been a magazine on that Bren gun we might have got a shot at him as he went over the hill!'

During September 1940 the Battle of Britain was taking place and the whole of the south of England afforded a grandstand view of the aerial fighting. We were able to recognise instantly the difference in sound between the German aircraft engines and the British Merlins.[7] New guns arrived for the batteries from the Central Ordnance Depot. I do not remember which mark of gun/howitzer they were but they had plain barrels and were not fitted with the muzzle brake and flash eliminators of the later marks. With the guns came new limbers and Quads. The Quad[8] was a very ugly vehicle but very practical. Manufactured by Morris Commercial Vehicles, they were capable of towing limber and gun over very rough terrain when engaged in four-wheel drive. The gunners were visibly more happy to be operating British 25 pounders than the obsolescent French 75s. Each Quad was able to accommodate a complete gun crew with all their kit. The arrival of the new guns was the trigger for a move to the south coast in readiness to oppose the imminent invasion of Britain by the German Wehrmacht. The regiment moved overnight to the Worthing area and RHQ was established at Lancing College, which had been evacuated by the students at the end of the spring term. The walls of the ablutions bore notices: 'Soap is a munition of war. Do not waste it.' After laying lines out to the batteries, radio was shut down as usual. As a double line of communication we established visual links with lamp stations. Most of our time was occupied with digging gun pits and slit trenches on the golf course. I removed my shirt to try to keep cool. At the end of my stint I replaced my shirt to find that my back was red raw with sunburn. I was on duty as flying picket that night and suffered torture with webbing and small pack, respirator and rifle rubbing my shoulders. I daren't ask the MO for calamine lotion for fear of being charged with SIW – self-inflicted wound. I certainly learned a lesson and I was never foolish enough to expose my back or shoulders to the sun again.

Serjeant Freddie Peebles was posted to Div HQ while we were at Lancing. His replacement was 2318218 Serjeant Bill Delicate, a reservist. Serjeant Delicate had barely hit civvy street before he was

---

7 Rolls-Royce Merlin engines powered some of the most famous British aircraft of the war, including the Spitfire, the Hurricane, the Mosquito and the Lancaster.

8 Morris C8 Field Artillery Tractor.

recalled. He was a small wiry man with a ready smile and neat quick gestures. He remained SERJEANT always and no one ever called him by his Christian name. He was every inch a regular soldier, vaguely distant, firm but kind. While everyone liked Freddie Peebles, there was something missing militarily. It was only after we had left the section that we, the recently joined personnel, realised the his job in civvy street had been a postman in Stirling and several of the Signalmen had also worked in the same office. It was hardly likely that he could command real discipline. This problem occurred in many Territorial units. I remember one case in particular where a lieutenant was in civilian life the employee of a lance bombardier. Under circumstances such as these it was virtually impossible to run a unit on proper military lines and we newcomers got the distinct impression that the situation was about to be changed by posting out large numbers of personnel from the regiment as a whole. As soon as conscription of 20-year-old males was imminent, large numbers of young men made a headlong rush to join the Territorial Army, where they received training at weekends and evenings. In most cases the instructors were not regular army personnel, so it was a case of the blind being led by the blind. Andrews and Stevens on duty in section office one afternoon were able to look at the personal records of almost the whole section and were amazed to find that half the operators were only holders of Group E qualifications. If this sort of situation existed in every TA unit of the army, it was no wonder that we had been chased out of France in such a short time. The militiamen among us were extremely glad that we had waited for call up and had received an extended period of training. Since the 3rd Division was a regular unit it was clear to most of us that such a situation could not be allowed to continue.

As the summer of 1940 receded, so did the danger of an invasion by the Hun. In late October the regiment moved to Dorset. RHQ located at Dewlish House, an old mansion in a hamlet of the same name. Dewlish is near Milborne St Andrew, a village a few miles south-west of Blandford Forum. This Dorset market town was also the 3rd Divisional HQ. For the first few weeks of our stay in Dewlish the signal section occupied a derelict cottage next door to the pub a few hundred yards from the RHQ. The Signals and RHQ vehicles were parked along the roadside opposite the pub and our billet. The guard for the HQ and vehicle lines used one of the pub outhouses as a guardroom. Since the guardroom was as cold as a mortuary, most of the off-duty sentries and pickets spent most of their time in the bar. As the winter progressed and the frost became harder, our only source of water froze and washing and shaving became impossible without a long walk to the HQ billets. Finally we (the Signals) were moved into the servants quarters in the attic bedrooms of Dewlish House. The signal office was established in the butler's pantry, which was very comfortable and warm. Unofficially the signal office became a sort of recreation room. Serjeant Young gave us boxing lessons and to clear the use of the premises with the OC I used to hold Morse classes every night. The only operators who were keen to increase their speed and upgrade their qualifications were the ex-Prestatyn operators, with the exception of Atholl Stuart and Charlie Fraser. Stuart had been a newspaper compositor and Fraser had worked as a GPO technician. In late November the copy of 3rd Div Sigs Part 2 orders arrived as usual by Don R and there in black and white, among the section called Ranks and Appointments: 'Promotions. Sigmn Morris DC 2361401 to L/Cpl with effect from date.'

Chapter 4

CLOCK MENDING AND AQUATIC SPORTS

During the last few days in January 1941 I was buying goodies from the mobile WVS shop when I was brought a message to report to the section office. On arrival there I found the OC and Serjeant Delicate with grave faces. The OC handed me a telegram saying that my father had died the previous evening. He also handed me a pass and a rail warrant to cover eight days' compassionate leave. It just so happened that Serjeant Delicate had to collect some stationery from Warminster and could give me a lift that far on my way to Bristol. I did not believe a word of the story about collecting anything from Warminster and knew that transport being laid on was an act of generosity on the part of the OC. He had done the same thing with Hodgkinson when Coventry was bombed by allowing Hodgkinson to use a motorcycle and a three-day pass to find out if his parents were still alive. They were but the house had been destroyed. I arrived at Bristol Temple Meads station just as an air raid started. It was the first time I had been present during an air raid and I was surprised at how calm I felt in spite of the awful din of anti-aircraft gunfire and clatter of spent shrapnel falling on the roof of the station. I don't think that the falling bombs were very big and were probably mostly incendiaries.[1] The train finally arrived in the station fifty minutes after the all-clear had sounded. When the train left there was only one other person apart from me in the compartment and after having wheedled out of me the purpose of my journey, the old boy, a civilian of about fifty, suggested

1 The Luftwaffe conducted six major bombing campaigns on Bristol between November 1940 and April 1941. Bristol was the fifth most heavily bombed British city.

that I stretch out on the seat and get some sleep. With the luxury of the soft seat and the pleasant warmth of the compartment I was soon asleep. When I woke up much later I discovered that there were six people on the seat opposite, all sitting squashed up against each other while I occupied a whole side to myself. It seemed that my companion of the previous night would not let anyone wake me. I was profuse in my apologies and immediately made room for the other passengers to spread themselves out. By this time we were well north of Shrewsbury and it was quite daylight. The further north we travelled the deeper the snow seemed to become. At Chester there was about four inches on the level fields. I wondered what it would be like in the lanes around my home. I was soon to find out when I walked home from Caerwys station and encountered drifts completely filling the lane from hedge to hedge. I was almost home when I suddenly wondered how the hearse would be able to negotiate the journey to the church. When I finally arrived I found Tony Meade was already there and had been able to offer moral support to my mother before my arrival. Tony had arranged a flight from his Squadron to Sealand FTS[2] and had then hired a taxi as far as it could take him and then had only a short distance to walk to complete the journey. The local District Council did sterling work in clearing the road from the house to the church. There being no snowploughs, every shovelful had to be thrown over the hedge into the adjacent fields. At the outskirts of the town the cortege was met by a contingent of the Home Guard, which preceded the hearse to the church.[3] After the service and interment the firing party sent a volley or two over the grave. I could see by the kick of the rifles that they were not firing blanks but live ammunition. Enquiries made afterwards proved that no blank ammunition could be obtained and it was decided to use the proper stuff in spite of the fact that they could have killed someone a few miles away.

Early 1941 was largely occupied by Divisional exercises or schemes as they were called at the time. As a result, the entire regiment was often away from Dewlish for periods of up to ten days, leaving behind only a skeleton cadre to look after the billets and man the telephone exchange. As a junior NCO I was often detailed to stay with the rear party as NCO in charge. The exchange had to be manned for 24

---

2 RAF Sealand, in the north-east corner of Flintshire near Chester, was Number 5 Flying Training School during the Second World War.

3 Pete's father was the commander of the Caerwys platoon of D Company of the 3rd Flintshire Battalion of the Home Guard.

hours a day so at least one operator had to remain within earshot of the signal office. To make life easier, all three of us would bring our bedding down and sleep in the signal office. This arrangement gave the off-duty pair plenty of time to wander around the buildings and rooms that made up Dewlish House, a privilege denied to us when the officers were in residence. During one exploration we discovered a large cellar almost below the signal office. One part of this basement area was shut off by a stout door, above which was a small grille with bars placed vertically and spaced about four inches apart. The opening was bow-shaped with the centre portion over the door about six inches high. Shining a torch through this hole revealed a very extensive wine cellar with many rows of racks bearing hundreds of bottles all lying on their sides and in most cases covered with the dust and cobwebs of years. The very presence of the cellar presented a challenge that could not be ignored. It was obvious that on no account must the door be forced open. We decided that none of us liked wine and in any case if we wanted a drink we could always go to the local in Dewlish village. Still the challenge remained. After much thought, I borrowed the Adjutant's fishing rod from his room and fitted on the reel. After making a loop or noose on the end of the line I was able to lasso the neck of a bottle on the nearest rack and by pulling gently brought it quietly to the floor. After that it was easy to draw it to a position under the grille. It was then possible to hoist it up and pass it through the grille. Having taken the bottle to the signal office, it was duly opened and tasted. It may have been a very rare vintage to a connoisseur, and priceless, but to us it was ghastly and had to be disposed of quickly down the sink in the signal office (Butler's pantry). The bottle was pushed well and truly down a rabbit hole well away from the house.

The challenge having been overcome, the matter was forgotten until about three weeks later when a special parade of all ranks and all arms of the RHQ was called. The second in command stalked about in front of the parade until the RSM had called the roll and declared that all were present. As far as we knew, the only person missing was the operator on duty in the signal office. When all was ready, the 2i/c told us that a crime of the utmost gravity had been committed. The wine cellar of Dewlish House had been broken into and a large amount of valuable wine and spirits stolen. Until the culprits owned up and faced the necessary charges, all leave and privileges for the entire HQ would be stopped and route marches over and above the six-mile run would be introduced. Furthermore, the entire HQ would be confined to the immediate vicinity. The major continued to rant for a good fifteen minutes until he was sure that every man had got the message. Finally he told us that we had just twelve hours for those responsible to come forward and confess. As soon as we were dismissed, the rear party of three weeks before got together and decided that our small adventure could not possibly have caused such a furore. As the 2i/c had said 'a large quantity' had been stolen, we decided to remain silent. The following morning at our own first works parade our OC told us that the guilty party had confessed and was being dealt with summarily to avoid a court martial. The following morning there appeared the news that a serjeant and two bombardiers had been reduced to their permanent rank of gunner and awarded several weeks in the Shepton Mallet glasshouse. Several gunners received stiff doses of jankers for receiving stolen property.[4]

The last few of the old NCOs were posted and the section had lost all of the lacklustre behaviour. All the NCOs were now either regulars, reservists or militiamen. There was no using Christian names when speaking to NCOs and the sort of discipline that had been taught at training camp prevailed. At the same time we lost our OC, 2nd Lieutenant Smith. He was replaced by 2nd Lieutenant English, himself a militiaman, who had trained at Whitby as an operator before being selected for OCTU (Officer Cadet Training Unit). Although his Christian name was John, the Scottish members of the section called him Sam. I think that the reason for this was that there was at the time a Scottish footballer named Sam English.[5] Every officer since the dawn of military history has received a nickname and Mr English was called 'Sam' behind his back until he left the section.

I cannot recall accurately when the regiment left Dewlish but it was probably late February or early March. After a spell in Bournemouth the regiment moved to Shorwell in the Isle of Wight by way of the ferry from Lymington to Yarmouth. The RHQ was a very pleasant country house surrounded by stabling and other farm buildings. The stables were surmounted by a small tower-like structure with a four-dialled clock permanently pointing to a quarter to two. Almost every afternoon most of the section would dress in denims and run down to the beach at Atherfield Point and into the sea without undressing

---

4 Jankers: an imprecise bit of slang for military punishment such as confinement to barracks, being given tedious and pointless tasks, and frequent uniform inspections.

5 Sam English was a Northern Irish footballer who played for several clubs in the 1930s but was best known for playing for the Glasgow club, Rangers.

and then run back to the billet, allowing our fatigue clothes to dry on us as we ran. Apart from relieving the boredom by violent exercise, it had the effect of making us very fit. At the beginning of September 1941 the regiment left for Otterburn artillery practice camp in Northumberland. I was detailed to stay behind at Shorwell as part of the rear party – myself and two operators, the section cook and one or two gunners of RHQ. I was the only NCO and I assumed that I was in charge of the rear party, although I received no specific orders to that effect. The only vehicles left behind were the CO's Z car, a Humber Snipe shooting brake, and one motorcycle. During the waiting period two of us reconnoitred the clock tower with a view to winding it up and getting it in action. The two weights (clock and chime) appeared to have been cast from concrete in ten-gallon oil drums with a large ring cast in at the top of each to facilitate hooking on to the weight cables. These came from drums in the clock mechanism, exactly after the style of a grandfather clock. Eventually we discovered that the failure of the clock to perform was that three teeth were broken off one of the large cast iron gear wheels in the drive sequence. Had the LAD (light aid detachment) been left behind with the welding equipment and had we been able to remove the gear to the workshop for them, it might have been possible to effect a repair. It looked pretty hopeless but after having slept on the problem we decided to try another tack. We filed off the broken teeth down to the level of the periphery of the mean diameter of the remaining teeth. We were lucky in that the area was quite accessible and caused no strain or pain at all to get through the operation. The next stage was to mark out and drill four holes in place of each missing tooth. The holes were tapped and bolts screwed in tightly and cut off to the length of the original teeth. It was a tedious job drilling twelve holes with a hand drill but eventually all the bolts were screwed in and filed to the right length. Before starting work we had already cleaned off large quantities of dust, chaff, pigeon dung and the filth of years from the gears and general area surrounding the mechanism. Below the clock was a long wooden chute designed to keep people and animals away from the weight wires and so forth. At the bottom of the chute was a door to give access to the cables for maintenance, the hinges of which screamed in agony when the door was opened or closed. They needed lots of oil. The clock bearings were cleaned with paraffin and a paint brush and liberally oiled. Finally the winding pawls were lifted from the ratchets and the cables lowered to the bottom of the 'cupboard' and the weights hooked on. The large winding handle was placed on the square shafts of the cable drums and the weights were wound up to their maximum height. At last we gave the pendulum a swing and a splendid even ticktock was heard as the escapement wheel rotated.[6] When we descended for tea the clock indicated ten past two although it was actually half past four. The clock was going but it was not set to the correct time. After tea we had another look at the machinery and could find no obvious way of setting the time. In the end we had to free the escapement and allow the clock to advance under control to the correct time when the escapement was replaced quickly.[7] We ended up about a minute fast so the pendulum was stopped until the correct time showed on the dials. At the hours the bell struck well enough but sounded muffled as though cracked. On investigation a bird's nest was found between the bell and the side of the tower. When this was removed a lovely sonorous note rang out over the whole farmyard. The next morning at breakfast we had a slight contretemps with our colleagues about the bell waking them every hour. We went and watched the clock movement. Not a hell of a lot to see, but fascinating in view of the fact that it had previously been so much scrap iron. Had we been detailed to repair it, we would have been moaning like banshees.

A few days after the regiment returned, a splendid Red Label Bentley[8] drew up in front of the house just as the clock was striking twelve. The driver, an elderly gentleman in a deerstalker and accompanied by a spaniel, hearing the clock strike, turned and looked long and hard at the clocktower. I was standing in the signal office at about two o'clock that afternoon when I saw the Colonel accompanied by the old gentleman and the 2i/c come out of the officers' mess and stroll around the stable yard, occasionally looking at their watches and up at the clock tower. As the minute hand arrived at the hour the mechanism did its usual 'whirr' and the bell

---

6 The escapement in a mechanical clock was invented in medieval times. In the case of this clock, the escapement was driven by the suspended weight, like a grandfather clock, with each swing of the pendulum advancing the escape wheel over one of its teeth. The wheel's teeth releasing and being stopped give clocks their tick tock sound. The regular movement advances the clock's hands at a regular rate.

7 If the escapement is freed while the weight is driving the pendulum, the hands will advance quickly, without the tick tock, because the gear train is driving the hands without check.

8 The Bentley logo included the letter B and the colour surrounding the letter varied. A black surround showed it was a sporty car; red showed it was luxurious; and green indicated something in between.

rang twice. The three gentlemen nodded to each other and returned to the mess. Later the RSM sent for me and asked me who had been tampering with the clock. I had no option but to tell him that it was Signalman Smith and I who had been amusing ourselves while the regiment were at Otterburn. The RSM looked very savagely at me and told me to make sure that Smith and I presented ourselves at defaulters parade at 1000 hrs the next day. I found Smithy and told him of the orders from the RSM. We both feared the worst but reasoned that we could always remove the weights and stop the bloody thing. After all we had done what we had set out to do and no one could take that pleasure away from us. Next morning went very slowly until 1000 hrs, when we took up our station outside the orderly room door. When the last of the defaulters had been wheeled out by the RSM he said 'Right you two it's your turn now.' Smithy whispered that we couldn't be on a charge since we had no escort so it was probably only a bollocking coming our way. The RSM marched us in and the regimental 2i/c told us to stand at ease. He proceeded to tell us that we had been very remiss to tamper with someone's property without express permission. Having delivered the mildest of bollockings, he went on to say that the gentleman of yesterday was the owner of the estate who had paid a visit to the family home to collect something or other from one of the locked rooms upstairs. He was very surprised to see the clock going and hear it striking since it had not been working since during the 1914–18 war when he, the gentleman, had been a subaltern in the Hampshire Regiment. The 2i/c said that the owner was very pleased to have the clock working again because all the local clock repairers had said that a new wheel would have to be cast at great expense, entailing complete dismantling and re-assembly of the entire mechanism. As the RSM called us to attention prior to marching us out, the 2i/c handed me an envelope saying that the owner had left it for the clock menders. When Smithy and I got back to the signal office and opened the envelope we found a brand new white five pound note inside, nothing else, just the fiver. We were both cock-a-hoop because it meant that we could leave our pay in credit for three weeks. We were also ordered to silence the chime as it was keeping the entire HQ awake. This was accomplished very simply by removing the weight from the chime cable.

In January 1942 the regiment made the long drive in convoy to Fort George at the northern end of the Caledonian canal. The fort stands on a promontory which juts out into the Moray Firth between Nairn and Inverness. The fort itself was a grim barracks beyond a tiny village called Ardisier.[9] It was here at Fort George that we were initiated into what we came to call 'aquatic sports'; that is, the training required to invade Europe from the sea. It was a long and arduous process and all we really got out of it was superb physical fitness and the knowledge that eventually we would be at the forefront of an attack on the Hun. Initially experiments were carried out in the waterproofing of vehicles and equipment. Exhaust pipes and induction tubes to carburettors were extended, breather vents were piped away above the intended water line. Any vulnerable holes were filled with waterproofing compound. A whole host of techniques were tried out and a free rein given to anyone with ideas that might help to achieve perfection. When a vehicle was considered ready for test, it had a winch cable attached to its rear pintle hook and was then driven down one of the sloping slipways into the sea under its own power until it was immersed to the desired depth. If the engine kept running for fifteen minutes it was considered a successful trial. If the engine faltered or stopped the truck was winched out and checked to find the fault. The same type of experiments were being carried out on tanks by the armoured unit working on the same slipways. Little did we know at the time that tanks would eventually 'swim', all 39 tons of them.[10]

As far as the signal section was concerned, it was not only our vehicles that had to be protected. Wireless sets were fitted with waterproof bags and all leads in and out of the bags had to be sealed with the gooey compound. The sets mounted in vehicles were particularly difficult to cope with as the mounting brackets for the sets had to be put inside the waterproof bag and then screwed to the operating surface. Then the set was placed on its mounting and the bag pulled over the lot and sealed up with compound. Changing frequency was a nightmare as the bag had to be unsealed, frequency flicked and then resealed with all speed. The bags in question were made of waxed canvas, double sewn and

9 Fort George was built after the Battle of Culloden in 1746 as a secure base for the forces of George II. It took a couple of decades to build and by the time it was finished the Jacobite threat had subsided, but it has served the British Army ever since. Among its features are a museum and a dogs' cemetery.

10 A large subject. Amphibious tanks were indeed used on D Day – Duplex Drive or DD tanks, nicknamed Donald Duck tanks – which could 'swim' at about four knots. Trials of DD tanks began around the time Pete was in Fort George – May 1942. On Sword beach, where the sea on D Day was reasonably calm, the DD tanks worked well but on Omaha beach 29 amphibious tanks were launched offshore and 27 sank.

fitted with a draw string at the mouth. They came in various sizes to accommodate various bits of equipment. The ones used for manpack 18 sets were fitted on a frame after the manner of a Bergen rucksack.[11] It required a fair amount of ingenuity to achieve watertight conditions and have the set operating at the same time. The trick was to form the top of the bag around the antenna and mike and headphone leads with a wad of compound around them and then pull the drawstring up really tight. The wad of compound stuck around the aerial did cause the performance of the set to deteriorate considerably and I cured most of the trouble with a large chemical laboratory rubber bung on the aerial rod to keep the compound away from the radio frequency component. This idea was adopted throughout the regiment – subject to bungs being available.

As the weeks went by we became so used to working under waterproof conditions that it became second nature. In the early spring we moved entirely to Rothesay on the Isle of Bute and it was here that we really began to learn about 'aquatic sports'. Fantastic equipment such as midget submarines and fast motor launches and frigates lay cheek by jowl with LCTs (landing craft tank) and the tiny LCMs (landing craft mechanised) and a host of other wonders. The purpose of our visit to Bute was to learn about 'run-in' shoots – that is, to fire our guns at targets on land as the LCTs carrying the guns were running in to make an assault landing. With wheeled field guns, limbers and quad towing vehicles this was an extremely difficult operation. The quads and limbers had to be facing the ramp of the LCT so that they could be driven off in a hurry. During the shoot the guns had to be facing the target; that is, the wrong way round for towing. To complicate matters further, extreme care had to be taken not to have anything in the line of fire on the LCT. After a great deal of trial and error, a troop and a half of guns[12] were driven on to the LCT and the limbers and quads were literally manhandled through 180 degrees while the guns were left facing forward. When the shoot was complete the guns had then to be turned and hooked up to their respective limbers ready to be driven off as soon as the ramp door was dropped on the beach. The whole procedure was frantically exhausting and fraught with danger. A field

11 Manpack 18: the 18 Wireless Set. Bergen rucksack: standard-issue backpack with metal interior frame to make carrying heavy loads more comfortable.

12 A troop in this context might comprise four field guns, so this might mean six guns.

gun leaps about like a wild horse even with the spade on earth but on the steel decking of an LCT the guns would recoil for yards. All very frightening. We admired the gunners very much and were glad to be safe if not so warm in our little LCM observing fall of shot.

In the early days of this training the LCM was in the hands of a naval Petty Officer and under training with the PO was an RASC junior NCO.[13] The much bigger LCTs were always under the command of naval personnel. In the case of the run-in shooting, this was very necessary as great skill was need to keep the craft head on to the target in a choppy sea. The target for most of this shooting was a tiny island called Inchmarnock in the Kyles of Bute. It was, of course, totally uninhabited and didn't even boast a sheep as population. It was a long sail from Rothesay around the north end of Bute to Inchmarnock and those with seasickness suffered badly. The gunners went out a troop and a half at a time but we were out every day until our faces were raw from spray. The observation officers that we accompanied were under training and they alternated with the gun troops and none of them really got used to the sea journeys to the island. We on the other hand did it almost every day and attained sea legs that lasted us throughout our service on little boats.

Coming back from a shoot late one afternoon, we were smitten with engine trouble. The type of LCM involved was powered by a Scripps V8. This was a Ford V8 engine modified for marine use with special manifolds and carburation. The RASC cox was a very worried man as darkness fell and told us to keep a sharp look out for other shipping that might run us down. When he finally got the engine running again it was quite dark and we didn't even know which way we were pointing. We knew that we were on the eastern side of Bute and couldn't go out to sea or anything dangerous. It was decided to press on slowly until we either ran aground or sighted something familiar. After half an hour's sailing we spotted a lamp sending Morse over to our port side. It was going far too fast for any of us to copy and was quite obviously an Aldis lamp in the hands of someone pretty skilled. The only lamp available to us was an Army Lamp Daylight Signalling Mark III. One of the operators held it in his hands and kept the sight on the distant flashing station. To attract his attention I kept sending a series of 'A's which was the Signals calling letter. When the other station finished

---

13 The Royal Army Service Corps was responsible for, among other things, land and coastal transport. In 1965 its functions were divided among other Corps and the RASC ceased to exist.

his traffic with the station that we could not see, he turned his lamp full on us and gave us 'K' (invitation to transmit.) Quite sedately I told him that we were an Army LCM and that we were lost and could we come in. In reply we got a stream of signals far too fast for any of us to read. We took a chance and went flat out towards the light that came on every few minutes to give us a bearing. After every one of his flashes I gave a brief blink in reply. Eventually we fetched up at a jetty at the landward end of which was a hut with windows facing out to sea. The cox tied up the LCM and stayed aboard while a couple of us went up to the hut. Our knock on the door was answered by a Petty Officer who invited us inside and offered us tea, which we declined saying that there were three more of us in the LCM. He sent one of his ratings to fetch the others from the LCM and told us that the boat would be quite safe where it was. I enquired who was sending so damned fast that we couldn't read it. A WREN about five feet one high in her stocking feet popped her head up from behind a desk and said that she was the telegraphist on duty.[14] We didn't dare ask what they were doing because there was so much secret work being carried out in the area. One could end up in the cooler for just asking the time of day. The PO pointed out on his wall map just where we had landed up, which was on the point of land between the eastern Kyle of Bute and Loch Striven just below the village of Altgaltraig, literally miles from anywhere. There was not a star in the sky, no moon and the PO was not prepared to lend us a compass. He strongly advised us not to set out in the darkness as we were certain to get lost and run out of fuel. Far better to start at first light and be sure of success. Although we had wireless, we were forbidden to use it for any purpose other than the shooting exercises. In any case the base would be shut down hours ago. We stayed.

As the sky started to lighten next morning we started the engine and the PO pointed us in a south-easterly direction. By keeping the wake behind us dead straight we kept going in the right direction until it got light enough to see our destination at Rothesay. The RASC cox dropped us off at the jetty and moored the LCM for refuelling. We were absolutely starving and hung around the cookhouse until breakfast was ready. After breakfast I reported to the OC, who informed me that I was on a charge not of his doing but on the order of the 2i/c. It seems

14 The Women's Royal Naval Service, popularly and officially known as the WRENS, was formed in 1917 and disbanded in 1919, then re-established in 1939. The service remained active until 1993 when it was integrated into the Royal Navy.

that I was guilty of not reporting back to base at the appointed time, prejudicial to good order and all the usual military bullshit. When the RSM wheeled us into the august presence of the 2i/c himself I listened to the charge being read out and a long rigmarole about duty and crap about the responsibility of being an NCO and an example to the men. Finally he asked me what I had to say for myself and I told him that until a person had been out on an LCM in pitch blackness without compass or stars on a choppy sea no one had the right to accuse me of dereliction of duty. I could feel the RSM prodding me gently in the back with his cane and I turned my tirade into a form of apology and did a mock cringe. This seemed to mollify the old boy and he looked very severe and handed me down a reprimand, which is nothing serious but still goes on the charge sheet. After he marched us out the RSM told me that if I had kept my mouth shut I would have got away with a bollocking. The only time we went out with no officer with us and the flaming engine packed up. When the 2i/c finally went out to observe a shoot he was sick all the way there and all the way back. The old mal de mer is no respecter of rank and I have seen Brigadiers and Major Generals shoot tigers left right and centre, groaning and wishing they could die just like everybody else. Don't believe the old crap about a nip of whisky to prevent sickness, spirits just make it come up quicker. Some of the gunners on the large LCTs suffered very badly from sickness. The early type of LCT was an ungainly brute and seemed to snake in the water along its length. The very sight of this happening was extremely sick-making. When fully laden in the heavy sea it was almost impossible to keep them going in a straight line and many were marked where they had been sideswiped. It was a never-ending source of amazement that the things didn't break up in a rough sea. I was fortunate in never having to travel far in one of them. I was always in a proper ship like a frigate, or on an LCM.

In May 1942 several of the section were sent on detachment to a small camp of Signals at Largiemore on Loch Fyne. It turned out to be a training centre for a new breed of signals known as 'Beach Signals'. These it seemed were to be landed first in any invasion to provide communications for the Beach Master and his staff. The Beach Master as the name implied was master of all he surveyed and had the task of maintaining order in the landing and dispersal of units and formations as they came ashore. An extremely important job. The personnel under his command had at the time no experience of any sort of the sea. Why we were chosen to give them instruction was beyond our comprehension; surely it should have been the Navy. The exercise chosen was to transfer from a small assault boat, known as 'R' boats, to a larger vessel anchored in the loch with a scrambling net hanging over the side and away from the ship's side by about a foot. We had to rush in at about six knots and leap off the R boat and grab the net and climb up to the deck of the larger craft. Why it was necessary for Beach Signals to do this was beyond us but as the saying went while we were doing that they couldn't clobber us for anything else. Our boys spent a very pleasant morning out on the loch practising ourselves, first without kit and finally with a small pack with bricks to the weight of an 18 set. We became quite proficient and could jump off at almost the full speed of an R boat. No one got the slightest bit wet.

The following morning training was due to start and we took out our first four victims. One of the first requirements of Beach Signals was the ability to swim. After that they had to be either linemen or operators. Most of them were able to leap off the boat with gay abandon and obvious enjoyment but occasionally one had to be coaxed. After two days one of the eighteen trainees had not made a jump and failure of the course was looming for him. I made him stand between myself and another instructor and told him to wait for the R boat to rise on top of a wave and then jump outwards and grab. Simple. In we came on the next circuit and up rode the R boat a yard from the net. We all jumped together. My colleague and the trainee caught on beautifully but I missed it completely and hit the water with a hell of a splash. Boots, equipment and bricks took me down at a frightening rate and I struggled desperately to unhook my belt catch. Eventually it came undone and I dropped all my kit off and swam up as hard as I could. When I broke surface I was gasping for air and scared stiff. Someone grabbed me and fastened a line to me. One of the matelots had dived over the side and brought a rope with him. Finally I was pulled to the net and I was able to scramble up. Being cheerful in front of the trainees and acting as though it happened every day was not easy. I wondered if I would have to pay for a new set of kit. As it happened I claimed some from the Beach Signals 'Q' bloke quite easily. The officer in charge of the training session, who never left the deck of the static ship, insisted that as wet as I was I should immediately do another jump in case I lost my nerve. The weather in May was not very warm and I was glad to get the jump over with and cadge a ride back to the billet for a change of clothes.

The jumping on and off boats lasted for a week until the officer i/c the course was satisfied that all the trainees were acclimatised to the sea and small boats. The whole course was then moved to a hutted camp at Pollokshields very close to Glasgow. Here we had to supervise the classes of Beach Signals operators in advanced Morse reading and line laying with an innovation called 'assault cable'. This was a new telephone cable that appeared to be made of soft iron wire insulated with a single layer of some brown substance which was not bakelite and not rubber. Years later we would have recognised it as plastic. This was intended to be laid as an expendable 'one-off' line, used for a short period and then abandoned. It was laid from hand-carried reels of one third of a mile each. For the purpose of training it was recovered for re-use but it was very prone to kinking. It was at Pollokshields that I saw my first contingent of American troops. We met some of them in the local pubs, where they seemed very keen to learn all about the British way of life. It was obvious that they had been thoroughly briefed and certain subjects were carefully avoided. At the start of an evening in their company they seemed reticent and reserved but as the beer took hold they brought out the photographs of 'Mom and Pop' and became just homesick kids. They had seen nothing yet! By our standards the money they received was enormous. They even hired taxis with gay abandon to take them into central Glasgow for an evening's entertainment and then another taxi back to camp. As a corporal B1 operator I was receiving eight shillings (forty pence) per day. Just the price of a taxi ride from camp to the city. The American uniforms were much smarter than ours and they could ring the changes of combinations of tunics and trousers and also had two or three types of headgear and boots. As a result of more money and candy and chewing gum to throw around, and more glamorous uniforms, the poor British Tommy was a long way behind in the race to entertain the local girls and fights took place most evenings at the local dance halls. Prolonged bad feeling did not exist and by and large the GIs were a warm-hearted and generous bunch of boys. They had a tremendous range of commodities available to purchase from their PX,[15] anything from silk stockings to tinned pineapple chunks. Cartons of 200 cigarettes, Camels, Chesterfields and many other brands. Fat King Edward cigars and pipe tobacco like Edgeworth flake or ready rubbed. Prince Albert in flat oval tins, designed for easy filling of the pipe. There was never an air of 'make do' but always 'throw it away and get a new one'. The amount of transport they had was incredible. It appeared to us that every soldier had his own personal vehicle whether it was a giant six-wheeled GMC truck or a small runabout called a Jeep.[16] We

15 The store on a US military base – it stands for Post Exchange.

16 GMC: General Motors Company. The Jeep was a quarter-ton vehicle, four-wheel drive and highly manoeuvrable.

are all now quite familiar with the ubiquitous Jeep but when we first saw them running about the roads around Glasgow, very often on the right-hand side of the road, we were green with envy. They were built to a standard specification by several manufacturers, mainly Willys-Overland and Ford. During the whole war I do not remember a single occasion when I saw an American riding a motorcycle.

I was due for seven days' privilege leave and I wrote to my friend Tony Meade, now a Squadron Leader, to ask him if he could make his leave coincide. He replied that this was impossible but if I could be outside my nearest aerodrome at 1000 hrs on the morning of the day my leave started he would give me a lift home. I was not sure what he meant by the offer but I agreed to be there. Saying nothing to anyone, I quietly caught a lift on the road by the drill hall and arrived at the airfield a few minutes before the appointed time. A few minutes later an Airspeed Oxford[17] came in to land and presently Tony came striding out of the main gate with his face wreathed in smiles. I saluted him smartly for the benefit of those present and we walked into the guardroom, where Tony informed the guard commander that 'he was collecting this NCO for liaison duties with the RAF.' We then proceeded to the aircraft which refused point blank to start its port engine. I think the pilot wore out two sets of ground crew on the inertia starter handle and after doping and cranking for a while the beast finally started. Tony was not flying the aircraft and was sitting on the floor with the rest of us in the back. He had asked me in his letters to get him a couple of 36 grenades (Mills bombs).[18] I don't know what he wanted them for but was only too pleased to oblige. As soon as we took off he shouted to me 'Have you brought my grenades?' I took one out of my webbing and tossed it to him. He missed the catch and it rolled across the floor of the aircraft. All the airmen who had come along for the ride leaped away from it like startled deer and all went as white as ghosts. Tony picked it up off the floor and put it in his pocket. The second one he caught like a professional cricketer. There were of course no detonators in the grenades. These I carried in a tobacco tin and gave over separately, two 3-second delay and two 7-second delay, with details of which colour was which. Grenades are quite safe

---

17 Twin-engined monoplane, manufactured by Airspeed throughout the 1930s, used for training aircrew.

18 The Mills bomb was designed by William Mills in Birmingham in 1915, the first in a series of fragmentation grenades used by the British Army in the First and Second World Wars.

if unfused and we used to practise throwing with live 36s on a grass surface. The trip to Sealand was uneventful and rather uninteresting since I was unable to see out of the small and very sparse windows and had no clue where we were. Finally we landed at Sealand and Tony saw me through the main gate on to the road. That was the last time I ever saw him, a true and loyal friend with whom I had been brought up like a brother. He was killed after two complete tours of operations in a crash on landing in an aircraft which he was not even flying.[19] Outside the gate of Sealand airfield I was able to hitch a ride home with ease. Leave was not really very enjoyable. My father was dead, none of my contemporaries were around and I had no car to use. I borrowed a bicycle and was able to visit a few old haunts but all the old magic had gone and I was not sorry to rejoin the regiment.

---

19 The Commonwealth War Graves Commission's records show that James Anthony Meade died aged 27 on 16 July 1943.

Chapter 5

8TH ARMOURED BRIGADE

In early November 1942 I was promoted to serjeant and in the same directive was posted away from F Section, 3 Div Sigs. I was extremely sorry to leave the section since all my military career had been spent in the company of friends such as Andrews and Stevens with whom I had joined up exactly three years previously. However there are many advantages in being posted on promotion to senior NCO. A corporal lives with the men and while discipline can be maintained in a properly run section, an underlying current of familiarity is unavoidable. If a newly promoted sergeant stayed with his old unit this familiarity would remain and would be detrimental to his performance as an NCO. On the other hand, a posting on promotion meant that a clean break could be made. You could move into a strange serjeants' mess without feeling in any way inferior, which could never happen if a move from 'men's mess' to serjeants' mess happened in the same unit. My new regiment was the 147th (Essex Yeomanry) Field Regiment RA and they were stationed at Cambuslang near Glasgow. The three batteries were 413, 431 and 511, which were located at various sites nearby. The OC signal section was a Lieutenant Max Phair, who was on leave when I arrived. I was greeted by the section serjeant Jock Moir, a diminutive thickset Dundee man who I took to immediately. His technical serjeant had been posted away some weeks before and he was glad to see me so that I could take some of the work off his shoulders. The line section was under the charge of Corporal Jack Halford, a brawny high-spirited Mancunian. His favourite expression to coax his men to greater efforts, even in beer drinking, was 'come on yer likkle jockey.' The two electricians were Corporal Harry Liley, from Hechmondwike, and his assistant Sigmn Matthews. The operators were headed by Corporals Whate from Newark on Trent and Coles from Burley in Wharfedale. Cliff Coles was a keen ornithologist and he and Whate were considerably older than the rest of the section, probably in their mid-thirties. After the war I visited Clifford Coles at his newsagent's shop in Burley on several occasions before his death in 1985. The regimental commander was Lieutenant Colonel Phayre[1] and I don't recall the name of the second-in-command but do remember that Cliff Coles christened him Toffee-arse and this he remained to all the RHQ personnel. It was quite strange to hear the accents of the Essex people in place of the broad Scots which I had become so used to. While the gunners were mainly from the Essex area, the Signal Section were mostly Mancunians from the remnants of the 42nd Armoured Div, which had been disbanded. The RSM was a genial shopkeeper from Colchester, a pleasant enough man but he lost interest in conversation after the initial handshake. The other warrant officers in the mess were the RQMS and Mr Rawsthorne, who was in charge of the Light Aid Detachment. The RHQ serjeants' mess was never more than 12 to 15 strong and had its own cooks and kitchen facilities. The mess furniture was ample and comfortable, quite unlike anything that I had encountered during my few days in the serjeants' mess at 76 Field Regiment. There everything had been spartan and general issue. Every Sunday a poker school was maintained as a ritual. It was a good thing that I had played quite frequently before I started soldiering and for this reason I was able to hold my own among the sharks. The main loser was the survey serjeant, a wealthy farmer from Halstead. He seemed quite content to lose four or five pounds every Sunday to his less well-off colleagues.

Less than a month after I joined 147th Fd Regt, a move took place to Muir of Ord, a very small place a few miles north-west of Inverness. I was amazed to be told that all personnel were to travel by train because all the transport was to be loaded with the furniture from the Officers' and the Serjeants' messes. Previously I had imagined that the majority of the stuff had been taken over with the billet but no such luck. I had never seen such a collection of odds and ends cluttering up a regimental headquarters. Every vehicle was loaded to bursting point with creature comforts. Even to a hall hatstand from the lobby of the Officers' mess. When I saw an elephant's foot umbrella stand being placed in a place of honour in the back of the CO's Z car, I knew I had witnessed the ultimate in regimental bullshit. Being a newcomer I was unable to protest too strongly at the way in which the wireless trucks and signal office wagon were being used as a sort of Pickfords

1 Robert Arthur Phayre, DSO.

removal service but I wondered what would happen in the event of a sudden move at a few minutes notice, which I had become used to at 76 Field. It seemed incredible that all the personnel of an RHQ should have to travel to a new location by train in order to make room for furniture and other paraphernalia that had been collected over a period of three years. The probable reason for the lack of in-built regimental discipline was the non-affiliation or membership of a parent unit such as a division or a brigade. At that time the 147th Field Regiment was an independent unit under the aegis of AGRA (Army Group Royal Artillery). This was a group of artillery units of all calibres, capable of being used in multi-purpose roles, as and when deemed necessary by an Army commander. These regiments were not attached permanently to any division but came under the command of units on a temporary basis when needed.

Our arrival at Muir of Ord station was late at night and was followed by a march with full kit to the billet a couple of miles away. A member of the advance party had been waiting at the station to show us the way. On the way the inevitable singing started, led by Corporal Whate. It consisted of one phrase only, an endless repetition of 'Blue bells are blue bells and blue bells are blue'. After many lusty choruses of this tuneful but monotonous ditty, I decided that it was time they were taught the Signals hymn as sung by 76 Highland Field Regt. After calling for silence I gave them my reedy falsetto rendering of the anthem:

'We are the Royal Signals
What f***ing use are we?
We cannot f*** we cannot fight[2]
We're full of misereee
And when we get to Berlin
The Fuhrer he will say
Hoch hoch mein Gott
What a bloody fine lot
Are the boys of the Signals Corps ...'

After two goes at it the whole section took to it like ducks to water. Serjeant Moir remarked that it was a pity they couldn't learn the contents of the training manual as quickly. On arrival at the billet a brew up awaited us followed by a mad scramble by the men to get the best bed spaces. Serjeant Moir had kept me half of his room on his

---

2 Pete's asterisks.

orders given to the advance party. At Cambuslang Serjeant Moir had occupied a room of his own and I very soon found out why the other serjeants had banished him to solitary sleeping. He ground his teeth! This might not sound a very serious fault in such a great character but I found it quite impossible to even contemplate the mildest of snoozes with such a racket going on. After a couple of nights, totally sleepless, I collected all the loose kit in the room and assembled it by my bed. When the cacophony started I picked up the first thing that came to hand and shied it at the wall above his bed, whence it dropped on him. Three minutes of blissful silence ensued and then it started again, grind, squeak, squeak, grind. When all my ammunition was exhausted I took a 'lamp, electric, hand' and went over to his bed and looked down at the recumbent sleep assassin. His lower jaw was moving in an exactly similar fashion to a ruminant animal chewing the cud, with perfect rhythm. Next day I moved out and joined the two corporal operators. When I asked for their approval for my move they said I'd been very stoic in sticking it for three nights and I was very welcome.

Muir of Ord was very isolated and lacked any form of entertainment for the troops, not even a WVS[3] tea wagon visited us. Gambling on cards and crown and anchor[4] became rife. The senior NCOs turned a blind eye to the gambling in the absence of any form of amusement. Housey housey or lotto was the only gambling allowed by King's Regulations and then only when supervised by a Warrant Officer. The drive up to the billet at Muir of Ord was not suitable for tracked vehicles and so the CO's tank was left on a strip of concrete outside a large corrugated iron building about half a mile from the RHQ. The building was totally plain, about thirty feet high with no windows and a large vehicle door at one end. In this sliding vehicle door was a small personnel door which opened on to the concrete apron on which our tank stood. After first works parade each morning it was my practice to send a couple of operators, L/Cpl Stan Lees and Sgmn Bill Dick, down to the tank with the driver, who was a gunner, to carry out maintenance and generally get lost and keep out of the way. At about ten thirty each day I would ride a despatch rider's bike down to see how they were progressing and smoke a pipe and yarn generally. Always there would be a brew of tea going, which made for a pleasant interlude. Invariably, standing in the small door at the end of the shed

---

3 Women's Voluntary Service.

4 A simple dice game using a die with, instead of numbers, the symbols of a crown, an anchor, and the four playing card suits.

would be a small man in a cloth cap. After several days the tank driver offered the old boy a brew of tea, which he accepted with alacrity. When invited to drink with us the following day, he approached with a mug in his hand and enquired 'are ye for a wee dram?' He sloshed a liberal dose of whisky into each mug of tea and had his own filled up with tea from the driver's brew can. Eventually we discovered that the building was a store where whisky was kept to mature and the old chap was the custodian of many thousands of barrels of spirit. He took us inside to look at the serried ranks of barrels from floor to ceiling and wall to wall. I mentioned it to Mr Phair, our OC, and he expressed an interest in joining us the next morning. I suggested that he wear a 'jeep coat' which had no badges of rank. As we stood around waiting for the water to boil, the old boy came out with his mug as usual but stood some distance away until he was reassured that the newcomer was not hostile. The OC was treated to a conducted tour of the building. It was strange that Mr Phair always happened to be in the vicinity of the tank at 1030 hrs each day. That tank was the best-maintained vehicle in the RHQ. The tank itself was a standard Sherman from which the gun had been removed and replaced by a dummy barrel on the front of the turret. The space provided by the removal of the gun and ammunition racks was filled with map boards and an extra radio set for lateral communication to whichever brigade we became attached to. I don't think the Colonel was particularly enamoured of the claustrophobic conditions in the tank and most often the Adjutant was told to make use of it. In theory I was the Adjutant's operator and so had first claim to ride in the only armour in the RHQ.

The end of January 1943 brought news of a probable move southward again and speculation was rife as to when and where. The RHQ sanitary orderly (an Essex man) was certain that Colchester would be the next location. He was to be proved slightly out in his prediction but not much. It finally filtered out of the Orderly Room that the destination was Brandon, a small village close to the border between Norfolk and Suffolk, but actually in Suffolk, thereby making the sanitary orderly only one county adrift in his clairvoyance. I was horrified when the ritual of loading all the junk began again, each wagon bulging with the awful stuff. The guns were loaded on to flatcars at a local station for the journey south. This was considered common sense since such a long road journey would cause far too much wear and tear not only to the tracks but also to the roads. The regimental move occupied a whole train apart from the vehicles and personnel that travelled by road. Under the conditions prevailing at the time the journey took over eighteen hours, not counting the time spent waiting in various sidings for higher-priority traffic to pass. The entire section was pretty jaded when we finally arrived at Brandon but not too tired to notice the incredible flatness of the terrain. We could literally stand on the top of a truck and look into the next county.

The Regiment, soon after our arrival at Brandon, became affiliated to 8th Armoured Brigade. This Brigade had fought with distinction in the desert campaigns and was very battle hardened. While still AGRA troops, we were attached to the Brigade for training, so closely in fact that we wore the fox mask insignia on our shoulders and were issued with the black berets of armoured troops.[5] The 8th Armoured Brigade was made up of three very distinguished formations – the 4th/7th Dragoon Guards, the 13th/18th Hussars and the 17th/21st Lancers. It seemed fitting that such a Brigade should have its own armoured artillery regiment of self-propelled guns in support and we were proud to be attached to and affiliated with such a fine unit. As a regiment we did not see a great deal of our parent Brigade and we assumed that they were off somewhere engaged in 'aquatic sports' on the south coast. The 13th/18th Hussars were to become the leading exponents of the 'swimming' tanks and had Shermans fitted with a pneumatically supported skirt for buoyancy and screws in the water for propulsion. These screws were driven by the normal engine of the armoured fighting vehicle, AFV. The flat eastern side of England was in those days plastered with aerodromes both British and American and every place of entertainment was crowded with airmen. They called us 'pongos' and we always referred to them as 'Brylcreem boys'.[6] They had much nicer boots than ours, much lighter in weight and no toecaps and much easier to polish. At every village hop one would find dozens of airmen lined up to dance with the local maidens. In the gents toilets one would find rows of RAF boots where their owners had left them after donning their dancing pumps. Two of us would make for the gents and heave all the RAF boots in sight out of the window to be picked up by our colleagues waiting outside. On parade the RSM

---

5 Black berets were found to be of practical use to troops working on armoured vehicles because they would not show oil stains. Their use was officially adopted by the Royal Tank Regiment in 1924 and other armoured formations followed suit.

6 Brylcreem is a British brand of hair-styling products for men. There's been at least one film and one television play about servicemen in the RAF called the Brylcreem Boys. Referring to soldiers as 'pongos' began in the Royal Navy rather than in the RAF – there are several theories about the term's origin.

asked our Section Serjeant how we had been issued with different boots. Serjeant Jock Moir mumbled something vague about 'special Signals issue' and it was left to blow over. In fact the boots were no more comfortable than our own 'ammos', it was just the satisfaction of 'Brylcreem baiting'.

A few weeks after our move to Brandon, Serjeant Moir was posted and his replacement took a long time to arrive. I was able to move into Jock's quarters and establish myself away from the senior corporals. Both were splendid fellows but they liked their privacy and I liked mine. It was mid-March before Teddy Edwards arrived as a replacement for Jock Moir. Teddy was a chemist from South Wales. I was very glad to see him as I hated administration and I had been doing his job for the three weeks since Jock's departure. The first evening after his arrival we took a Jeep and went to a pub a few miles distant where we could discuss the Section in private. As newcomers to the Section we were both able to take a long hard look at the peculiarities of the regiment as a unit. I had been part of the lean, hard efficiency of the 76 (H) Field Regt, which had received its polish from Lieutenant Colonel Shoesmith, and Teddy had just returned from the Middle East campaign. We were both able to see glaring instances of slackness and inefficiency. In my long talk with him Teddy didn't give much away about himself and apart from his being married I wasn't able to learn a great deal. I didn't even discover whether he was in retail chemistry or research or whatever. He was even reticent about his activities in Egypt. Over the years I had learned not to pry if a man was not immediately forthcoming with personal details. I had brought a nominal roll of the Section with me and we went through each man and I gave Teddy my own assessment of each one as they impressed me personally. One man's meat, however, is another man's poison. I could only give my own opinion. I did make it quite clear to Teddy that I was very glad that he had joined us and that I was prepared to cooperate with him to the full. We both agreed at the outset that everyone had a better chance of staying alive in an efficient section. The officer commanding the Section, Lieutenant E.M. Phair, had been a master at Epsom College for a considerable time. I thought that he was rather too soft in as much as he tended to treat the men like fourth and fifth formers rather than mature soldiers. After all, the vast majority of them had at least three years' service behind them and like any squaddie would take advantage of a soft touch if possible. Max Phair was at times far too lenient for the good of the Section. We could never decide whether the Regimental Commander, Lieutenant Colonel Phayre, was a good leader surrounded by idiots or whether the others were efficient and led by a nut. I had warned Teddy about the amount of gear that the Regiment carried about with them and we both decided that the Signal Section would be pared down to fighting weight regardless of what the rest of the Headquarters was going to do. When loading started for the next move to the south coast to continue with assault training both Teddy and I supervised the loading of each truck. Any article that was not on the G1098 scale of issue was discarded among howls of protests from the troops. We rummaged around in each vehicle and found all sorts of ridiculous articles such as bedside table lamps and large civilian radio sets that had been loaded in spite of our express orders to the contrary. Serjeant Teddy Edwards gave me a direct order to put the offending men on a charge. This I did and they were tried by the OC the day after we arrived at our new location. This put the OC in a very awkward position since his pick-up had been loaded to its utmost capacity with all kinds of non-military paraphernalia. We had achieved exactly what we had set out to do and put the OC in a position where he had to listen to what his senior NCOs were saying. He gave each of the culprits seven days confined to barracks, not for carrying non-army gear but for disobeying a direct order from the Section Serjeant. People were beginning to get the message. Confinement to barracks was an easy ride physically but it meant that the stigma went on the soldier's history sheet and who the hell cared about that unless he was preparing to set a foot on the promotion ladder.

At a Section conference attended by the OC, Teddy and I, together with the four corporals – Cliff Coles and Eric Whate, Operators, Jack Halford, Line Section, and Harry Liley, Electrician Signals – Teddy explained at length what we were trying to accomplish in getting the Section down to fighting weight. Teddy and I had both been in sections where nothing was carried other than the bare G1098 scale of equipment. Collapsible beds and civvy mattresses were definitely out! This last jibe was a direct tilt at the OC since we had seen his batman, Pugsley, carrying these things into the officers' quarters after our move from Brandon. Teddy contended that soft living would have to end when we went into action and it would come as a hell of a shock unless the Section started to harden off immediately. All present could do nothing but agree and it was resolved that no further odds and sods would be accumulated by the troops and that an example would be set by the NCOs. When Teddy had finished speaking and we had all nodded agreement, the OC's face was quite impassive and it was impossible to tell whether he would be carrying out the good intentions or not. We could easily find out what was going on in the Officers' Mess from Driver Pugsley. We the NCOs had every intention of whipping the Section into shape since we had all agreed that the assault on the mainland of Europe could come at any time. It would be better for us to be efficient and ready for real action at all times.

The Regiment moved to Bournemouth at the beginning of April 1943. For me it was the second time to have been posted there. Our main concern was the practising of assault landings. The landing craft would be loaded in the morning and afternoon on a couple of days a week. The crews would embark and then the whole fleet of landing craft would cruise around all night and make an assault on the beaches as dawn was breaking. Most often it was possible to get ashore without 'getting yer feet wet'. This was up to the RASC cox of the landing craft in question. If he was in a funny mood or had been bollocked by a Regimental officer during the night he would lower the ramp while still forty or fifty yards from the tide line. It was the responsibility of the cox to extricate his craft from the beach in order to return to an LSI[7] to embark more troops to reinforce the assault. Depending on how steeply the beach shelved, it was possible to drop the ramp above the waterline on some occasions.

One of the greatest tragedies of the war occurred during one of these night exercises off the south coast. A flotilla of American LSIs and LCTs were caught well off the coast by a group of German E boats.[8] The resulting sinkings caused hundreds of GIs to be drowned. Needless to say the whole matter was hushed up and never appeared in the local or national press. For a long time after the event, bodies continued to be washed up along the coast. Most of the Signal Section were allotted to various LCTs which carried the SP guns and a mixture of armoured and soft-skinned vehicles. The idea was to avoid putting

---

7 Landing ship infantry.

8 German *schnellboots*, or fast attack boats, were designated E-boats by the Allies – E for Enemy. During Exercise Tiger at Slapton Sands in Devon at the end of April 1944, 749 Americans were killed by E-boats based in Cherbourg. It would be an interesting piece of research to establish when and how the details of the Operation Tiger actually emerged. One account of Exercise Tiger is contained in *The Forgotten Dead*, a book by a local hotelier, Ken Small, whose campaign to commemorate the GI s included raising a Sherman tank from the seabed and using it as a memorial. In the immediate aftermath of the German assault, ten American servicemen with high security clearance were missing. The men had knowledge of the plans for D-Day and General Eisenhower ordered that the men's bodies must be found before the invasion could begin.

all our eggs in one basket. Senior NCOs all travelled on different craft. In theory I was supposed to be the Adjutant's operator but since the CO always wanted the Adjutant to be in personal attendance two other operators were always available. These were L/Cpl Stan Lees and Sgmn Bill Dick. Lees worked laterally to Brigade while Dick was in constant touch with RHQ and the three batteries. In this way the CO had instant control of regimental fire power. During any assault we travelled in the same LCM (landing craft mechanised). These were tiny craft capable of carrying a Bren gun carrier and a motorcycle and about ten bodies. In practice we found that the larger craft were the most likely to be shot at and we were quite happy to continue to sail in our little boats, to which we had become accustomed by many hours of observing fall of shot around Inchmarnock in the Kyles of Bute. It was quite surprising that so few vehicles were 'drowned' in driving ashore off the landing craft. We had mastered the art of waterproofing and could land vehicles like three-ton trucks in four or five feet of water. Tanks and SP guns had a great advantage in that they were tracked and had a much greater purchase on the sandy bottom. On a real assault all waterproofing and snorkels could be ripped off after landing to improve the aspiration of the carburettors. On these exercises we had to preserve the efficiency of the waterproofing or 'drown'. It was quite alarming to drive down the very steep ramp of the LCT and not know whether the bottom was there or not. We of the LCM department were more than happy to walk ashore in the wake of the Brigade commander, who rode in the Bren gun carrier on which our CO also cadged a ride. The Brigadier's dispatch rider took pot luck on whether he could get his machine ashore.

During the winter of 1943 the Regiment visited artillery practice camps at Okehampton in Devon and Sennybridge in South Wales. Practice camps were always a good opportunity for signals exercises, during which live fire orders could be passed from OP officers observing fall of shot or from infantry troops as far forward as battalion requiring support. Air Observation Post (AOP) aircraft were also used to familiarise the operators and pilot with the modus operandi. The AOP officer attached to the Regiment was a Royal Artillery captain who had been trained by the RAF to fly light aircraft. It was rather incongruous to see RAF brevets on Khaki battledress but they were worn with obvious pride, particularly with service dress or mess kit. The aircraft were of several different types and were capable of flying from very limited airstrips. All were totally unarmed and very vulnerable to even rifle fire from enemy on the ground. Having flown many hours as operator in Lysanders from Larkhill I had a very real fellow feeling for the AOP boys, who in my opinion were incredibly brave when enemy fighters were looking for blood. We were to witness later a pilot flying round a clump of trees much to the frustration of the pilot of an ME109.[9] The same officer was later to reduce height to avoid enemy aircraft and fly into the trajectory of shells from his own guns. So died a very gallant officer.

The tempo of training was kept up all through the winter and into March 1944. By this time the whole of the south of England was like a huge garrison town with troops of several nationalities occupying every building in sight. The Americans seemed to be mainly over to the west, in vast numbers, in Cornwall, Devon and Somerset. Canadians, Free French, Poles and contingents of smaller nations all crowded cheek by jowl. We had no way of knowing what the rest of England looked like or whether the concentration of soldiery was as heavy further north. Security was intense. Lectures covered every aspect of the subject. Mail was strictly censored. The troops were well aware that their safety and even lives could depend on tight security being maintained. For this reason all ranks had enough sense to ease the burden of censoring officers by writing only of trivialities and family matters, and not even referring to regimental comrades by name. We knew that a huge assault was coming but we did not know where and we did not know when. We knew that our brigade would be on the initial beach landings by the very nature of our long training. We also knew that the assault would be up a sandy beach. We spent hours poring over school atlas maps trying to pinpoint likely areas where we might land.

We received new vehicles both soft and armoured. The soft trucks were mainly three-tonners, ours being Austins but Bedford and Commer lorries came to other units. Standardisation of vehicles was aimed at in units to make spare parts and repair availability less complex. The light armour in the Signal Section comprised a Bren gun carrier for the line party, and two International half-tracks[10] for 19 sets to maintain links to the Batteries, Brigade and Division. Since we were AGRA artillery we might be attached to any unit in the 2nd Army so

9 Messerschmitt Me 109, Nazi Germany's, and probably the world's, most-produced fighter plane. More than thirty thousand were built from 1936. The Spitfire was slightly faster and had a tighter turn but the Me 109 could climb much more quickly because of its fuel-injected engine.

10 The M5 half-track made by International Harvester was, as the name suggests, an armoured personnel carrier with large tyres at the front and tracks set at the rear.

we had to play the Brigade and Divisional links by ear and come in on a strange net as an outstation as circumstances demanded. When all the new vehicles had arrived and had been waterproofed the old trucks stood all forlorn under camouflage netting awaiting disposal.

Early in May 1944 the CO's party, comprising the Colonel and Adjutant, a Bombardier clerk/orderly, myself and Lees and Dick the two operators, together with a Bren gun carrier driver and a DR, boarded a Navy frigate HMS *Nith* at Southampton and were signed on as crew members.[11] I was allotted hammock space in a petty officers' mess which had twelve occupants. I made the number thirteen. Instantly all twelve Naval personnel of the mess drew lots to decide which of them should move into other quarters so as to avoid the dreaded number thirteen. I volunteered to sleep in the passage outside but they would not hear of it and it was settled among themselves. I couldn't sleep in a hammock, having tried it before, and opted to sleep on the floor under the messroom table. Once settled on board we met the Brigadier's party and were given a long briefing as to what was to happen on the assault. At last things were beginning to move. We were told that we, the command party, would be going in on the *Nith* until three miles out from the beach. At H hour minus fifteen minutes we would transfer to our usual LCM for the run in. We were scheduled to hit the beach at H plus 30 minutes, just as our guns were doing the run-in shoot from the LCTs. The Dual Drive (swimming) tanks of 13th/18th Hussars of 8th Armoured Brigade should by this time have gone up the beach to clear any opposition from the immediate beach area. The division we were going with was 50th (Northumbrian) and the assault brigade would be 231 Brigade. Up to now we did not know that the Brigadier with whom we had so often 'gone up the beach' was indeed the commander of 231 Bde. All the bits and pieces were beginning to fall into place. [12]

---

11 HMS *Nith*, launched in September 1942, was originally dedicated for convoy escort missions. Sea trials indicated she could also be suitable for amphibious operations. She was the Brigade headquarters ship for the 231st Infantry Brigade on D-Day, responsible for coordinating the Brigade's landing at Jig sector of Gold Beach. In 1948 the frigate *Nith* was sold to Egypt, where she was renamed the *Domiat*. During the build-up to the crisis over the Suez Canal in 1956 the *Domiat* was sunk by HMS *Newfoundland*, which rescued 69 of her crew. The light cruiser *Newfoundland* was later to be sold to the Peruvian navy.

12 The commander of 231 Brigade on D-Day was Brigadier Sir Alexander Beville Gibbons Stanier, DSO and Bar, MC, 2nd Baronet of Peplow Hall.

The following morning we moved back to camp near Fawley with the knowledge of how and with whom we would attack but without a clue as to when and where. The same procedure of boarding the frigate *Nith* took place again in mid-May and this time we went over the side of the ship on a scrambling net down to our LCM. All went well except for our CO who was rather portly and encumbered with map case, pistol, binoculars, and God knows what else. Everything got caught up in the net and a couple of matelots had to help free him and rather unsuccessfully hide their mirth at the same time. The Brigadier tactfully gazed out towards the Isle of Wight until all were aboard. That time we travelled home in the LCM and did a tiny landing of our own near Fawley and walked back to camp on our own flat feet. It was not our place to advise the CO about the kit he was trying to carry. Admittedly he would probably need his map case and so forth but surely he didn't need binoculars when the Adjutant carried a pair. Also in the party we had several Sten guns and at least one Thompson .45 calibre sub machine gun. So why did the CO need to carry a combless .38 Enfield pistol?[13] As I have said it was not our place to interfere but I did remark as much to the Adjutant who told me that he had already suggested that the OC lighten his load and had received an offhand reply.

Stan Lees, Bill Dick and I had long since got the loading of our kit down to a fine art. We assumed that after the first few hours ashore we would either be casualties or have joined up with the rest of the Regimental Headquarters and its transport upon which the bulk of our personal kit would be carried. The two operators, being responsible to the Brigade for passing requests for fire support, had as their main concern the No 18 backpack sets. These were in waterproof bags and carried after the style of a Bergen rucksack with aerials and microphone and headset leads brought out through rubber bushes. Over the actual headphones we stretched French letters and tied the surplus around the leads with thin string. The same procedure was carried out with the microphone, the rubber being thin enough to keep out any water and still be capable of transmitting sound. In this way we were never switched off, even when wading ashore on a wet landing. Our Army

13 The comb on a gun is that part of a rifle or shotgun which rests against the shooter's cheek as they aim. The comb can be adjustable to suit different users to enhance their accuracy. In this context I take 'combless' to be a necessary characteristic of a pistol, meaning that it is by definition less accurate. However, the .38 Enfield revolver was the standard British sidearm of the Second World War and it surely can't have been unusual for officers leading their men into battle to carry one.

and our personal watches were also carried in our breast pockets tied up in issue French letters. We had adopted this idea way back in the early trials at Fort George with great success. When the Brigadier first saw our sets done up in this way he was very amused but still passed the tip on to his Brigade Signals officer. As previously stated, the two operators carried nothing but their sets which gave them almost complete freedom of movement. In a Bergen rucksack I carried the personal kit of all three of us. This only consisted of spare socks, mess kit, shaving tackle and a few odds and ends vitally necessary. I also carried my pistol and the two Sten guns of the operators. Having once been in the drink over the side I made sure we had belt buckles that would undo with great ease and that no arms were slung in a way that would prevent them being discarded instantly if we fell in. Further issues of kit were made during the last days of May. Felt-soled assault boots were a great joy. These were light, comfortable and did not slip on the deck of a boat. A flat tin of Players cigarettes was also issued. The tins had a flip up lid and had a piece of sticky tape around to keep them waterproof. I had to find room in my rucksack for three lots of emergency rations consisting of compressed sweetened oatmeal, boiled sweets and malted milk tablets. I asked Lees and Dick if they wanted to carry their own rations and Dick said 'If you get hit Serj we'll bloody well starve and we won't shave for days either!'

We could feel that time was getting short and when new batteries were issued for the packsets it was a sure indication that action was imminent. Dry batteries were always treated like gold and getting them out of the Q-bloke was rather like asking him for blood. Woe betide any operator who left his set switched on when not in use. An order came to do maintenance on the sets. This to my way of thinking was pure nonsense. Poking about inside the waterproofing could only do more harm than good. I told my operators to leave things alone while everything was still working and just pretend to be busy with the sets. Since the 18 set had valves with 1.5 volt filaments they were very vulnerable to shock and we had trained our operators to be aware of this fact with the result that the sets were treated with great care. I never remember a packset being out of use due to rough handling. Those in use by the Infantry did come in for much more rough treatment. If an infantryman was called upon to throw himself into a ditch or slit trench for self-preservation he was not going to worry about the wireless set on his back. Most infantry units were using 38 or 58 sets by this time and these were worn on the front of the body after the style of a large ammunition pouch with the aerial sticking up over the shoulder.

When the first days of June arrived and we were issued with 'scrip', or currency issued by the allies for use in France, we knew for certain that our destination was to be French territory. The issue of the scrip was a signal for everyone to start playing poker for quite high stakes. It seemed like Bank of Toytown money and the good players soon had many thousands of francs to their credit. All this in spite of repeated warnings of dire consequences if the scrip was lost, misused or traded with before we reached the other side of the Channel. While security was still very strict, we were being given more and more information all the time. This was because we were in a sealed area and by this time it was impossible to get in or out of the camps. On the afternoon of 4 June, Lees, Dick and I were taken by road to join HMS *Nith*. When on board we signed on as crew members and met up with the Brigadier's party and went below to a briefing by our CO. We were told that 50th (Northumbrian) Division would be assaulting Gold beach, located almost opposite Bayeux in Normandy. The beach was about 100 miles due south of our present position. We already knew the order of battle from previous briefings. 231 Brigade was to assault the beach at 0700 hrs supported by tanks of the 13th/18th Hussars and artillery of the 147th Field Regiment. On our immediate left on Juno beach the Canadians of the 3rd Canadian Infantry Division were to land at the same time as ourselves. Further to our left 3rd British Infantry Division was to take Sword beach. On our right, further to the west, the Americans were to land on two beaches, namely Omaha on our immediate right and Utah, the most westerly of the landing areas. Omaha beach was to become known as 'bloody Omaha'.

Our briefing by the CO was long and detailed. He showed on large-scale maps exactly where we were to go ashore and the immediate objectives of 231 Bde. 50 Div was to take Bayeux by nightfall on the first day ashore. On our left 3rd Cdn Inf Div and 3rd Br Inf Div were to advance on Caen. Mention was made of large-scale parachute and glider-borne landings but here details were rather vague and the drop zones were not revealed. We were not privy to this information because it transpired that we would not link up with the airborne forces. Gold beach, our Brigade landing area, was divided into three sections, Item, Jig and King. Our section, Jig, was the longest and faced the village of Arromanches and almost reached Port-en-Bessin, the former being right in the line of our Brigade advance. We were told that the beach was sandy with low sandhills beyond and a sandy track running parallel to the beach a hundred yards inland. This track was the primary objective for the first wave of infantry and would probably act as a path for lateral communication and we were told not to cause any congestion on it. Finally the CO became less military and mused that this type of briefing was going on all over the south of England at this very moment. Just before he finished his address he informed us that the first day's casualties had been estimated to be about 25 per cent. After delivering this cheerful piece of news he wished us all the best of luck and said that any further information would be passed on to us as soon as he received it. In view of the fact that we were no longer alongside the dock but out in the Solent we did a few sums and calculated that the distance could be covered with ease. We decided that 5 June would be the big day!

We decided to get our heads down early on the evening of the 4th but anyone who has been aboard a small Naval ship will realise that sleep is virtually impossible under the table of a petty officers' mess. I gave up the idea of sleep and fished out my pipe intending to fill it with tobacco. To my disgust I found that the stem was cracked where the mouthpiece fitted into the bowl section. In consequence the pipe was unsmokable. One of the POs who was playing Mah Jong saw my problem and took the pipe away to return half an hour later with a very neat brass band turned and fitted to the stem, making the job stronger and more attractive than the original. That pipe was to last for years after the war, brass band and all. When I did eventually doze off, the mess, which was no bigger than the average small kitchen, had become very hot and sleep was not restful. The thoughts of what might happen on the following morning had become less harrowing since the main engines had not been used and the time available to cover the 100 miles to Gold beach was just not great enough. We, the Army personnel aboard, had noticed on previous occasions that the Navy never seemed to eat breakfast but had an early dinner about midday. Just before dinner 'up spirits' was piped and the men were issued with their rum ration. I am not sure what the dilution rate was for the lower ranks but Lees and Dick started to talk rubbish with eyes glazed and speech slurred. The POs and senior Army people received a less dilute ration and I gasped when it hit the back of my throat and shortly afterwards I too began to slur my words to the vast amusement of the assembled POs. They told us that it was all a matter of getting used to it! What with the lack of breakfast and the aperitif effect of the rum I was absolutely ravenous and could, as Corporal Jack Halford would have put it, 'have eaten a baby that had died of smallpox.' I enjoyed my dinner.

During the afternoon of the 5th we were given another briefing by the CO. This took the form of a refresher to the previous talks. He did add what we took to be a few observations of his own. The nub of the position was that the moon and the tide suitable for the landings would only last for a few days and unless we went soon the whole thing could be delayed for another month when conditions would again become suitable. The same thought passed through everyone's mind. 'Let's go now and get stuck in!' The CO ended his chat by wishing us luck again and bade us check our arms and equipment. We had all checked and cleaned our arms a dozen times already. I carried a Luger Parabellum pistol that one of my uncles had brought home from the 14-18 war. It had been kicking around our home ever since.[14] When the Sten guns came into use the 9 mm ammunition was an exact fit for the Luger. I had left my issue small arm, a Sten, in the Regimental transport because I was carrying the two Stens of Lees and Dick. I had always fancied a Colt .45 automatic as issued to the GIs. Wishful thinking of course.[15] The operators asked if they should check the nets but I told them to leave the bloody things alone since all the fiddling in the world would not improve them and might upset the netting. We just mooned about the deck and got a lungful of fresh air. We had not had a great deal of time to take in the salient points of HMS *Nith*. We knew she was a frigate only because we heard the matelots say so. We could see that she carried no heavy armaments such as a 4-inch gun. All we could see were lots of Oerlikons and multiple pom-poms.[16] The weather was overcast and quite a strong breeze was blowing. It had not occurred to us that the weather was holding up the operation. We did not know when things were scheduled to start so we could not know if there had been a hold-up. One thing that the Army was good at was waiting and the longer the delay, the further away were those 25 per cent casualties. Just as it was getting dusk the screws started to turn and the ship moved very slowly down the Solent between Ryde and Pompey. A

---

14 The Pistole Parabellum, designed by Georg Luger, was a semi-automatic pistol produced in several variations from 1898 to 1949.

15 The Colt M1911, designed by John Moses Browning, was used by American troops throughout both world wars.

16 The Oerlikon, a 20mm anti-aircraft and anti-tank cannon, is a gun with an interesting history. It was produced in Germany during the First World War but the Treaty of Versailles banned the production of such weapons in Germany so the patents and design works were transferred to Switzerland. The Oerlikon is named after the suburb of Zurich where it was manufactured. The British-made QF (quick-firing) 2-pounder guns were nicknamed pom-poms because of the sound they made when they were discharged. They were 40mm anti-aircraft guns made by Vickers and used by the Royal Navy.

mass of shipping of all sizes and types were being swallowed up by the oncoming darkness. Goodbye England! The build-up of excitement made sleep very difficult and I was separated from my operators by being in the Stoker POs' mess and they in the seamen's mess. I missed being able to assure them that all was going to be well with us. I must have dozed fitfully because when I woke the movement of the ship suggested that it was quite choppy outside. Then I must have nodded off again.

Chapter 6

D-DAY AND THE BATTLE OF NORMANDY

Bonjour Normandie! At 0430 hours on 6 June the loud hailers on HMS *Nith* called all hands to stand to. I grabbed my kit and moved to our assembly point on deck, where Lees and Dick joined me. I made sure that all our gear was present and that the operators were carrying the correct sets. A swap over of roles could cause chaos. It was still quite dark and the sea was pretty rough. The rest of our party was assembled close by and someone suggested that we should divest ourselves of the back packs since it was nowhere near time to board our LCM. Lees said in a voice loud enough for all to hear 'Just like the Navy to send us ashore without any bloody breakfast.' I'm sure that in the heat of the moment no one had thought of food but once the subject was broached it became of paramount importance. Our CO spoke to the First Lieutenant and the First Lieutenant spoke to the catering officer and the catering officer spoke to the PO cook, who probably detailed a cook to feed us. Fifteen minutes later all the army people received a greasy fried egg between two pieces of bread and a mug of cocoa. Dick commented 'This should come up nicely.' This was not very kind because the CO's orderly room Serjeant Clerk was not a very good sailor and was already looking rather green about the gills. We wondered what the officers were having for breakfast in the wardroom.

As it gradually became light the sight that met our eyes was almost beyond description. Ships, ships and more ships. The lighter it became the more ships came into view, all sailing in the same direction, south. Overhead we could hear aircraft above the cloud. There seemed to be a continuous stream of them. Suddenly there came the most appalling, devastating and mind-bending crash of gunfire as several battleships quite close to us opened up with salvo after salvo of their main armaments. Broadsides of shells that weighed almost half a ton each went screaming off to land God only knew where but we hoped squarely on the German coastal guns. What we didn't know was that the airborne boys were at that very moment dealing with the coastal guns. Normally in June it becomes light shortly after four o'clock each morning but it must be remembered that British Double Summer Time was in operation and it was still light at almost eleven o'clock at night. For this reason it was still dark later in the mornings. By 0545 hours it was fully light and we could see the coast about four miles away. Smoke was rising from some point ashore and it could have been caused by the Naval shellfire or the RAF bombing. Looking northwards we could see the tremendous collection of shipping that was following us.

Shortly after 0615 hours we prepared to board our LCM. It was on the port side of *Nith* and fairly sheltered but still bobbing up and down like a cork. Lees, Dick and I were down the net and on the LCM in a few moments, as were the more able members of the party. The last to descend were the Brigadier and our CO. We noticed that there were two matelots halfway down the net to render assistance should the need arise. Craftily the kit of our CO had been lowered into the LCM on a line. He descended unencumbered. Many bawdy catcalls were passed between the matelots and soldiers as we prepared to let go – suggestions as to what the Navy would do to the mademoiselles had they been in our place. As we left the side of the ship under our own power a Lieutenant Commander shouted through a megaphone 'Three cheers for the landing party!' There followed a truly Naval, caps off and waving three cheers that could be heard loud and clear over the thunder of gunfire. On our LCM there wasn't a dry eye. Some hairy-arsed gunner muttered to cover his embarrassment 'What a bullshitting shower of bastards.' The stoker petty officers of our tiny mess on *Nith* had made me promise to send them a card to inform them of our welfare. From our lowly position in the LCM we were unable to see what progress was being made by the 'R' boats carrying the assault infantry and beach Signals party. According to the time schedule, our regimental run-in shoot should be about to start, also the 'hedgehogs' – low-trajectory rocket launchers designed to cut a swathe up the beach to destroy any mines or obstacles in the path of the infantry. Sure enough, almost dead on time the swoosh of the rockets and staccato cracks of the 25-pounders on the LCTs started up. Through the French letter covering my watch I could see that it was

0610 hours.[1] The infantry and first of the DD tanks should be ashore by now. Later we found that the DD tanks had not swum in but had been taken right to the beach and driven off on the heels of the infantry, which must have been very comforting for the footsloggers.[2] By now we could see the beach defences. Lots of steel RSJs and bits of pipe welded together to form lethal-to-boats obstacles. The nasty ones were a post with an 88mm shell strapped to the top and a detonator plate pointing seaward. All kinds of other diabolical nasties were waiting for the unwary.

From about a hundred yards out we could see the odd body lying on the sand above the waterline and a brewed-up tank just short of the sand dunes. The Brigadier yelled to us 'Don't stop to help casualties, get clear of the beach.' The RASC cox was looking for a clear way in between the obstacles and stalled his engine (Scripps modified Ford V-8), which steadfastly refused to restart. By this time the LCM had drifted broadside on to the tide and as I looked over the side I could see an 88mm postmounted shell about to brush the side. I leaned back as far as I could against the Bren carrier and the shell exploded almost under my feet. The decking upon which we stood was about a foot above the actual skin of the LCM but the detonation made my feet smart through the felt-soled assault boots. The inrush of water into the lower compartment made the starting of the engine an impossibility and the Brigadier called to the cox to lower the ramp. We had drifted bow-on to the beach again and could see the shit flying ashore. As senior officer the Brigadier sat on the end of the ramp and lowered himself into the water. At his mid chest his feet touched the bottom and he yelled 'All right Phayre, get the party ashore.' The Colonel went next and being a shortish, plump officer he was only just in his depth. Even in such a dire predicament we all giggled at the figure he cut with his steel helmet knocked over his eyes. We all followed off the LCM which had by this time settled by the stern and was a total loss taking the Bren carrier and motorcycle with her. Another slight snag arose for the Colonel. There was a small dip in the bottom between us and dry land. I could see the Brigadier almost above his breast pockets in water.

---

1 At the beginning of the paragraph, yet to board the LCM, it was shortly after 0615. At this point Pete probably means 0710. The war diary of 147th Field Regiment says H Hour was 0730 hrs, and in his briefing (see above) Pete's CO said 231 Brigade was to assault the beach at 0700.

2 A reminder that Duplex Drive tanks, nicknamed Donald Duck tanks, were amphibious 'swimming' tanks developed by the British.

This meant that the Colonel would be totally awash. Fortunately the Adjutant and the Serjeant Clerk were both fairly tall and took him by both arms and virtually carried him to water that was more shallow. The air in our waterproof bags helped to keep the operators afloat but tended to impede forward progress by lessening the grip of our feet on the bottom. Finally we reached the edge of the water. The weight of our water-sodden clothing and gear was incredible and we were literally forced to our knees for the first few stumbling yards. The beach was fairly well pitted by craters from what we afterwards assumed to be mortar bombs but we didn't stop to look. I told Lees and Dick to follow me and then made a dash for the dunes from which reasonable shelter we watched the CO strolling up the beach too buggered to even trot. As soon as he joined us he told Dick to call up the Batteries and find out who was ashore by this time. We received replies from 413 and 511 but no word from 431. They were all ashore, we were assured by the gun position officer of 413 Bty, who claimed that he could see parts of 431 Bty quite near his position.

The Brigadier was anxious to join his headquarters and went off to do a recce along the road running parallel to the beach. We were told to follow and halt near the roadside and keep our heads down. We needed no telling as there was a fair amount of naughties flying around. On the way to the road we passed several dead jerries and one of our infantry lying on a wheelbarrow with both his legs blown off just above the knees. He was dead and we assumed he had stepped on a mine but it could have been a shell or a mortar bomb. We found the sandy track and were delighted to find a fair ditch on the landward side of it. We dropped into the ditch and saw a barbed wire fence between the ditch and a scrubby field. Hung at intervals on the wire were red notices bearing a skull and crossbones and the legend 'Achtung Minen' and 'Attention des Mines'. We got out of the ditch smartly in case some crafty kraut had sown a few mines in the bottom of the ditch. While we waited I suggested that the boys get the seawater out of our weapons and we all shook the water out as best we could since none of us had even a dry handkerchief. At this time there appeared a lonely-looking American soldier, quite dry and carrying a map case and little else. The poor lad seemed almost in tears and I asked him if he had lost his outfit. He replied that he was attached to 50 Div for liaison duties. I told him that the commander 231 Brigade would be along shortly and he seemed to be less upset. I casually unhitched my water bottle to have a drink of water and after taking a swig I almost choked. It was full of Naval rum! The boys on the *Nith* must have doctored it while I was asleep. We had good swigs all round and soon the young

American was talking fluent rubbish, as Lees and Dick had done on *Nith*. I made sure that neither of my operators had too much. I pulled out my pistol to give it a final shake and to check the magazine for freedom from sand. When the American saw it was a Luger he went mad with delight and asked me where I had got it from. After glancing at Lees I said that it had been taken from a German officer. The Yank marvelled at our having captured a German after only being ashore a few minutes. He pulled out a stack of notes from his breast pocket, a mixture of dollar bills and pound notes, and thrust them at me. I told him that I would trade it for his Colt .45. He wrenched out his pistol so quickly that I thought he was going to shoot me and the deal was done. I wonder what yarns he spun to his buddies when he joined his own outfit.

The Brigadier and our CO returned and told Dick to call 413 Bty and get an SP (self-propelled) gun to report to our present position. While we waited for the gun to arrive I offered the officers a pull at my water bottle after explaining the reason for my having the rum. They had a long pull and blessed the stoker POs of HMS *Nith*. Serjeant 'Pip' Palmer arrived in his SP and the CO explained that a nest of snipers had been holding up the advance on Arromanches. We followed behind the SP for about a hundred yards to where we could see a house facing us two hundred yards beyond. The sort of house that a child draws, two windows upstairs, two windows and a front door downstairs. The Colonel told Pip Palmer, 'One round HE (high explosive) through each bedroom window. Open sights, in your own time. Fire!' As Serjeant Palmer was loading an HE round the whiplash crackle of bullets striking the front of the SP gun armour made us all duck behind the bulk of the gun. The gunners inside were well protected from small arms fire so Palmer was able to take time with his sighting. The SP lurched on its tracks as the gun went off and we peeped out from cover to see the distant house wreathed in a cloud of dust. Again came the splatter of bullets on the SP and this time we heard the very high speed chatter of the gun that later we would come to call 'Spandau'.[3] The second round of HE went through the other window and a few seconds later tiny figures came through the cloud of dust some with their hands in the air and others reeling as though drunk. I looked at my watch through its rubber cover. It was barely 0900 hours.

---

3 The MG 42, a general-purpose machine gun extensively used by German forces in the second half of the Second World War. As Pete indicates, it had a distinctive sound that led to it being nicknamed 'Hitler's buzzsaw'.

There was a fair amount of traffic coming in on the Regimental net, rendezvous coordinates and requests for fire from OP officers with the leading infantry. The CO told me to get a firm position for us to meet the rest of the Regimental HQ as it came through. A Bren carrier arrived to collect the Brigadier and our CO. As he climbed over the side of the carrier the CO told me to take my party to the RHQ position. I told him that I had no map, so shoving his map into my hand he drove off with the Brigadier. I knew immediately why he had given me his map. It was a soggy mess and barely readable, but it did help us enough to work out in which direction to walk. After several backtracks to avoid mined areas and being advised by the infantry boys to keep our heads down at certain places, we finally joined up with the rest of the section. It was splendid to see the other members of the Signal Section all together again. What with being in separate camps before leaving England and travelling on different craft, some of us hadn't met for the best part of a month. Most of the section had come ashore dryshod and only one member, namely Lineman Thackeray, seemed to be missing. He was last seen standing on the roof of a drowned three-tonner with water lapping around his feet and waving his arms about. We knew that Thackeray could not swim and we could only hope that some returning empty landing craft had stopped to pick him off. Since the Signal Section had not lost any vehicles, it could only be assumed that Thackeray had been seasick and had cadged a lift on one of the trucks that had been lost by the RHQ. Now that we had joined up with the headquarters halftrack wireless vehicles we were able to close down our backpack sets and get rid of the waterproofing from all our gear. Our clothes had pretty well dried on us and our main need was food. Requests to the cooks produced a tin of bully and a packet of biscuits. Ambrosia indeed. The rest of the section had been in vehicles all through the landing and had access to food that they had carried with them. Lees, Dick and I had eaten only an egg sandwich since the previous day.

It was impossible at our level to know how the attack was going or if we were likely to be driven back into the sea. We did glean some information from the requests for fire. Most of these were given uncoded to save time since the recipients of the shells were the enemy. We could pinpoint where the shells were falling and so tell roughly where the front troops were located. The enemy must have got over the initial surprise of the landing because he was starting to throw stuff back at us in the shape of shells, probably 88mm, and multiple-barrelled mortar bombs. These were particularly frightening because they screamed as they approached but as someone remarked the noise won't hurt you! Soon the order came to move forward. This was mainly to make room for more units to come off the beaches. By midday we found ourselves almost halfway between Arromanches and Bayeux. On the way up we had passed quite a number of dead German troops and a few khaki-clad figures huddled by the roadsides. The occasional trickle of prisoners with their hands clasped on their heads came slogging back towards the beach, bound for PoW cages in England. Our new location was well separated from the area occupied by the gun positions. This was a great asset since the return shellfire was directed at our guns and therefore left our area unstrafed, more or less. The new position was well forward and we would be able to give fire cover for a substantial advance beyond Bayeux. For this reason the powers that be in the RHQ ordered the cooks to prepare a hot meal. This consisted of shoving dozens of tins into a dixie of water and bringing it to the boil. As the tins came out each man opened his own and either emptied it into a mess tin or spooned it directly out of the tin. The latter method was favoured by most since it did away with cleaning the mess tin afterwards. It was the much-maligned Maconochie stew. Personally I was crazy about it and couldn't get enough. The best part was the tea. We had not had proper Army tea for days. Much as we admired the Navy, their tea was awful and their cocoa like dragon piss. Cliff Coles stuck his head out of the back of his halftrack and shouted '*Comment ca va, Chef*? Bienvenue a la belle France.' For weeks now Cliff and I had been making exchanges in schoolboy French or what is known today as Franglais. He had said that as soon as he came across a genuine Frenchman he was going to find out what they had done with his aunt's pen. Ever since his first year at Otley Grammar School some rotten sod had mislaid the old girl's plume and he was going to bring the French to task for the misdemeanour.[4]

During the afternoon the soft vehicles joined up with us and, with the exception of the vehicles up at Tac HQ with the Colonel, we were complete as a section. We now had spare clothes and boots. The assault boots were quite comfortable but hardly robust enough for digging slit trenches and we were glad to put on our ammos. We began to dig our slit trenches under the shade of trees on the periphery of the field, all nice and tidy and hidden from the air. When a couple of mortar

4 Ou est la plume de ma tante? – Where is my aunt's quill – was a phrase used in elementary French language instruction as early as the nineteenth century. It was probably used because it helped to show the different pronunciation of French vowels. An example of an English phrase traditionally taught in French schools is 'My tailor is rich'.

bombs arrived and burst in the branches of the trees, scattering the area underneath with shards of red hot shrapnel, we realised that out in the open was the place and we did some more feverish digging. Fortunately no one was injured but we learned a valuable lesson. The danger had not occurred to Serjeant Edwards because there were no trees in the desert. A continuous rumble of tracked vehicles, mainly tanks, was kept up as more and more were unloaded from landing craft. The amount of room in the bridgehead was limited and until the periphery could be pushed out it was going to be pretty crowded. The armour of the 8th Armoured Brigade, our parent unit, was almost the first ashore and had been in the thick of the advance all day. The Dual Drive Sherman tanks of 13th/18th Hussars were designed to 'swim' in from a couple of miles out but since the sea had been rough they had been brought right up to the beach by the landing craft pretty well at the same time as the assault infantry. This could have been why our trip up the beach had been so easy compared to other landings. Later we were to learn that the Americans at Omaha beach had launched their DD tanks three miles out and had lost more than 75 per cent of them. The Americans had also spurned the use of other British 'funnies' of General Hobart.[5] Among the funnies was the flail. This was a Churchill tank with a boom out in front upon which was a spindle furnished with lengths of very heavy chain. The spindle was driven from the tank engine and revolved at fairly high speed so that the chains thrashed against the ground ahead of the tank, exploding any mines in its path. The Brigadier had led us up the beach in the path left by the flail. No doubt many lives were saved by the use of this marvellous device. Another of General Hobart's brainchildren was called a fascine. Here an enormous bundle of logs was carried on a couple of arms above the front of the Churchill. On encountering an anti-tank ditch, the bundle of logs was dropped into the ditch and the tank proceeded on its way across the ditch followed by as many more AFVs[6] as necessary. Also there was the AVRE.[7] This was a Churchill with an enormous mortar about the size of a household dustbin mounted forward of the turret. This was able to throw a huge charge against a pillbox or strongpoint which usually disappeared in a cloud

---

5 Major General Sir Percy Cleghorn Stanley Hobart was a British military engineer who commanded the 79th Armoured Division during the Second World War and designed many specialised armoured vehicles.

6 Armoured fighting vehicles.

7 Armoured vehicle Royal Engineers.

of dust. Another diabolical (for the enemy) device was the 'Crocodile'. This was a flamethrower capable of projecting a terrible jet of flame over a hundred yards. The chemicals were carried in a trailer which was towed behind the tanks and pumped to the nozzle mounted on the turret. Such were the devices offered to the Americans. The only one they chose was the least effective, the Dual Drive tank. The result was the bloody slaughter on Omaha Beach. The troops were unable to move off the beach until almost dark and then at terrible cost.[8]

As the afternoon of the 6th wore on a few civilians started to emerge from wherever they had been hiding. Animals needed tending and food had to be prepared to feed families. Near our location several cattle had been hit by shrapnel or small arms fire. Those not already dead were shot to put them out of their misery. What had started as an ordinary day for the local people had turned into a nightmare that they would never forget. Unless the Germans counter-attacked in great strength and retook the area, the occupation was over for these people. During conversations with some of the French civilians we encountered later we were told that the German occupation troops had behaved very correctly. Cliff Coles emerged from his halftrack for a stroll and a breath of air, another operator having taken over from him. We walked past a small but beautifully kept cottage where an elderly gentleman was milking a goat in the garden. I told Cliff that now was his chance. Cliff cleared his throat and the old boy looked up from his milking. 'Bon soir monsieur, avez vous la plume de ma tante?' The old chap inclined his head, smiled gently and replied slowly and with great clarity. 'Bon soir, corporal. Mais non. La plume de votre tante est dans le bureau de votre oncle.' Cliff's face was a study. Of

---

8 A number of factors contributed to the American losses at Omaha beach: strong German defences; ineffective pre-invasion bombardment; ineffective air support; navigation difficulties amid strong currents and heavy seas; and a lack of cover. It's true that most of the DD tanks were lost and it's also true that the Americans did not adopt any of the other specialised tanks developed by Hobart. But they did have good reasons. They would require extra training and support, and most of the funnies were based on Churchill tanks which the Americans didn't have. General Eisenhower was in favour of the DD tanks but left the decision on the other funnies to General Omar Bradley, who did request 25 flail tanks and 100 Crocodiles but in the end decided there wasn't enough time to train the tank crews. No doubt the American losses would have been reduced if they had used Hobart's Funnies but Pete is wrong if he's implying that Bradley's decision about the funnies was the main reason for the carnage.

fifty million Frenchmen, he chose a retired schoolmaster who had for fifteen years taught French at Lancing College in Sussex. We told Mr Phair, our OC who was himself a master at Epsom College. He roared with laughter and told Cliff that he now knew what it was like to be hoist with his own petard. Which sounds very painful.[9]

Attached to our RHQ was a Royal Navy lieutenant equipped with a halftrack, an AB driver and a Petty Officer telegraphist. These people were with us to act as an OP[10] for battleships lying about ten miles off the coast. Any concentration of enemy armour or difficult strongpoint could be dealt with by these enormous guns. When a call for fire came into the RHQ it was passed to the batteries to be acted upon. If the firepower of the Regimental guns was insufficient to dislodge the cause of the problem, the FBO (Forward Bombardment Officer) would go forward in his halftrack and size up the situation from a Naval point of view and then call down fire direct from the ships. To be on the receiving end of those half ton shells must have been beyond terrifying. As they passed over our position they made a noise very akin to an express train. The sequence of events was always the same. A flash in the sky to the north followed by the express train, then a rumbling roar as the sound of the guns reached us. This was closely followed by the flash in the sky of the bursting shells and finally the dull detonation as the sound of the shellburst reached us. Each broadside was equivalent to several bomber-loads and far more accurate. Each time the FBO party came back to RHQ the matelots would join our operators and talk wireless and guns. They were all volunteers and did a marvellous job.

As Cliff and I wrapped ourselves in our blankets and crawled under his halftrack total weariness closed in on us and we went unconscious, remaining so until some mortar bombs fairly close to the RHQ woke us. It was already light and we could hear the cooks' burners running for tea or perhaps breakfast. A mug of tea and half a tin of bacon between two men, biscuits ad lib. Almost immediately the order came to mount up and we advanced a few miles to give support to the 2nd Essex, who were about to assault Bayeux. RHQ was established in an orchard. Calvados, a department of Normandy, is famous for the

---

9 The phrase was coined by Shakespeare in *Hamlet*. A petard was a small bomb, late medieval or early Renaissance, used to breach doors or gates. Hoist of course means lifted – in this context a past participle rather than a noun. Thus the phrase literally means 'blown off his feet by his own bomb' while the metaphorical meaning is to fall victim to your own plot or device … so Mr Phair's application of it was neat.

10 Observation Post.

apple brandy of the same name and large orchards were kept for the apples. We were spared a lot of digging at the new position because the infantry who had vacated the position had left good slit trenches. The small trees were a menace in as much as they made any incoming shells or mortar bombs explode well above the ground like airburst shrapnel. The guns were firing intermittently for most of the day and during the afternoon of the 7th we heard that the 2nd Essex had taken Bayeux and were pressing on beyond. The axis of advance seemed to be almost due south along the Bayeux-Caumont road. When the RHQ moved forward we by-passed Bayeux and occupied a position south of a junction which we came to know as Jerusalem crossroads. As we drove past we saw no fewer than nine Daimler scout cars that had been knocked out in the immediate vicinity of the crossroads, also a couple of Sherman tanks that had been brewed up close by. There had obviously been a terrific scrap for the area.[11] It was fairly open country and the siting of anti-tank guns was easy. Further south the roads plunged into 'Bocage' type countryside which proved to be a tankman's nightmare.[12] Since we were pretty well up with the leaders of the advance, the OC considered it worthwhile laying out lines to the batteries. Shortly after our arrival the line parties from 8th Armoured Brigade and 50 Division brought in lines from their respective HQs. It was a pretty hazardous business to lay lines along the main roads since the number of tracked vehicles travelling south was enormous and since the weather had become rather more warm the dust was increasing and reducing visibility to a few yards. The wireless links were kept open for fire orders and where possible the lines were used for administrative traffic.

During the night several lines went 'dis' and the line parties were pretty stretched to keep them working. Jack Halford asked me to go out with him to clear a fault on the line to 50 Div starting at our end, the Divisional line party starting at the other end. As we suspected a break was located near Jerusalem crossroads. I held on to the end of the cable from our HQ while Jack searched around in the dark for the other end of the break. It is possible for a vehicle to pull the end of a cable for many yards and it took Jack a few minutes to find our

11 It was the scene of bitter fighting when a German armoured column sought to retake Bayeux shortly after its capture. A Commonwealth War Graves Commission cemetery was begun there on 10 June 1944.

12 Bocage: pastureland divided into small hedged fields, interspersed with groves of trees.

cable. I bared the end of the cable and connected it to the D5 (Don 5 field telephone), shoved in the earthpin and called the exchange at our HQ. Straight away the exchange operator answered and I told him the position. At the same time a battery of medium guns about fifty yards to my rear fired in unison. The fright I received left me shivering with terror and when Jack returned with the other end of the line I was unable to speak for several minutes. As soon as Jack had spliced the line together the exchanges at both ends answered our call. Before we returned to RHQ we looked at a tank silhouetted against the sky. As we walked around to the front we could see by the light of Jack's hand lamp through the open hatch doors two figures seated in the driver and gunner seats. When we looked closer we could see that the figures were burnt corpses. No features or clothes, just an awful shape. Jack reached through the hatch and pushed one of them gently with his crook stick. It oscillated back and forth in a nodding fashion as though it was made of rubber. The mediums went off again and gave us another dreadful fright. I was very glad to get on the back of Jack's BSA and return to RHQ.

On the 9th we settled in the inevitable orchard at a place we knew as Point 103.[13] We were at the top of an almost imperceptible hill and had extended the slit trenches left by the infantry as we were likely to be resident for a couple of days. The cooks had brewed up and a hot meal of some sort was being served. Visiting us from one of the batteries was their BSM (battery serjeant major), whom the RSM had invited to have some food before he returned to his battery. Most of us were sitting in our slit trenches eating as the BSM walked across the orchard to join the RSM at his jeep. We all ducked when we heard incoming 'moaning minnies'.[14] After the explosions we looked up and saw that the BSM had gone. The blast had stripped all the foliage from one of the apple trees and replaced it with shreds of khaki cloth. The BSM had literally been blown to pieces and later we had the doubtful pleasure of disentangling intestines from the branches of the tree. The rest of the bits were shovelled into a sack and buried. I wonder what the War Graves Commission made of it when they disinterred the remains. Later that evening – it did not get fully dark until almost

---

13 At this point on 9 June the 8th Armoured Brigade had advanced two miles further into France than any other Allied unit.

14 Nickname for the rockets launched by the German Nebelwerfer launcher, so-called because of the shrill noise the rockets made in flight. Nebelwerfer translates as 'smoke thrower'.

Pete with corporal's stripes, undated. He was promoted to serjeant in November 1942.

On the sea wall at Weston-Super-Mare, 1940. L to R Pete, Serjeant Freddie Peebles, unidentified corporal.

L to R, Andy Andrews, W.T. Smith, Pete. In the foreground are three '18' radio sets. Andy is holding aerial rods.

The Caerwys platoon of the Home Guard preceding Pete's father's hearse to the parish church in January 1941.

At the time of 'aquatic sports' in Scotland, probably taken at Muir of Ord.

At Fort George. Pete is wearing a forage cap. He noted: 'Both the chaps on my right were killed at Caen.'

Pete and Rose Gurney on their wedding day, 25 August 1941. Pete's sister Margery is on the right.

147 Field Regiment Signal Section Hanover, 1945, Pete front row, third left, Teddy Edwards on his left.

147 Field Regiment Signal Section on parade, Hanover, 1945, Pete far left.

Corps Commander's Parade, 147 Field Regiment Signal Section.

Picnic on a trip to the Harz mountains, late May 1945. L to R Tommy Jay, Pete, Teddy Edwards, unidentified driver, Frank Orme, Jack Halford, Driver Smith – wearing Pete's tunic – and Harry Liley.

On a trip to the Harz mountains. The self-propelled gun is German, 88mm. Pete notes: 'I'm not in it as I took it.'

Pete (left) and Lofty Meyer during the building of the Dive Inn.

On the roof of the Dive Inn. L to R Ginger Howes, Lofty Meyer, Pete, the Germans Bobby Kiendorf and Wilhelm Thiel, unidentified signalman. Pete notes: 'X on extreme left is the balcony of my room.'

One of the glasses removed by Pete from the Nazi 'hochhaus' in Cologne.

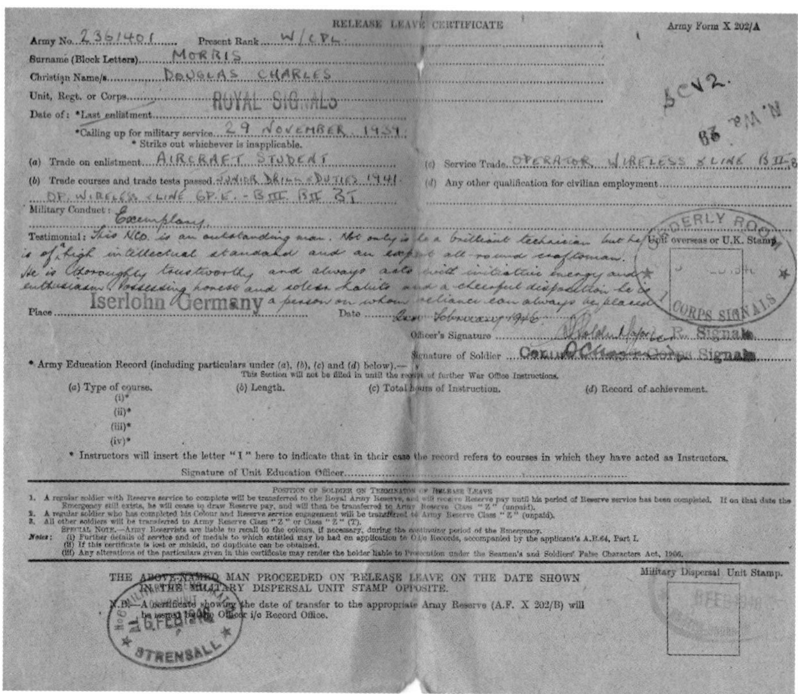

RELEASE LEAVE CERTIFICATE

Army Form X 202/A

Army No. 2361401 Present Rank W/CPL

Surname (Block Letters) MORRIS

Christian Name/s DOUGLAS CHARLES

Unit, Regt. or Corps ROYAL SIGNALS

Date of: *Last enlistment

*Calling up for military service 29 NOVEMBER 1939

* Strike out whichever is inapplicable.

(a) Trade on enlistment AIRCRAFT STUDENT

(b) Trade courses and trade tests passed JUNIOR DRILL & DUTIES 1941 OP. WIRELESS & LINE GP. E. - B III B II B I

(c) Service Trade OPERATOR WIRELESS & LINE B II

(d) Any other qualification for civilian employment

Military Conduct: Exemplary

Testimonial: This NCO is an outstanding man. Not only is he a brilliant technician but he is of a high intellectual standard and an expert all-round craftsman. He is thoroughly trustworthy and always acts with initiative energy and enthusiasm. Possessing honest and sober habits and a cheerful disposition he is a person on whom reliance can always be placed.

Unit overseas or U.K. Stamp

ORDERLY ROOM 1 CORPS SIGNALS

Place Iserlohn Germany

Date February 1946

Officer's Signature ... R. Signals

Signature of Soldier ... Corps Signals

* Army Education Record (including particulars under (a), (b), (c) and (d) below).—

This Section will not be filled in until the receipt of further War Office Instructions.

(a) Type of course. (i)* (ii)* (iii)* (iv)*

(b) Length.

(c) Total hours of Instruction.

(d) Record of achievement.

* Instructors will insert the letter "I" here to indicate that in their case the record refers to courses in which they have acted as Instructors.

Signature of Unit Education Officer

POSITION OF SOLDIER ON TERMINATION OF RELEASE LEAVE

1. A regular soldier with Reserve service to complete will be transferred to the Royal Army Reserve, and will receive Reserve pay until his period of Reserve service has been completed. If on that date the Emergency still exists, he will cease to draw Reserve pay, and will then be transferred to Army Reserve Class "Z" (unpaid).
2. A regular soldier who has completed his Colour and Reserve service engagement will be transferred to Army Reserve Class "Z" (unpaid).
3. All other soldiers will be transferred to Army Reserve Class "Z" or Class "Z" (T).

SPECIAL NOTE.—Army Reservists are liable to recall to the colours, if necessary, during the continuing period of the Emergency.

Notes: (i) Further details of service and of medals to which entitled may be had on application to O. i/c Records, accompanied by the applicant's A.B.64, Part I.
(ii) If this certificate is lost or mislaid, no duplicate can be obtained.
(iii) Any alterations of the particulars given in this certificate may render the holder liable to Prosecution under the Seamen's and Soldiers' False Characters Act, 1906.

THE ABOVE-NAMED MAN PROCEEDED ON RELEASE LEAVE ON THE DATE SHOWN IN THE MILITARY DISPERSAL UNIT STAMP OPPOSITE.

N.B.—A certificate showing the date of transfer to the appropriate Army Reserve (A.F. X 202/B) will be issued by the Officer i/c Record Office.

Military Dispersal Unit Stamp.

16 FEB 1946 STRENSALL

A page from Pete's Soldier's Release Book: 'This NCO is an outstanding man'.

Pete around the time he was writing his memoir. On his breast pocket is the Royal Signals badge depicting Mercury, nicknamed 'Jimmy'.

eleven o'clock – we were told that an armoured counter attack was coming in opposite our position. The gun positions were told to have AP (armour piercing) ammunition ready for use as well as HE. We were all well below ground level. All that is except the on-duty people, who were mostly in light armour and fairly safe from shrapnel. One of the off-duty operators, Bob Bruce, got out of his slit trench and stood relieving himself against the rear wheel of a three-ton truck. When a mortar bomb burst on the other side of the truck, a piece of shrapnel pierced the jerrican on the nearside of the storage rack, crossed the back of the vehicle, pierced the oil container on the offside and entered Bruce's buttock. We took him to the RAP (regimental aid post) and handed him over to Bombardier Spurling, the MO's orderly. Bruce returned to the section nine months later with the piece of shrapnel on his watch chain. They had not removed it straightaway by surgery but had let it work its way to a point near the alimentary canal and at the opportune time had fished it out via his rectum. The Naval FBO went forward to see whether he could see any concentration worthy of his big guns. He was in our full view when he got out of his halftrack and stood looking forward with his binoculars. We saw the bomb explode very close to him and when the dust cleared we could see that he had been hit. I shouted to Corporal Halford to come with me and together we ran out to bring him in. As we approached we could see him on his knees grubbing about on the grass. He stood up when he saw us coming. Jack wrapped a length of spun yarn around the stump of his left arm and used his pliers to wind up the improvised tourniquet, blood flying everywhere. The AB driver of the halftrack must have been dazed and only when we were halfway to the RAP did he start his engine and move the halftrack. As we handed the FBO over to the doctor, who had barely finished attending to Bruce, the incredibly brave fellow said to Jack Halford 'Corporal, will you take the watch off the hand you will find in my trouser pocket?' It must have been his hand he was looking for as we ran out to him. As we went back to our slit trench we heard the MO arranging to have the FBO taken back to the beach for transit to England.

Altogether Point 103 was a very frightening and unlucky place for the RHQ and the slit trench that I was sharing with Jack Halford was half full of dog-ends and match stubs by the time we left.[15] During the

15 The fighting around Point 103 and the village of St Pierre, to its south, in the week of 9 to 15 June was some of the heaviest experienced by the 8th Armoured Brigade.

night we were on the receiving end of a heavy stonk of shelling. The shells were either airburst or bursting in the tree branches because a large amount of shrapnel was coming downward. A large piece buried itself in the side of our trench two thirds from the bottom exactly between where Jack and I were sitting. We heard it come in with the most evil 'whirrr-thunk' as it slammed into the earth wall. We dug it out when it became light and Jack kept it as a souvenir. The counter-attack was repelled but in the repelling the 17th/21st Lancers took a tremendous battering and for a long time were not a viable fighting force. One troop of our SPs was firing at the enemy armour with open sights in an anti-tank role. With the FBO out of action, we did not receive any assistance from the big guns of the battleships. Since the range was getting stretched, the use of the Naval guns was to be discontinued in any case.

We were not sorry to leave Point 103 and move to a place called Le Pont Roc. This seemed to be some sort of agricultural collective with a collection of storage buildings and a few houses. The civilians were still in residence and the children greeted us enthusiastically as we drove into the yard. It was late afternoon by the time the signal office had been established and the line party had brought in the lines from the three batteries. The wireless net was kept open and our Air OP had joined us having flown over from England and found a landing strip. Everything seemed to point to our spending a few days at the new location since we even had the signal office in one of the buildings. One of the families occupying a house in the complex was called Poisson. A young son of the Poisson menage rejoiced in the name of Claude and like children the world over was imbued with an insatiable curiosity. He rattled out questions in Normandy patois and could not understand why we could not give him answers at the same rate. Monsieur Poisson told him to speak very slowly in his best French and to wait for us to formulate a reply in schoolboy French. The result was hilarious and Claude would jump up and down in his impatience. Eventually we were able to communicate quite satisfactorily and I'm sure he learned a great deal from the 'Tommees Anglais'. He was particularly fascinated by the AOP, whose code name or call sign was 'Cheeky Charlie'. Every time the AOP flew near the RHQ Claude would perform a war dance and shout 'Sheekee Sharlee' at the top of his voice. He was also very fond of the boiled sweets from the ration packs.

A few sneak patrols of the enemy had been reported over the past few nights and it was decided to establish a forward listening post out in front of our position. The OC and I went and selected a position about 150 yards directly in front of the regimental position. A line was run out to the site and a telephone installed. The idea was to give the RHQ prior warning of any intrusion near our position. As we walked back to the signal office I casually asked the OC who was going to man the post overnight. I never expected the reply I received. 'Since all the other NCOs have been doing shifts since we landed I thought that perhaps you and Corporal Liley would like to do it.' As dusk deepened into night Harry Liley and I went quietly down and settled ourselves in the hide. We tested the phone and told the operator on the exchange not to call us as the ring or buzz of the D5 would be heard for yards. We would call him if necessary. I cautioned Harry not to light his stinking pipe since only the nearby victims realised how viciously pungent it could be. I told him to be content with self-heating soup or cocoa milk. We decided that I should have the first sleep and accordingly I curled up and nodded off, to be awakened an hour later by a couple of salvoes from our own guns about a mile behind us. We took it in turns to sleep for an hour or two at a time. I must have been sound asleep when I felt an urgent shaking of my arm and I woke to find a hand across my mouth to prevent me speaking. Harry whispered very close to my ear. 'There is something out there.' Sure enough I could hear a stealthy movement in front of me in the pitch darkness. Harry clutched my arm, fearful that I should attract attention to our position. When I became fully awake I recognised the sound as that of a cow grazing, the sweep of the tongue as the grass was gathered in a bite and then the soft sound of the tuft being quietly wrenched from the ground. Altogether a comforting sound to a countryman. I told Harry that as long as the cows were grazing quietly there would be no Germans about. Harry came from Heckmondwike.[16] When it got light enough to see a few yards I told Harry to light up his pipe while we listened to the dawn chorus of artillery and mortar fire.

By this time we were pretty well stinking of stale sweat since the weather was very warm and we were unable to take our clothes off for any length of time. There was a stream a couple of hundred yards to our left and Cliff and I did a recce one very warm afternoon with an idea of having a good soap down. I remained on watch for any intruders while Cliff went back to the truck for soap and towels. Nothing stirred and on his return we stripped naked and sat in the stream, which came up to our midriffs. Absolute bliss! We were sitting with our backs to the bank from which we had entered and we did not notice the three

---

16 Presumably Pete mentions Harry's home town to suggest he was no countryman; Heckmondwike is about ten miles from Leeds.

girls approaching until we heard their voices right behind us. We had been busy soaping and rinsing our sweat-stained shirts and 'drawers, cellular, short' – quite busily engaged. The girls did not seem to be going to move and by this time had sat on the grass and were chatting to us in half French, half English of about the same proficiency as ourselves. By this time Cliff and I were just about frozen in spite of the warm weather. Our towels and dry clothing on the bank looked very inviting and at last we decided that we had had enough and mutually decided to stand up and make for the bank and bugger the modesty. As we reached the bank the girls picked up our towels and proffered them to us as though they encountered stark naked men every hour of the day. They seemed very interested in our Lifebuoy soap and picked it up and smelled it again and again. Since we could get soap from the ration packs, we made them a present of both cakes. They seemed quite delighted. We did not realise that soap was practically unobtainable in the occupied countries. We were still very naïve.

Our stay at Le Pont Roc came to an end a couple of days later when we moved forward to a new position at a farm with the batteries fairly close at hand. I went with the line party to lay out to the batteries and at one particular place we had to build a pole crossing to clear the gateway entrance to a delightful cottage. As we were making the crossing an old couple came out and offered us cider, which was most acceptable in the heat of the afternoon. Presently the old people were joined by a strikingly lovely granddaughter of about 17 or 18 years of age. When we had finished our drink we wished them good afternoon and went on with our line laying to the battery concerned. Teddy Edwards and I had put our beds in a dry pigsty. Sometime during the night we were literally lifted out of beds ands deluged with the thatch from the roof by the most almighty explosion somewhere close by. The duty lineman came up and said that the line to one of the batteries had gone out and that he was going out to find the fault. The bang had wakened the whole RHQ and Jack Halford and I decided to go with the lineman to see what had happened. As we approached the cottage where we had met the old couple we could see the still smoking crater exactly where our pole crossing had been in front of the cottage. The cottage itself had completely collapsed and several gunners were looking for the old people in the rubble. As it became daylight they were discovered both dead and in each other's arms. A couple of gunners found the granddaughter wandering stark naked and in a semi-coma several hundred yards from the cottage. The gunners had wrapped her up and taken her to our MO for a check-up before leaving her with neighbours. We never did discover what had caused the explosion but were told by Brigade that the Jerries were dropping parachute mines along the front.

At this position it was very distressing to see cattle maimed by shrapnel. They were so frightened by the noise of fighting and their wounds that it was very difficult to get near enough to get a clean pistol shot to put them out of their misery. The unwounded cows were distended with milk and any of the boys who could do so spent every spare minute milking the poor beasts to relieve the pressure on their udders. The civilians in this area seemed to have vanished and the stock was completely untended. Further back towards the beach the advance had been so rapid that the civilians had not had time to make up their minds whether to abscond before the retreating Germans or risk death by staying put in their homes. Boiled chicken was on almost every private menu for a couple of days. The cooks had been forbidden to deal with any civilian poultry but we could boil them ourselves without attracting the attention of the powers.

At first light one morning the CO's driver/batman was taking tea for the CO when a mortar bomb exploded close to where he was walking. A splinter of shrapnel pierced the flip-top cigarette tin in his left-hand breast pocket and buried itself halfway through the New Testament behind the tin. Not a drop of tea was spilt, he said. I actually saw the cigarette tin and Bible but didn't believe a word of the tea story. He was of course an old soldier who had been with the CO for about ten years. The mobile showerbath unit caught up with the Regiment at this location and established itself about a hundred yards from the HQ near a convenient collection of slit trenches which had been dug in a large nettle patch. We went in batches of ten to have a hot shower and several of us were walking away having completed our turn when mortar bombs started to fall. We dived fully clothed into the slits to be followed by the chaps out of the showers all bollock naked and steaming. The thought of being hit by shrapnel when naked was far worse than being struck when fully dressed. The nettle stings were accepted as part of the hazard. That was the only time I saw a mobile bath unit during the whole of my service.

For the whole of July we fired our guns in support of many different units, both armoured and infantry, gradually moving south through the bocage countryside. The slightest movement of armour caused clouds of dust and even soft vehicles stirred up enough to be seen for miles. The roadside signs 'Dust means Death' were well intentioned but useless. Another nightmare was the way the armoured vehicles hooked our lines off the hedges and fences and chopped them to ribbons. Jack Halford and I conceived the idea of stringing the lines from the now unenergised and useless electricity poles along almost every road. For a large part of the line to Corps HQ we actually used the electric cable on the insulators as our telephone line, bridging any missing spans with our own cable. It certainly kept the lines away from tanks et cetera and did not need to be recovered when we moved. The bocage of Normandy around Caumont, although very beautiful, was extremely difficult for tankmen. Even the infantry had it that if someone on this side of a hedge sneezed, a German on the other side said '*gesundheit*'. The narrow sunken lanes with high hedges reminded us very much of Devon. The small irregular fields were easy to defend and difficult to attack. Many of the lanes were too narrow to accommodate a tank or SP gun and made it necessary to travel on the exposed fields at each side. To cross a sunken lane at right angles was a hazardous undertaking since the high banks and low roadway could act as a very effective tank trap. The most effective weapon at the disposal of the allies during this part of the campaign was the rocket-firing Typhoon aircraft.[17] They always seemed to be stooging around 'up there' and their attention could be attracted by firing a red smoke shell on to a strong point or another form of hold-up. Within minutes of spotting the red smoke at least one pilot would dive out of nowhere and loose a couple of projectiles at the target. As the aircraft dived we could see the rockets leave their racks under the wings leaving a trail of smoke in their wake. We seldom saw them actually explode but often saw the devastation that they caused when we overran the site that had been the target. I saw on several occasions a Tiger *panzerwagen* with the turret blown out of the hull and lying yards away from the overturned chassis. The explosive used in these devices must have been possessed of tremendous power. I spoke to several panzer troops later and they all without exception were terrified of the Typhoons. On a very minor scale the power of the PIAT bomb (projector infantry anti-tank) was terrific for the size of the projectile. It did however take

---

17 The Typhoon was a single-seater fighter-bomber, manufactured by Hawker Aircraft. In June 1944 the RAF Tactical Air Force had eighteen squadrons of Typhoon rocket-firing planes in operation and they did play a large part in the Battle of Normandy. But the weapon was not as accurate as Pete implies. The RAF historian Dr Alfred Price says a direct hit on a tank would destroy it, but the rockets were too inaccurate for that to happen often. More severe, Price says, than the physical damage was the effect of the attacks on the enemy troops' morale, a point Pete underlines.

a very brave man to get near enough to an enemy tank for the PIAT to be accurate enough for a direct hit.

By the time August arrived lots of new troops were coming up from the beach area and taking their share in the action. They spoke of the marvels of the Mulberry Harbours and how they had driven straight off the boats and to an assembly point without even dismounting from their transport.[18] We had never heard of such wonders and could not imagine how a harbour to accommodate ocean-going vessels could have been provided so quickly. Never having been back to the beachhead since 6 June, we imagined that all was the same as we had left it. A virgin beach with a few craters and corpses. Neither could we imagine the vast dumps of stores, fuel, food and vehicles that had been building up over the past few weeks. Aerodromes had been built to accommodate fighters and Typhoons together with the personnel to fly and maintain them. In fact we had seen nothing except countryside that had been devastated by the stupidity of thousands of men throwing chunks of metal at each other and wrecking lots of beautiful machinery in the process. The small town of Caumont had been the subject of a huge air raid and as we passed through the rubble I noted that the highest part of a structure of any kind was a corner of the church tower that stood no more than twelve feet high. It has been said that General Montgomery[19] had insisted on the destruction of Caumont. I wonder if he ever saw what he had done with the once lovely little town.[20]

The Americans had broken out of the Cherbourg peninsula and General Patton's tanks were sweeping into Vire and Avranches, cutting off the Cherbourg area completely, and then swinging south and east to an area south of Falaise. At the same time the Canadians were driving south from just east of Caen and the British were coming south from Caumont, all converging on the German escape route east of Falaise. Many of the beleaguered German units escaped to the east

---

18 The Mulberry harbours were prefabricated in Britain in great secrecy and towed across the Channel. One was placed at Omaha Beach, the other at Gold Beach. Mulberry B, at Gold Beach, was in use for ten months after D Day, by which time the capture of French ports rendered them unnecessary.

19 Promoted to Field Marshal on 1 September 1944.

20 There was intense fighting around Caumont, as the Allies tried to exploit a weakness in the German line. The town's situation on high ground, on a road junction, made it an obvious target. Its destruction was probably inevitable.

before the bottleneck could be closed to trap the remainder in the slaughtering grounds around Falaise. During the two days of August when the exodus was taking place we poured thousands of shells into the tightly packed Germans. Ours was only one of many regiments doing exactly the same. Field, medium and heavy artillery all pounding away from almost 360 degrees of encirclement. Thousands got out of the ring but many more either died or were taken prisoner. When at last the firing ceased and no more of the enemy tried to flee eastwards we were given the task of supervising large batches of prisoners who were made to bury their dead comrades. The all-pervading stench of death and the sight of bloated corpses was frightful.[21] Many of the German transports were horse-drawn and the dead animals had to be towed away and buried also. The prisoners were totally exhausted and were grateful for even a few broken biscuits and a cigarette end. They were issued with a tin of bully and two packets of biscuits per man and all the water they could drink. They seemed to think that this was generous treatment since they had not been issued with any official rations for several days. Most of them were very young and had the pallid look of exhausted terror. Those who were not around the sixteen-year bracket were much older, possibly fifty years old. We learned afterwards that they were ex-Russian prisoners of war who had been given the ultimatum 'fight for us or die.'[22]

During the time that we, those not responsible for transport, had been burying corpses the drivers and fitters had been very busy maintaining the vehicles ready to pursue the enemy across France northeast towards Belgium. Other armoured units had been harassing the rear of the German retreat and 8th Armoured Brigade had to drive very hard to catch up with the fleeing enemy to take over from pursuers in order that they might re-arm, refuel and rest. When we took over the close pursuit role and were close behind the rearmost Germans,

---

21 The battle of the Falaise Pocket was the decisive engagement in the battle for Normandy in which Allied forces surrounded German Army Group B, consisting of the Seventh Army and the Fifth Panzer Army. Most of Army Group B was destroyed, opening the way to Paris and the German border. Historians differ in their estimates of German losses but up to a hundred thousand troops were caught in the encirclement. Up to fifteen thousand were killed, up to fifty thousand were taken prisoner, and up to forty thousand escaped.

22 It is true that many of the German troops in Normandy were Ostlegionen – Eastern Legions – conscripts and in some cases volunteers from Russia, Turkestan, Mongolia and elsewhere.

the repartee on the Brigade wireless net was most entertaining. With the Brigadier at the microphone the conversation went something like as follows:

'B squadron report your position, over.'

'Position B squadron 123456, I say again 123456, over.'

'Roger B Squadron, I now have you visually. Press on. I say again, Press on. You are driving like a lot of bloody old women, over.'

'Sir, with all due respect.' A tendency here to lose his temper. 'With all due respect this bloody Sherman is doing 32 miles per hour.' And now risking a court martial. 'If you can do any better please get up here.'

'Roger B squadron, that's the spirit, keep pressing on.'

So it went on for mile after weary mile, driving, stopping, firing. It was not much fun for us but it must have been dreadful for the Germans. Occasionally they would leave an anti-tank gun or a hull-down tank to hold up our advance but any small defence was immediately knocked out by the Typhoons. So it went on day and night, never halting for more than an hour. The RASC boys did a marvellous job keeping us supplied with fuel considering that the tanks did not do 'miles per gallon' but 'gallons per mile'! During one short stop Jack Halford and I dismounted to investigate a German horse-drawn vehicle which was lying on its side in the ditch with the dead horse still in the shafts. It seemed to have been an orderly room or administration wagon of some sort. It had all sorts of stationery and forms scattered about. Under the rear shelf was a padlocked cupboard. Jack reached up to his truck and got a shovel with which he belted off the lock, hasp and staple in one go. Neatly stacked inside were wads of French banknotes, all done up in paper bands in thousand franc bundles. We flung it all into the front of the line truck just as the convoy started off. Later after consulting with the OC and Teddy Edwards it was decided to pay the section with the money and let the boys leave their pay in credit. At the rate at which we were able to spend money, the hoard lasted several weeks. On approaching a small town which was located in a shallow valley we could see some German transport leaving the town on the eastern side of the road that climbed up out of the valley not more than a mile away. A troop of our guns deployed themselves, still on the road, and fired several rounds each over open sights.[23] It was not often that the gunners saw their own shells bursting on the

23 Firing at a target you can see directly, using the basic sights of the gun without any calculation of settings.

target. After passing through the town they were able to see the results of their handiwork at close quarters. The gunners didn't like it much. Dead Germans, dead horses and burning trucks is not a pretty sight at any time. We always thought that the RAF bomber boys could lay waste to a city, kill several thousand people and yet not have to look at the result. Small recompense for the low survival rate of the bomber crews. Chacun a son gout! Neither bomber boys nor infantry would go near one of our tanks in action. I avoided the RAF after seeing a rear gun turret on a Wellington years before.

At one stop for refuelling at a village during the headlong rush to the Seine, Driver Smith reported that his Bren gun carrier would not start and the OC asked me to stay behind with Smith to wait for the LAD (Light Aid Detachment) to overtake us. The LAD always travelled at the rear of the column to pick up any stragglers and make running repairs. It was an easy matter for us to locate and clear a blocked fuel filter and get the V8 Ford engine running again long before the LAD were expected to arrive. As Smith was putting his tools away a commotion started among the inhabitants of the village in whose square we were parked and presently a pair of young women were brought out amid much screaming and yelling and forcibly tied to chairs in the centre of the square. We stood up in the carrier and were able to see a burly man approaching the women with a pair of sheep shears in his hand. He stood before the unfortunate pair and harangued them in rapid French far too fast for me to understand. Finally he moved to clip the hair from one of the victims but she thrashed her head about to prevent him doing so. He caught her a belt across the face and she stopped moving. Smith bent down and picked up his Sten and was about to fire a few rounds over the heads of the crowd but I was able to stop him and told him that it was none of our business and that the two women had obviously been collaborating with the Germans in some way or other. We watched as the hair was cut off right down to the scalp with the sheep shears. Finally they were untied and allowed to run off to howls of abuse from the entire population of the village. Several of the men surrounded us and insisted that we repair to the local bistro and drink cognac and calvados with them. After toasting *la belle France* and *Vive les Anglais* ad nauseam we returned to the carrier just as the LAD entered the village. On the seat of the carrier was a cold roast chicken and a newly baked loaf. Smith and I drove and dined in turns. We had not had bread or fresh meat for weeks and it can be imagined how delicious the food tasted. While across the Channel the people of the United Kingdom were severely rationed, France seemed to have abundant food and wine, in spite of the heavy demands of the Germans to feed the population of the fatherland.

We were rather surprised at the enthusiasm with which the villagers received us but after discussing it with Smith as we drove to catch the Regiment we realised that this part of the country between Caen and the Seine had not been host to many British troops and those that the locals had seen were driving through at high speed in pursuit of the retiring Germans. Furthermore their countryside had not been used as a battleground. Merely the occasional few shells or mortar bombs used by the German rearguard to try to delay their pursuers. This happened mainly at bridges over a stream or railway cuttings when the Royal Engineers were putting down a Bailey bridge to span the gap where the original had been blown by the Hun.[24] Back in the Calvados department of Normandy the populace were obviously resentful of the liberating troops. After four years of occupation by the well-behaved German army, the people had become used to their situation and accepted their lot. Suddenly all hell was let loose and their way of life totally changed. Their farms and homes destroyed, shops and businesses annihilated. Complete villages with ancient churches totally flattened. While the people of Normandy had looked forward to their liberation, few of them realised what the act of liberation would entail. We saw a farmer standing with tears streaming down his face while he gazed at his bloated cattle with their hoofs pointing to the sky. His burnt hay ricks, looted poultry houses and uninhabitable farmhouse. Those of us who cared to think about the situation could readily understand the feelings of animosity of the French people towards us. There was, however, nothing we could do about it and were glad to move away.

We did not realise that the local spirit of Normandy, known as Calvados after the department, could taste so palatable. In the barns and outhouses of the area we had occupied around Bayeux and further south the troops had come across kegs full of spirit tucked away out of sight and covered with the dust of years. If a soldier, I don't care what his nationality, comes across a bottle, barrel or keg he will open it in the hope that the contents will be alcoholic. Most of the kegs that we found in Normandy were full of unmatured Calvados spirit, raw

---

24 The Bailey bridge was a portable prefabricated truss bridge designed by the British civil engineer Sir Donald Coleman Bailey and developed in 1941. The Bailey bridge had features similar to earlier designs, and even breached a patent, but Bailey was knighted for his contribution to the war effort. Montgomery said 'Bailey bridging made an immense contribution towards ending world war two.'

and quite unpalatable. It tasted like diesel fuel mixed with low-grade petrol with a soupçon of carbonised sump oil to give it body. The good Lord alone knows how the poor people of the region blended or matured the stuff to make it drinkable. The officers and serjeants received an issue of gin and/or whisky each month so did not need to sample the Calvados spirit as found. The lower ranks tried a tot or two in the same amount as one would of any other spirit. The result of drinking the stuff was remarkable, rather akin to having a grenade explode in the brain, a grenade with a long-delay fuse. A charming and mild-mannered boy named Fosker was sitting with his colleague Jones after drinking about a third of a mug of Calvados spirit. As the Colonel walked past the back of the half-track towards the room of a cottage which we were using as an ops room, I was passing a telephone line to Jack Halford through the open window. Fosker leaned out of the back of the truck and yelled 'Hey Fatty you're a silly old bugger!' The CO turned about and glared at Fosker who repeated 'Yes you. You're a silly old bugger.' The Colonel, instantly realising what had happened, turned to me and said in a tired quiet voice 'Serjeant Morris. Put Fosker under arrest.' Being under arrest meant nothing physically since we had no guard room and no one to guard a prisoner. The stigma was the drunk charge on one's conduct sheet. This remained a permanent record. In the case of Fosker it never came to a hearing because I didn't mention the incident until a week later when I asked the CO what he wanted to do about Fosker being still under arrest. I was told to send for the prisoner, whom the CO took for a quiet walk across the farmyard, where Fosker received the most monumental bollocking. Later I was told to tear up any paperwork that I had regarding the incident. Had Fosker been anything but a conscientious worker, he would not have stopped bouncing until he hit the glass house. Another incident concerning Calvados spirit was when one of the drivers had pulled into a position, parked his three-tonner and then pulled off the 5 gallon water can from its stowage and emptied the whole of the contents over himself, all the while shouting 'I'm on fire! I'm on fire!' Fortunately no officers were present and Teddy Edwards, who had been riding in the truck with the driver concerned, told us that for three hours the chap had drunk nothing. Corporal Whate took some of the awful stuff and held it in the bottom of his mess tin and put a match to it. It burned with the same flame as that of methylated spirit but more smoky. God knows what it did to one's guts but it produced a terrible hangover. Calvados, the true apple brandy, I found to be a very acceptable drink and I preferred it to the grape-based Cognac.

The pursuit of the retreating Germans was carried out in a series of leapfrog bounds by one unit and then another. We had been in the van of the pursuit and then had relinquished the lead to some other unit and we had pulled off the main line of advance to refuel and have a night's uninterrupted sleep. Teddy and I were having a late noggin with our OC (his whisky naturally) and he told us he was wrestling with the problem of writing to the wife and parents of Bobby Hartley, who we had lost a few days previously. What can one say to people under such circumstances? Signalman Bobby Hartley was the 2i/c's operator and travelled in the Major's half-track with the batman and all their kit and Bobby's 19 set. The Major travelled in the front with the driver and a DR followed behind on his motorcycle. The 2i/c and his entourage would swan about mainly in a reconnaissance role but sometimes as OP or liaison with other units. The last time I saw Bobby was just before they left to recce a route for the regimental advance for the day. He told me that he felt a bit ill or 'shaky inside' as he described it. I gave him a swig of whisky and told him that I would find another operator provided that he would report sick and see the MO. He declined the offer and said that he would be all right later. The operator I had had in mind to replace him was myself. You just can't buck the inevitable. The 2i/c was looking for a gun position to occupy later, along the side of a fairly well-defined valley. The Major had dismounted to get a better view of the other side of the valley with his binoculars. Suddenly there came an awful crash and the half-track burst into flames. The driver shot out of his door and into the ditch together with the Major and the DR. Each side of where Bobby was sitting were two 40 gallon petrol tanks, through both of which an armour piercing projectile had passed allowing the fuel to run down into the footwell of the vehicle. It was hoped that the shell passed through Bobby as well and killed him before he could be burned to death. The rest of the party were pinned down in the ditch by small arms fire from across the valley until the opposition was driven off. When we passed the wreck later it was still smouldering but there wasn't a trace of Bobby who had been consumed in a flaming well of almost 80 gallons of petrol. We could well understand the difficulty in which the OC found himself. What the hell do you tell the wife and parents? Your son/husband died bravely? Poor Bobby never had time to be brave. Just shut in a steel box without a chance of escape from the flames. The 2i/c's batman had been left at Tac HQ to tend the Major's kit. Lucky him! When our advance took us past the burned out wreck of the half-track we could see the holes left by the shell. Clean through both sides of the light armour, through both tanks and across the place where Bobby would have been sitting opposite his set. Someone had placed a little posy of wild flowers on the bank alongside the wreck.[25]

The continuous tension of travelling and being continually on the move without sleep and regular mealtimes began to have effects on us that varied from person to person. Those of normal morose outlook became more distant and gloomy while those like Jack Halford became even more jocular and frivolous. During an overnight stay at a farmyard one of the linemen was noticed to be missing. It was not until his steel helmet was found outside the entrance to a stone dog kennel built into the stone steps that led to a granary above a stable was it realised that he had crawled into the dog kennel. There had been no particularly heavy shelling or mortaring of our position and the man in question was not of a nervy disposition. The fact remained that for all Halford's coaxing and cajoling, the fellow steadfastly refused to budge. His colleagues took food and tea to him but nothing was touched. Seeking advice from the MO, Jack Halford was told that 'he'll come out when his belly is empty in a few days' time.' The regiment moved out and continued the advance. The OC forbade Halford to stay behind with the patient or leave a motorcycle for him. It had been decided to designate him as a patient since anything else would leave him vulnerable to a charge of desertion in the face of the enemy. It was two days later that he turned up on the pillion of a DR from Brigade. His hair was snow white. Not from the trauma of his two days plus incarceration in the dog kennel but from the flour that had seeped from the granary above. On being questioned by the boys as to why he had done it, the reply was vague and along the lines that he wanted a rest and was determined that he was going to have one. From then on he never lost a wild-eyed look but he was a dedicated lineman and could be relied upon to do his job.

25 The Commonwealth War Graves Commission's records show that Signalman John Robert Alexander Hartley was killed on 6 August 1944. He served with the Royal Corps of Signals with the 147th Essex Yeomanry Field Regiment, Royal Artillery. His grave, along with more than two thousand others of British servicemen, is maintained by the Commission at Banneville-la-Campagne War Cemetery in Calvados, Normandy.

Chapter 7

ARNHEM[1] AND BEYOND. INTO GERMANY

The relentless pursuit of the Germans continued, with armoured units always in the vanguard, Brigades and Divisions leapfrogging one another. August passed quickly in a blur of activity that was extremely hectic. On 1 September Arras was captured and we reached the Belgian frontier just north of Lille. German resistance stiffened noticeably and every possible obstruction was stiffly contested. In spite of this the Guards Armoured Division swept through us to take Brussels, where they were greeted by delirious Belgians. Celebrations and festivities were still taking place when we skirted the city to press on northwards and eastwards. Progress was being impeded by the

---

1 Over the next few pages Pete describes his experience of Operation Market Garden, which was an attempt by the Allies led by Field Marshal Bernard Montgomery to create a bridgehead over the Lower Rhine and open the way to northern Germany. It was one of the largest airborne operations in history, involving the American 82nd and 101st Airborne Divisions, the 1st Polish Independent Parachute Brigade and the British 1st Airborne Division. From a British perspective the Battle of Arnhem – 17 to 26 September– was the main engagement of Market Garden and it was disastrous. There were several reasons for the 'thorough caning' described by Pete but among them was the fact that the Germans were present in much greater force than Allied planners expected. Furthermore, Hitler – stung by the attack – poured reinforcements in during the course of the battle while the British troops were being picked off. In the end, of almost nine thousand troops in the British 1st Airborne Division, more than a thousand were killed and almost six thousand were taken prisoner. Fewer than two thousand made it back across the Rhine – in the condition Pete describes.

flooding of large areas due to the Germans breaching dykes in both Belgium and Holland. This trick was just as impeding to the German retreat as to our advance. The result was that on many occasions our leading elements were hard on the heels of German vehicles. Many of the roads were built on the top of embankments, which due to flooding were totally surrounded by water. By 9 September we were only 25 miles from the German border. By 11 September General Bradley's troops were fighting on German soil.[2]

On 25 September we drive like hell from the Dutch border north towards Eindhoven with explicit orders to push any stalled vehicles off the road with a tank. Nothing must stop the advance. We find out what all the panic is about when hundreds of aircraft and towed gliders come over, all heading north. The Guards Armoured are just ahead of us and taking heavy losses in tanks and scout cars. These we see as we follow up with the SP guns and our own armour. The 82nd US Airborne Division had taken the area around Eindhoven and opened the way for our armour. Likewise at Nijmegen and Grave the 101st Railsplitters Airborne Division of the US army had taken the bridges over the Maas and the Waal.[3] We sailed over these intact bridges in an endeavour to reach the last bridge at Arnhem. What we or the planners did not know was that the 9th SS Panzer Division were refitting just north of Arnhem and were giving our British Airborne boys a thorough caning. The Hun had thought up every sneaky device to delay our progress. As stated before, the roads were all up on embankments and at intervals along the route the German engineers had burrowed under the road surface and planted sea mines. These must have had some kind of sophisticated delay fuse since perhaps fifty vehicles went over before it exploded. When the explosion occurred it took out up to three vehicles and dug an enormous crater. Progress was only possible by bridging the gap with a Bailey Bridge. The rest of the column had to sit and wait for the Royal Engineers Field Company to complete the bridge. All the time we were shelled from either side since we were up a very narrow salient with our retreat frequently cut off by counter-attacks from both east and west. The result was that we had to be very sparing with

---

2 Strictly true, inasmuch as American troops reached the Siegfried line and began engaging the Germans in the six-week battle for the city of Aachen. But of course the Allies did not cross the Rhine until March 1945.

3 Apparently a slip by Pete. The Railsplitters were the 84th Infantry Division; they arrived in Normandy, and in Pete's narrative, later. The nickname of the 101st Airborne Division was the Screaming Eagles.

food. Armour, ammunition and bridging material were considered more important than soft vehicles carrying rations. Eventually we reached a small place called Elst, which was virtually cut off by water from the breached dykes. From this position the German positions beyond Arnhem were well within range of our guns and our regiment kept up a continuous barrage to try to take a bit of pressure off the beleaguered Airborne. It seemed that communications were lacking between the city and our relieving troops and at one stage the civilian telephone lines from Arnhem to Nijmegen were the only channel of communication with the Airborne Division. During this period of endeavouring to relieve the cut-off remnants of 1st Airborne, our food ran out completely. Local Dutch people informed us that there was a German stores depot several miles to our east. Several of us under one of the regimental subalterns went under the cover of darkness to recce the place and find out if there was any food available. The line party Bren gun carrier and one jeep with five of us soon found a quite extensive complex, seemingly unguarded, since a group of civilians were carrying off large quantities of stores. These people told us to be very quiet and careful since there were German troops at the far end of the depot loading horse-drawn transport. Two of our chaps were posted to warn us of any approach by krauts while we searched for rations. In the light of 'lamps, hand, electric' we soon found food. Whether it was good or bad we were unable to tell but just filled the jeep and carrier with greaseproof cases and sacks and then beat a hasty retreat. Examination of the sacks later revealed them to contain a kind of porridge meal with cabbage or something similar in small shreds. This proved to be quite palatable when the cooks had simmered it for a few minutes. The cases were marked on the outside with the legend 'Knackiebrot'[4] and each weighed five kilogrammes. On being opened they were found to contain slabs of biscuit-type material, segmented like a bar of chocolate. As we handed over our loot to the cook we broke off a dozen or so squares of the *knackiebrot* and munched them as we walked back to our trucks. They seemed very good to the taste and had succulent morsels in them which I took to be raisins. In the light of the operator's lamp in the half-track Jack Halford examined one of the squares more minutely and let out a bellow followed by a spitting and vomiting sound followed by more sounds of anguish. I broke one open with my fingers and discovered to my horror that the juicy bits were not raisins but maggots. When we told Mr Phair later

4 Probably Knackebrot – crispbread.

he remarked 'Ah well it's all good protein.' The crafty old devil hadn't eaten any.

The remnants of the 1st Airborne were beginning to filter through our position. Crossing the river must have been a nightmare after eight days of holding the north end of the bridge. They had been under constant attack from the 9th SS Panzer Division. Heavily outnumbered, scattered and short of ammunition and food, these boys had put up an incredible display of bravery and suffered 75 per cent casualties – killed, wounded and prisoners. They were all far too done up to be engaged in conversation about their trip south across the river. We found later that some of the survivors had swum across, while others had held on to the sides of returning assault craft which had been used to carry troops over in an attempt to reinforce the Arnhem party. If they had been able to capture the bridge at both ends. If we had been able to get through to them. If the 9th SS Panzer Division had not been in the area. If bad weather had not restricted air support and reinforcement. All these 'ifs' added up to a very gallant failure. Today one hears the armchair pundits giving their learned opinions about what went wrong and why. In almost every case the experts were nowhere nearer the battle than England and in a lot of cases still unborn.[5]

I recently heard a radio amateur criticising the communications during the operation. He claimed that the equipment was inadequate and flimsy. I did not enter the discussion but I could have told him that there is only so much equipment that a parachutist can carry and an 18 set on the shoulders is not one of them. The jarring received on landing by a valved wireless set of that era would shift the tuning off frequency and in many cases shatter the filaments of the valves. On landing, is an operator going to sit down and try to get a netting signal from his control station or is he going to get under cover possibly

5 The historian Anthony Beevor (born in 1946), author of *Arnhem: The Battle for the Bridges* said that Operation Market Garden was 'a bad plan right from the start and right from the top'. Brigadier General James M. Gavin, the commander of the 82nd Airborne Division, said 'there was no failure at Arnhem. If historically there remains an implication of failure it was the failure of the ground forces to arrive in time to exploit the initial gains of the 1st Airborne Division.' John Waddy was a major in the 1st Airborne at Arnhem. He was later Colonel SAS, doing much to develop the role of special forces. By the time of his hundredth birthday in 2020, Waddy was the last surviving British officer of the Battle of Arnhem. His view was that the strategic and tactical debate about Market Garden would never be resolved. Perhaps Pete had it about right; a gallant failure.

from the middle of a big field before he gets shot or mortared? The wireless equipment we had was extremely vulnerable to damage when the operators were ducking and diving for their lives. It is small wonder then that scattered units of the same formation were out of communication. The bigger sets in the glider-borne Jeeps were sometimes torn from their mounting when a glider crash-landed. The gliders had been under heavy flak all the way from the Belgian border right up to the dropping zone at Arnhem. Many of them had been hit and were barely airworthy enough to be manoeuvrable. Many and varied experiments were carried out by Royal Signals of the Airborne forces to determine the best way to deal with communications and which was the best type of set for each purpose. The small 38s and 58s were the best for dropping with parachute personnel but their range was very limited and battery life fairly short. Here again rose the problem of spare batteries, carriage and storage in a unit with such limited transport.

The disentangling of the crush of units in the corridor up to Elst took days and finally we found ourselves in a static role in the Limburg area of Holland. The village of Geverik seemed to be fairly untouched by war and the Heutz family on whose large farm we were billeted were a mixture of charm and kindness. Teddy Edwards and I carried our kit into one of the outhouses but were stopped by the senior Heutz and directed to an empty room on the ground floor of the house. This remained our home for the three weeks we stayed in Geverik. Several things remain perfectly clear in my memory of our stay in the Heutz household. Mr Max Phair, our section commander, was an inveterate pipe-smoker and was always looking for ways to augment his meagre supply of pipe tobacco. I have seen him crumpling up cigarettes and mixing the proceeds with his pipe tobacco to bulk up his supply. When he discovered many thousands of tobacco leaves hanging up to dry in the family greenhouse, his joy knew no bounds and he lost no time in striking a deal for some with farmer Heutz. The trick was to take several leaves and roll them up tightly and then wrap string around the bundle to compress them further. After several days of compression the bundle or 'prick' was undone and sliced thinly with a sharp knife. We all watched this process being carried out on the bonnet of his jeep and waited with bated breath for him to fill the last and only pipe that remained to him. The clouds of choking fumes that the stuff produced were most offensive, even to Max Phair, who it was claimed could smoke raw hemlock leaves. After the lighting ceremony Meneer Heutz was seen walking quietly into the house with a wry grin on his face. To add insult to injury, a few days later Mr Phair was standing on top of the threshing box watching the sheaves of oats being fed into the intake hopper when his pipe fell out of his mouth and into the gaping maw of the machine. Quickly he dismounted and ran around to the output end of the machine and thrust his cupped hand under the trickle of grain as it dropped into the sacks. A few bits of brown wood and vulcanite among the oats told those watching that his one and only pipe had not survived the trip.

Sitting one evening in the room allotted to us, I was cleaning my pistol, the same Colt .45 I had acquired on the beach. I had taken the magazine out and as usual unloaded the cartridges from it and stood all eight of them in a row on the table. I cleaned the magazine, oiled it and placed it on the table beside the eight rounds. I then dismantled the pistol completely, rodded out the barrel, oiled everything and reassembled the pistol. I then pulled back the action a couple of times, drew a bead on the light switch by the door and pulled the trigger. I was not prepared for the crash as the gun went off and the switch disappeared in a cloud of broken bakelite chips. Teddy Edwards came roaring into the room and must have seen my white face and demanded to know who I had shot. When I explained what had happened we both counted the rounds on the table. Eight of them were still lying beside the empty magazine. I never carried more than eight rounds on my person and the rest of the .45 ammunition was in the section transport as a supply for the Thompson sub-machine guns of the section. The pistol had been completely stripped and I had pushed the cleaning rod right through the barrel several times. The magazine was not loaded or even in the butt of the pistol. To this day I still ponder the possibilities of where that spare round came from. I had been handling firearms since the age of ten and had always been told never to treat them with undue familiarity. I always shudder to think of the possibility of one of the daughters of the house walking through that door at the moment I pulled the trigger. I might even have pointed the barrel at the ceiling and shot the old girl upstairs through the floorboards.[6]

The children of the Heutz family consisted of three daughters and two sons, all of whom were in their teens or early twenties. The girls

6 Pete told this story several times over the years, usually in the context of emphasising the need for great care in the use of firearms. 'Never point a gun at anyone, loaded or not.' He always insisted on the inexplicability of what happened when the only explanation is that he, for once, had been careless.

were all very domesticated and did not seem to have any occupation other than giving assistance to their mother in the running of the farm household and the poultry. The two boys were fully occupied in farmwork with their father. All the farm production beyond family consumption was, we were told, taken by the Third Reich at a fixed price determined by the local Gauleiter. The whole of the family were extremely kind to us and insisted on doing our washing in return for soap, which was quite unobtainable. Their main concern was what would happen to them should the British be driven out and the Germans return. All the people who were not strictly farmers could be conscripted into the German labour organisations and sent to almost anywhere in Nazi-occupied territory. Another fear of the mother was that her boys might be conscripted into the Dutch Army, now that Holland was almost free, and sent to fight in the Dutch East Indies against the Japanese. Secretly we thought that a few years in the forces might not be a bad thing for them. The people of Geverik gave a party-cum-concert for the Headquarters troops who were stationed in and around the village. A splendid party it was, with lashings of alcoholic drinks and food. All the latest British and American popular tunes came rolling out of the piano and accordion band. This proved to us beyond doubt that the radio receivers had not been handed into the occupying Germans as per orders. Failure to comply with orders of this kind was often punishable by long imprisonment and sometimes shooting. Anna, the eldest of the daughters, who spoke very good English, told us stories of the earliest days of the occupation when some of the local people defied orders to do this or that. The Dutch police would come and arrest the offenders and hand them over to the Gestapo representatives for the area. After that they just disappeared and were never heard of again.

As Winter 1944 approached we moved further south to a part of Limburg that was more urban than the pleasant farmland around Geverik. After pulling into a small town the vehicles were parked up and camouflaged in the usual manner with the inevitable crowd of inquisitive children crowding around each truck or AFV. There was something very different about these children. They were very quiet and just stood staring with large sunken eyes in pale faces. It was not until our cooks served out the food to us that we realised these kids were starving. I don't think one man of the whole headquarters had anything to eat that evening. The kids scoffed every crumb in sight. Most of them carried part of the food that we gave them home to brothers or sisters or parents. After breakfast next day a regimental order was issued to the effect that all ranks were to eat the rations provided or risk being charged with 'conduct prejudicial etc etc …' We were relieved of any further feelings of guilt by the arrival of lorryloads of rations which had been freed up by our advance. It seems that the Germans had taken our raids up to Arnhem rather badly and had stopped completely the already meagre rations allowed to the Dutch under their jurisdiction. It seemed incredible to us that the people of Geverik had so much and yet these urban Dutch had absolutely nothing. Each small advance by our troops liberated a village or two, wherein the people were lucky to eat turnip soup.

As the winter deepened into the coldest in living memory the scale of fighting slackened and units were less mobile. My keenest recollection was of the intense cold. Daytime mobility of the limbs made the hours of light passable but the nights were a long fight to keep up body temperature. The idea was to find a building which still had windows unbroken and few if any holes in the roof. It was impossible for everyone to sleep in the trucks since Jeeps were open to the elements and the half-tracks were used as permanent wireless vehicles with two sets in each manned twenty-four hours a day. This left the three-tonners of the cooks, stores and electricians which were either at B echelon or full of their own people or stores and rations. The Bren carrier was an open-topped vehicle jealously occupied by Driver Smith. He would spread over it a looted canvas and retire inside like a spider into its lair. The choice of putting most of the blankets and available bedding on top or underneath was a matter of individual preference. Too much on top resulted in the cold from the floor striking upwards into the flesh, whereas a protected bottom meant a frozen upper side. Bearing in mind that we were still in Holland and friendly territory, we were forbidden to loot the civvy houses for comforts. All the troops respected this arrangement and tried to imagine a similar situation occurring at home. Breaches of the pattern were punished not so much by officialdom but by the offenders being ostracised by the rest of the section. It was fairly important to know the sleeping places of most of the section since we the NCOs had to wake everyone at least one hour before dawn for the morning stand to. We had barely got warm enough to sleep when we had to kick the chaps awake to stand around in the pitch darkness waiting for the possible attack. To show a light was out of the question so we had to memorise where everyone was dossing down. Failure to wake an individual might result in the unfortunate sleeper being charged. For the same reason, the cooks were unable to start breakfast until the flame of the Hydra burner would not be too obvious. The Hydras were like a huge blowlamp which threw a jet of flame under collapsible stands on which the dixies were stood.[7] The first mug of tea on a frozen morning was the epitome of luxury. It was made from real tea and had real sugar in it and condensed milk. Quite delicious. For all the tremendous facility behind the American forces, all they could come up with for front-line troops to drink was lemonade powder.

Further south during October and November the Americans were blunting their spearheads against the formidable Siegfried line and building up for an almighty thrust into the Fatherland. Our Corps, the 30th British, had taken a severe hammering in the endeavour to relieve the Airborne at Arnhem. It transpired that our commander, General Brian Horrocks, had been told by Field Marshal Montgomery not to involve his Corps too deeply in any heavy action for the time being. The lull was not to last for long. November 15th found us in support of the 43rd Wessex Division with whom we had fought on several occasions earlier in the campaign. Also 30 Corps had been 'lent' the 84th Infantry Division of the US Army. These were raw troops newly arrived in Europe from the USA and had seen no action. We heard we were to attack Geilenkirchen, reputedly a tough part of the Siegfried line.[8] The weather had turned to rain and the ground was most unsuitable for tanks, particularly Shermans with narrow tracks. The Germans had learnt their lesson well on the Eastern front and had widened the design of their tracks to a point where even their Tigers could manoeuvre on the muddiest terrain. After midday on 16 November hundreds of heavy bombers went over, both RAF and USAAF. We feared for the infantry and armour massed on the start line since the American bomb aimers or 'bombardiers' were notoriously 'tit'-happy and had a nasty habit of dropping their eggs on their own and at times our infantry. Indeed the only American general to lose his life in France during the 1944 campaign was killed by bombs from his own aircraft.[9] In the case of Geilenkirchen, we heard later that as a result of warnings about inaccurate bombing the loads had been dropped too far from

---

7 The Hydra burners were fuelled by compressed petrol, and although like many pieces of British Army equipment they enjoyed longevity, they were eventually phased out for safety reasons.

8 The 84th Infantry Division, the Railsplitters, arrived in England on 1 October 1944 and landed at Omaha beach early in November. By 18 November the Division was involved in the attack on Geilenkirchen.

9 Lesley James McNair, Commanding General, Army Ground Forces – killed by friendly fire airstrike at Saint-Lô in Normandy on 25 July 1944.

the objective and the USAAF raid was only about 3 per cent effective.[10] Our regiment together with all AGRA (Army Group Royal Artillery) troops fired a prolonged barrage on selected targets. This firepower was added to that of the artillery of the 43rd British and 84th American divisions. The communication in the British artillery, particularly AGRA units, was so good that shells could be dropped on a selected target within sixty seconds of coordinates being given to the gun positions. This was a far better performance than that of either the German or American artillery. It was during this action that I first saw 'counter-battery' firing in operation. Troublesome incoming shells or mortar bombs were tracked by radar and the enemy gun positions plotted from the results. Immediately troop, battery or regimental fire could be returned and the source of the annoyance eliminated. This was of great comfort to pretty static units such as stores dumps and forward airfields but of little use to forward troops under sporadic harassing fire too intermittent to track properly. It was, however, a great technical achievement and the boffins deserved much more praise than they received. One such operator of counter-battery work was Staff Serjeant Ron Spencer, who had been our Section Serjeant with the 76th (H) Field Regiment of the 3rd British Infantry Division in 1942. At first the attack on Geilenkirchen went well but ran into trouble when the guns of the Static Westwall opened up and the Duke of Cornwall's Light Infantry ran into the 10th SS Panzers under General Harmel. The DCLI suffered a severe mauling and when the village of Hoven was re-taken by the Germans the DCLI were virtually annihilated. As an action the Geilenkirchen episode was not an outstanding success and spelled the end of mixing British and American units.[11] The 84th Division had failed to get through to Hoven to relieve the DCLI. There is no doubt that the opposition that the American infantry had met was almost impenetrable and those who have seen the Westwall 'dragon's teeth' will understand why the American Shermans were unable to get within firing distance of the German armour.

We withdrew to regroup and wipe our bloody noses. A great number of accounts of actions during November and early December

---

10 It is true that the Allied advance suffered from a lack of artillery support, caused not only by fear of inflicting friendly fire casualties but also by heavy rain, which made it more difficult to bring up armoured support.

11 The operation, code-named Clipper, did succeed in reducing the Geilenkirchen salient in the Siegfried line. It was suspended on 23 November and the 84th Infantry Division reverted to American command.

1944 tell of the appalling casualties taken by very raw American units that were expected to defeat battle-hardened German troops defending their homeland. Field Marshal Montgomery was criticised by the other allied Brass but he was well loved by the British troops. He would never throw his units into a fight unless he was sure of winning. El Alamein was the first example of this strategy. First a great build-up of strength in armour, artillery and stores, akin to winding up a huge spring and then suddenly the pent-up energy was released in a violent breakthrough. Above all Montgomery believed in artillery, masses of it. The barrage before El Alamein was reputed to have surpassed anything in history. Later we were to see even bigger artillery barrages. The failure at Arnhem has been held up as a mistake in strategy by Monty. It was in essence due to the faulty intelligence given to the British planners. There was reputed to be no German armour in the Arnhem area. In fact the 9th SS Panzer division was refitting a few miles north of the air landing area. Otherwise Monty would have had the Guards Armoured Division and the 8th Armoured Brigade over the Rhine by late September. It was widely held by our troops that the idea of a salient up the Rhine was, while thought up by Montgomery, only precipitated as retaliation to the wild and unauthorised forays by 'Blood and Guts' Patton. The escapades by Patton, though sometimes successful, were perpetrated by the greatest glory seeker of the whole war. Patton was shown in his true colours when he slapped an enlisted man across the face in Sicily, declaring that he 'wouldn't have yellow bastards in his outfit.' That time the publicity stunt went sadly awry and 'ole Blood and Guts' ended up with egg all down his tunic. Generals don't hit soldiers in hospitals.[12] It would be very difficult to imagine a British general dressing up with not one but two pearl-handled revolvers. It was a great source of amusement to us. Only those escapades that were successful and useful as morale boosters for the 'folks back home' were publicised. The failures never hit the headlines.

XXX Corps was in reserve around a large area including Dinant, Namur and eastwards to Liege. Our regiment was still in support of 43 Div near Liege when on 16 December all hell broke loose in

12 Patton in fact slapped two soldiers in Sicily, on 3 and 10 August 1943. They were in hospital with combat stress fatigue, or shellshock, which Patton didn't believe in. After the 3 August incident a war correspondent reported that Patton exclaimed that 'shellshock is an invention of the Jews'. When Eisenhower got to hear of the slapping incidents he strongly suggested that Patton should apologise, which he did – grudgingly.

the form of a terrific German breakthrough in the Ardennes. A large group of American troops including the 101st Airborne and 10th Armoured Division were surrounded at Bastogne. It was here that General McAuliffe made his famous reply of 'NUTS' when asked to surrender. McAuliffe's people were relieved on 26 December by the US 4th Armoured Division.[13] The German thrust carried enough momentum to punch a hole 50 miles deep into allied-held territory. No doubt the fact that the weather had been very bad for weeks was a contributory factor to the German success. It was during this period that our aircraft had been grounded. As soon as the weather cleared enough the Luftwaffe sent over several squadrons and destroyed up to 200 allied aircraft on the ground. The Ardennes battle was almost entirely an American show and by 28 January it was all over and the line straightened out. It had cost the Americans almost 77,000 casualties and had cost the Wehrmacht any further hope of large-scale aggression. From here on it was all defence. The German losses in men and equipment were enormous, equipment that could have been put to much better use defending a line east of the Rhine.

Christmas 1944 was passed quietly enough in reserve for us of the 147th Field Regiment and as usual the officers and serjeants served the men their early morning tea (gunfire) and dinner. The men received several bottles of beer each and most had saved up parcels from home to make the day a bit more special than the usual cold and dreary routine. Later the senior NCOs and the officers cracked a bottle or two of issue spirits which had been put aside from the monthly ration of duty free for those above the rank of corporal. The issue of spirits by rank rather than age seemed to me a most unfair method. Corporals Coles and Whate were much older than Teddy and me and dearly loved a drop of whisky. For this reason Teddy and I used to give the corporals more than half our ration. Cliff Coles ran a newsagent business in Burley-in-Wharfedale and Eric Whate a wholesalers in Newark. The other two corporals were unquenchable Jack Halford, a raw-boned loveable Mancunian who in civvy street was an undertaker; and Harry Liley, our Electrician Signals, who worked for a bus company in Heckmondwike when not engaged in war. Harry was seldom seen without a pipe in his mouth. The pipe was held together with black lineman's tape and reeked horribly. January 12th saw us in a small

13 Brigadier General Anthony McAuliffe was the acting commander of the 101st Airborne. His reply had to be translated to the German Commander, Heinrich von Luttwitz, as 'Go to Hell'. Pete does not mention that the 4th Armoured Division was led by Patton!

mining village in Belgium called Trebeek not far from the German border.[14] The Signal Section was billeted in a row of small miners' cottages along a terraced street. The people were as usual extremely kind and allowed us to sleep on their floors out of the icy coldness of the street. The womenfolk expressed their shame at not being able to feed us and kept telling us it was not the Belgian way to treat guests in this manner. We soon realised that they were living marginally above starvation level. We naturally gave the children every bit of extra titbit in the way of chocolate that we could scrounge.

On 14 January we moved over the border into Germany and occupied a bleakly situated row of state farms or smallholdings. We had the signal office located in one house next to Regimental HQ and the Signals billet was on the other side of the signal office. After we had established lines to the batteries and closed down the wireless links for traffic but as usual kept a listening watch, Jack Halford and I were sitting in the kitchen of our billet making a brew when we noticed that there was a chunk of the downstairs area that had no door to it. After walking around the outside a couple of times we realised that it had indeed no visible entrance. On re-entering the kitchen Jack suddenly saw that the door was obscured by a large kitchen dresser that had been placed in front of the opening. Moving the dresser was the work of very few minutes. Behind, the door had been nailed shut. Here again a claw hammer from the line truck soon removed the nails. Inside was a veritable hoard of food. Six sides of bacon were in prime condition. Large crocks of eggs in isinglass.[15] A sack of sugar. Several sacks of potatoes. Three cases of corned beef, 24 cans to the case. The room was fairly large and every nook and cranny was filled with food. We were halfway through our search when there was a hell of a bang from next door. We rushed out to meet the signal office staff reeling out of the front door covered with white plaster and dust. All four – two operators, a lineman and a DR – were holding their hands to their

14 I think Pete has had a rare lapse of memory here, or made an error in naming his country. The community of Treebeek (sic) near the German border, part of the municipality of Brunssum, is in the Netherlands, not Belgium. Treebeek is near to Sittard and Susteren, which Pete also mentions; and the area was a coal mining centre until the 1970s. It seems clear that even though Pete mentions Belgium several times in the next pages his unit was actually in the Netherlands.

15 Isinglass is a gelatin derived from fish swim bladders. In a water solution, it was used to seal the pores of eggshells, which were then stored in an airtight container.

ears and gasping for breath. Investigation showed that an 88 shell had arrived via the front window and exploded against the rear wall of the signal office. Not one of the four occupants had the slightest injury beyond deafening and a severe shaking up. We concluded that for a shell to arrive on that low trajectory it must have been firing in an anti-tank role. It was even suggested that the round came from one of our guns that had been fired by accident. When the signal office had been sorted out and new operators found for the exchanges, normality was restored and we were able to resume the stocktaking of our bonanza. There were four large crocks, thirty inches high, full of dripping complete with earthenware lids. We held a council of the occupants of the billet and decided that we would surrender some of the food to our regimental cookhouse for the benefit of the headquarters. The rest we would load on the line jeep and take it back to the street in Trebeek. The jeep when fully loaded was nowhere near big enough to hold the loot. Jack Halford told his chaps to unload the line trailer (10 cwt GS) and hitch it behind the jeep. Four of us crammed into the jeep and set off for the little street in Trebeek and knocked at the door of the house where I had stayed. The miner was delighted to see us and invited us in. Instead we took him to the trailer and pulled back the tarpaulin and shone a torch on the contents. Utter silence. He looked at us in dumb amazement and Jack motioned up and down the street to indicate all the residents and then pointed to the food. The miner went to several of his neighbours and brought them out to look at the stuff. One of the wives actually fainted when she saw the big crocks of dripping. We told them to get the stuff off the vehicles quickly and out of sight. Within a few minutes the jeep and the trailer were quite empty and the street quite bare of any telltale signs. We made it quite clear before we mounted up and drove off that the food was to be divided as fairly as possible among the street. When we got back all was quiet and we had not been missed. The following day Robinson, one of the DRs, called in Trebeek and on his return told us that the people were out in the street with several tables doling out the stuff to a queue of their neighbours. I don't know what it did to the Belgians but it gave us a hell of a lot of fun. Most houses in Germany had a picture of the Fuhrer above the mantelshelf in their kitchens or living rooms. It was the usual practice to wrench off the toilet seat and make a frame for the Fuhrer. Before we left the house with the secret room the boys inverted the Fuhrer and gave him the seat as well, making sure that he had a double insult for luck.

On 19 January F Echelon moved to Susteren with B Echelon at Schimmert in the most dreadful weather, freezing and driven snow.

I had occasion to visit 8th Armoured Brigade at Sittard and sustained three punctures. Driver Pugsley was not amused. We had two spares and ran the last one flat for ten kilometres. By the time we got back F Echelon[16] had moved to Saeffelen north-east of Sittard. There are lots of prisoners coming back, all looking starved and totally dejected. As I watch the prisoners a buzz bomb comes over very low heading in a west-north-westerly direction. I had never seen one so close before. We had, however, seen many V2 rockets climbing into the sky from western Holland before it was cleared of Germans. Just a trail of smoke going up and up until it disappeared into the cloudbase. No particular launch base as they are mobile and can be launched from almost anywhere. Had they been static like the V1s the RAF would have found and eliminated them.[17] On 24 January I was having a part welded by the LAD at a place 6 km south-west of Sittard when I received a flash from the welder and spent the next couple of days virtually blind. I managed to obtain a pair of dark glasses from Bombardier Capstick, the MO's orderly. The brilliant sunshine on the snow didn't help at all. On the evening Teddy came down about tea time and we pushed off to Geverik, where the family Heutz fed us again. On the 26th after a full belly we hear that Orme and James have returned from leave in the UK. They are the first pair to have been on leave and report that in spite of the dreadfully fatiguing and dirty journey, their leave was marvellous. Mr Phair, our OC, is also reported to be back from the UK but I have not seen him yet.[18] On the 27th I return to my old job at F Echelon, where Teddy has been relieving me for a week or two. I am very glad of the activity again since the idleness of B Echelon is very

---

16 In a field regiment, F (or Fighting) Echelon consisted of the reconnaissance parties, the Regimental HQ group and the gun groups. B Echelon contained the personnel and vehicles needed to collect and distribute stores. A Echelon linked the other two and contained back-up personnel and vehicles needed to maintain the unit's fighting efficiency.

17 The V2 rockets were transported on a *Meillerwagen,* a trailer with a hoist to place the rocket on its launchpad. The missile could be launched from practically anywhere, and the system was so small and mobile that only one *Meillerwagen* was ever caught in action by Allied aircraft.

18 In this section of his memoir Pete occasionally writes in the present tense. It feels in places as though he is copying material directly from a diary. For most of the memoir it is clear that he is writing from memory but around these pages some of his time and place references are too specific to be memorised. If he did keep diaries of his time in the army they have, most unfortunately, been lost.

boring. The cold is frightful. On the 29th the Regimental HQ moves to Moorveld near Beek. We are supposed to be due for a maintenance rest but it is too cold to sleep and it is impossible to hold a spanner. We are due for something big to happen soon. Speculation is rife that it will be a push through the Reichswald forest and up to the Rhine.

It has been a constant battle to keep the wireless vehicles supplied with charged batteries. These are 125 ampere lead acid accumulators, each 6 volts, two of which are needed for each set. The M-14 International half-tracks have no in-built charging equipment which could keep the batteries charged in situ. They need to be manhandled in and out of the trucks almost every day and replaced with the recharged ones. The discharged batteries were then taken to B Echelon for charging overnight. This entailed the lugging in and out of a jeep or weasel.[19] Pretty backbreaking work and mostly carried out in the darkness. At B Echelon the charging equipment consisted of 1260 watt dynamos driven by Jowett or Norman flat twin petrol engines driving direct or through twin vee-belts. Quite efficient but the engines were prone to break valve springs. Harry Liley and his assistant would sleep with their heads practically on the engine bed, totally oblivious to the noise of the exhaust and the vibration. Any change in note or if the engine stopped, they would both be instantly awake. Each M-14 was issued with a small charger called a 'chore horse'. This was a small petrol engine of about 125 cc direct coupled to a 12-volt dynamo which would put out in the region of 12 to 15 amps. They were quite suitable for their purpose but a Brigade Signals order had been issued to the effect that they should under no circumstance be used except in dire emergency and on the direct order of the OC Section. This order made a great deal of sense since there was no way they would have stood up to prolonged daily use. It was quite necessary to change the batteries every day. Since a voltage check is not a very accurate method of determining the state of a cell, I had the operators test the gravity of the electrolyte with a hydrometer. This helped Corporal Liley back at B Ech and prolonged battery life. I was determined to find a method of charging the M14 batteries in situ, thereby avoiding shifting mounds of gear in each half-track every time batteries were changed. I had cast an inquisitive eye on several small engines in Holland but the OC forbade me to liberate one from the Dutch.

19 The M29 Weasel was a small tracked all-terrain vehicle, particularly useful on snow.

On 1 February we move as a regiment to Moll just a few kilometres north of Bourg Leopold.[20] The billet we were left with was awful with rats running everywhere and ten children in the family. Teddy and I vow to get out tomorrow before our kit gets full of bugs. Here we do two days solid maintenance. The gin palace was missing on two cylinders due to broken valve springs. The LAD claimed that they were unobtainable except from the UK. Harry Liley and I fitted springs from the Jeep spares and to hell with the LAD. Also Cliff Coles's chore horse wouldn't start and we had to take off the flywheel to fit new points. The chore horses, although not used extensively, were started every few days to ensure their availability. Reveille at 0300 on 4 February and moved off at 0400 from Moll and land up in a most inhospitable billet in Eindhoven. They have a roaring stove in the kitchen and never ask us in to warm our hands. We sleep in a freezing room upstairs. We were glad to shake the snow of Eindhoven off our boots and drive off at 1230. Halted 13 km from 's-Hertogenbosch until after midnight and finally arrive 6 km south east of Nijmegen in part of the Reichswald forest. After digging in and camouflaging we get breakfast at 1130. We retired early to try to catch up on some sleep. On 7 February we are briefed on the coming assault.[21] We are in support of the 53rd Welsh Division who will be assaulting through the Reichswald forest and on into Germany around Kleve and Goch. We are told that the CRA[22] will be linked by radio to pretty well all gun divisions so that he can fire all guns simultaneously to give the Hun one hell of a shock before our attack goes in. A sharp thaw has set in and the place is a sea of mud, axle deep. We receive some heavy shells from Jerry but they don't do a lot of damage. 15th Scottish Division are also to engage in the attack and I hear that 1 Battalion Royal Scots are in the Nijmegen area. After some enquiries I locate my brother-in-law Captain Alastair MacIntyre with his company just outside the town and we have a long ragchew and a brew-up with a drop of whisky in it.

At 0500 on 8 February all the guns of several divisions, plus unattached AGRA medium regiments, tanks, Bofors and light

---

20 Sic. Perhaps Pete means Mol, which is north-west of Leopoldsburg. If so, the Regiment has moved into Belgium. This is entirely possible because hereabouts, in Limburg, a tongue of Dutch land including Maastricht is almost surrounded by Belgian territory on the one side and German on the other. Saeffelen, mentioned by Pete above, is actually in Germany.

21 It was code-named Operation Veritable.

22 Commander, Royal Artillery.

ack-ack – in fact every piece of ordnance – opened up at the same instant. The barrage was by far the most intense ever fired[23] and outstripped that of El Alamein several times over. It went on for 24 hours, one agonising cacophony that went on until our ears rang and our heads felt like bursting. It was bad for us; in our imagination we could see the Germans cowering in their slit trenches. It was still very cold, though not quite freezing and the gunners were in their shirt sleeves feeding shells and cases into the breeches as fast as the RASC could unload their trucks of ammunition. All the time the hollow sound of medium shells going over our heads from the 60 pounders and American Long Toms behind us.[24] Suddenly it stopped and only intermittent firing continued. Now the infantry would be leaving the start line to advance into God knew what. It was never possible for us to know or even find out what was going on in our immediate front. To forward troops the news seemed to come via the BBC news bulletins rather than from our own Brigade or Division. Occasionally a DR would glean some information on his travels. This sort of 'gen' or 'dope' was always embroidered until it bore little resemblance to the truth. We found it more sensible to wait until the resultant advance told us that our attacks had been successful.

After the barrage the Regiment left Groesbeek and I was determined to stay behind with a small party and the charging engines so as not to interrupt the topping up of the batteries. At 0400 on 10 February the bulk of Robinson loomed up out of the dark on his BSA to lead us to the new location. We passed through a shallow valley that had been fought over during the original airborne landings in September. It had been no man's land ever since and the whole valley floor was littered with skeletal corpses at which hungry dogs and perhaps foxes had been nibbling. In the bright moonlight it was most eerie. We were the only trucks on that bit of road as far as we could see and we had only Robinson's word that we were on the correct route. It turned out that we were not on the correct road and Robinson had got himself quite lost. I had not been told where the regiment was going and I had no map. I told Robinson to sort himself out and bloody well find

23 A large claim, and one not easy to verify. It was, however, likely to have been the biggest barrage fired on the Western Front in the Second World War. The biggest barrage of the war was probably that fired by the Soviet Army at German positions on the Seelow Heights, east of Berlin, in April 1945.

24 Field guns, British and American respectively, with shells about 150mm diameter and a range of 10 kilometres or more.

us. He suggested that he go off and ask someone where we were but I forbade him to leave us and swan off anywhere. We did not rejoin the Regiment until 1400 in the afternoon, by which time the OC was going around in ever decreasing circles due to having no batteries for the sets. Robinson received a king-sized bollocking and was threatened with being put back on the leave rota – a fate worse than death to a man due to be married on his next leave.[25] Robinson was a great character and had two loves, motorcycles and photography. We had not been in Holland long before he had got hold of a Leica 3C[26] complete with motor attachment and all the trimmings. We dared not ask how he had got hold of it or how much government equipment or petrol had changed hands. He never let it out of his sight and even wore it round his neck at mealtimes. The major snag, however, was that film was in very short supply and in consequence he would take only a limited number of exposures of the boys.

The advance of XXX Corps into the Reichswald forest had taken the leading elements beyond Kranenburg on the road to Kleve and the regimental F Echelon was just short of Kleve.[27] I was again detailed to stay with B Echelon. We established ourselves in a builder's yard near a cross roads about a kilometre beyond Kranenburg. The builder's yard was well stocked with timber and Harry Liley was able to roof in his truck under the canvas tilt with tongued and grooved boards. We called back Cliff Coles's half-track and put a new roof on that as well. Cliff had been sitting in a pool of water where the canvas had been ripped by shrapnel. The light-coloured wood made the inside of the vehicles much brighter. The whole job took three hours and when Cliff went back to F Echelon Mr Phair sent back Eric Whate with his M14 to be done also. On 12 February one of the DRs told me that the 15th Scottish were in the Materborn area so I borrowed a bike and rode over to find Alastair. He was in great form but had not enjoyed the very wet push through the Reichswald. We drank tea with my whisky this time. In the builder's yard I found to my delight a suitable engine for my proposed charging plant. A single-cylinder horizontal machine, water cooled with the usual cast iron pot around the cylinder. It had an

25 'Put back' here probably means put further down the list, so that the leave would be delayed.

26 Leica, a German company founded in 1869, introduced their IIIC camera in 1940 and continued to make it until 1951. It was a 35mm rangefinder.

27 Home of the fourth wife of Henry VIII, Anne of Cleves.

automatic inlet and push rod-operated valves and impulse magneto.[28] All mounted on two wooden runners. On these projecting runners I was able to bolt a dynamo from an SP gun which I scrounged from the LAD. A couple of twin-groove pulleys and vee belts completed the ensemble.[29] We flashed it up into a couple of spare batteries and were delighted to get up to 50 amperes into a 12 volt bank. A carbon pile regulator from Harry Liley's junk box gave us complete control of the output. We called up F Echelon and asked the OC to come down at his convenience. We discussed several ways to carry the beast and although one of the trailers, 10 cwt GS, would have been ideal, neither could be spared. It was finally decided to see if it could be mounted on one of the M-14s above the winch.[30] We transported the thing on the back of a jeep and found that it fitted behind the winch on Cliff's M-14 as though by design and didn't even need bolting down. A couple of heavy leads were run back to the batteries and within the hour the batteries of both half-tracks were on charge. Fait accompli! All that lugging and unloading of kit had been eliminated at one fell swoop. The engine needed some further silencing of the exhaust but this was easily accomplished with the aid of materials found lying about. There was a slight vibration transmitted through the one half-track but Cliff soon became accustomed to it. While at the builder's yard we saw a convoy of six RASC trucks parked on the Kleve side of the crossroads. The drivers and mates were being briefed by a lieutenant and a couple of NCOs right on the crossroads. Stooging across the sky came a JU252 (Jerry's only wartime jet fighter) and dropped a bomb on the crossroads, killing nine of those being briefed. The six trucks caught fire and since they were carrying mainly petrol caused a tremendous blaze. The type of bomb was such as we had never seen before and descended in three pieces. The bomb itself was encased in two halves of a fibrous covering. On ejecting from the bomb rack the casing split and fluttered down in two halves while the bomb plummeted down unseen as the observer was watching the other two bits. This was the fate of the RASC boys as they watched the aircraft and the bomb casing. The JU252 was so fast it could accelerate away from pursuing Spitfires as though from a Tiger

28 Basically, a small petrol engine. An impulse magneto is an ignition system.

29 The engine powers the dynamo via the vee belts working on the pulleys.

30 The M14 half-track had a winch in front.

Moth.[31] Later in the day a dozen German PoWs were set to digging graves in a field near the crossroads. The RASC guards gave them the impression that the graves were for the diggers. The prisoners were visibly relieved when the corpses were brought out of a building and interred.

On 22 February we moved to Hau, a couple of kilometres south-west of Kleve. We felt much better after a good rest at the builders' yard. We were located at a farm where we loot eggs for supper. The roads are full of transport and we learn that we attack at first light tomorrow. During the next morning (24 February) we move into Goch, which has been shelled by our artillery and bombed by the RAF. It is in a terrible state and bulldozers have to be called up to clear a way for our armour. Halford and I go up in the Honey tank[32] and halt just before entering the town square. We saw through the open door of a shop on our left a press camera lying on a table. As there was no movement of traffic, we jumped out and looped a length of D3 cable round the camera and, retreating to the Honey, pulled it off the table. Nothing exploded. When we examined it more closely we find that it is covered with blood and has a note attached: 'finder please deliver to 53 Div HQ'. Since we were in support of 53 Div this presented no problem. When we remount the Honey a mortar bomb drops on an SP gun at the opposite corner of the square and brews up some red smoke rounds. Clouds of red smoke ascend to the sky and as though by magic the Typhoons are sending the rockets and make a hell of a mess of the town centre. I pulled back on one stick and get out as fast as possible to where our chaps are parked at the entrance to the town. Halford and I start looking for a place for the boys to bed down and visit several houses in one street. One looks ideal until we find a hole in the ceiling of a room. It is a very round hole that was obviously made by a bomb that failed to explode. We got out very quickly. While looking at another house for billets Jack Halford discovered the body of a baby girl lying on a sofa in an upstairs room. She is quite dead but has no signs of injury. A beautiful blonde child and Jack sobs as though his heart would break. The troops have a habit of digging in the gardens

31 Either a lapse of memory or an error on Pete's part; there was no JU252; the Ju 287 was tested but never entered service. Pete probably means the Messerschmitt Me 262, the first operational jet fighter and fighter-bomber.

32 The M3A1 Stuart; the first American tank used by the British. It was highly reliable so nicknamed Honey, according to legend; but its firepower and armour were soon outmatched.

of these and other German houses for buried wine and valuables. Jack takes out a dresser drawer and makes a coffin complete with lid. He insists on getting the padre and having a small burial detail. With great reverence she was buried. Jack sat up all night making a sign in German and English: DO NOT DIG. BODY OF UNKNOWN BABY GIRL. Jack was completely convinced of the futility of war.

After the burial of the baby, I was detailed to find the HQ water tanker, which had gone back to the edge of the town to fill up at a small river which ran under a bridge in a smart residential area. At least it had been smart before the shelling and the bombing. The reason for the delay was a longish queue of other water tankers. I decided to wait for the driver to fill up. As I propped the BSA against a wall, the sound of a piano came through the darkness from a house across the road. With my 'lamp, hand, electric' I found the rather imposing doorway and entered the building, the strains of the Warsaw Concerto becoming louder all the time.[33] Through a door to the left was what had obviously been the drawing room and there I found a grand piano being played by an infantryman of 53 Div. His audience consisted of myself and two German corpses lying face down on the carpet which was black with their blood. The pianist said quietly 'put the bloody light out'. I put the light out but stayed a while to listen to the most moving recital that I have ever heard, before or since. Before the light was extinguished I saw that he had placed his sten on the top of the piano, from which he had wiped the dust, plaster and filth with the sleeve of his greatcoat. I felt my way out carefully and rejoined the tanker driver, who was just completing his fill-up.

On 25 February the road 'down' is closed to allow armour to come up. Our A Echelon get up to us just in time and at 2130 we are mortared and shelled heavily. Five of our chaps end up in the Regimental Aid Post but are not evacuated. I hear that 3rd Div is close and pinch a bike and find my old chum of Prestatyn days and 3rd Div Sigs, Andy Andrews. I found him in good fettle and promoted to serjeant. He gave me tea and whisky and I promised to look him up again. The following day Cliff Coles and I ventured up the steeple of Goch church. The first bit is a stone spiral staircase but the flight up to the top is a vertical ladder fastened to the wall. The whole idea was stupid from

---

33 A short work for piano and orchestra written for the British film *Dangerous Moonlight*, made in 1941. The film is about the Polish struggle against the Nazis in 1939 but it's also – of course – a love story. The composer was Richard Addinsell. Spike Milligan, not a bad musician, described the Warsaw Concerto as 'bloody awful'.

the outset because the Hun must have seen us through the slots in the tower. When he opened up with 20 mm light ackack guns[34] at the tower we retreated down like a pair of scalded cats, breathless and wiser. On 2 March we left Goch for a location 2 km short of Weeze but to get there we spent the night on the road held up by traffic jams. While we waited in the vehicles, unable to draw off the road because of steep banks on either side, enemy aircraft fly up and down the column machine gunning and bombing all and sundry. The weather had turned to frost again. We were all suicidally miserable and couldn't even brew up. The regiment sustain quite a few casualties but none of them are Signals personnel. At 0530 next morning we move off again to 3 km north of Kevelaer but on the way the M-14-1[35] has its radiator and pipe broken by shrapnel from a mortar bomb. The LAD take all day to fix the trouble. Finally we move on through Geldern to 2 km short of Issum, where we are shelled quite heavily. We loot lots of eggs, which I boil hard since I cannot eat them any other way without bread. While compo rations are very good, they tend to become monotonous. The A packs are without doubt the most toothsome but they always seemed to get picked out by the people at B Echelon before we get them up front. The only young men we see are not Germans but Russian, Polish or Lithuanian slave labourers employed to keep the German agriculture going in the absence of the male farmers. They appear quite indolent and now that we are present pay no attention to the orders of the matriarch in charge. They make no attempt to dissuade us from pinching eggs and the odd fowl.

There is a rumour that we are going out of the line. The regiment moves to Geldern and we find pretty good billets for the chaps. I take a turn on wireless watch to give the operators a chance to have a rest and stretch their legs. Halford's linemen get the lines out to the batteries and Brigade and we are able to close the wireless links down for maintenance. The juggernaut, as my charging machine has been christened, is running continuously to charge everything in sight. I find a new Pfaff sewing machine and after sewing all my flashes and stripes on a newly issued battledress, I am prevailed upon by pretty well all the section to do theirs. I find that Lance Corporal stripes are the very devil to keep in position while machining. It is easier to do them by hand. Someone suggested tacking them on first and then it was plain sailing. On 12 March I am detailed to take an advance

34 Anti-aircraft guns.

35 Gun carriage.

party back to Goch. The billets I found are not too bad. A sewage farm control room is reserved for a signal office and serjeants' billet. The main party arrive at 1500 and some jerry jet planes harass us at 1800. Ack ack is quite useless against them and the pilots know it and become very cheeky. I heat water for my evening wash and when my back is turned Teddy steals it and a blazing row develops. This is not the way for senior NCOs to behave in front of the men. The chaps ignore Teddy for days. I think we are all getting a bit edgy after the strain of the past few weeks. Advantage is taken of the lull to catch up on maintenance of all the gear and Liley and I make up new remote control cables for the M-14s. These are used when static and enable the wireless sets to be used remotely from an ops room or command post. Otherwise the officer concerned would have to present himself at the back of the half-track. It is so quiet and tranquil that we blanco our kit to keep it tidy.

On 17 March I am ordered to present myself at the Maas-Waal canal to witness water loading trials and a simulated crossing of the canal. They seem to forget that some of those present were on the assault of the beaches and we criticise loudly. The colonel in charge is not very enamoured of our behaviour. His outfit came ashore dryfoot at D plus 45. I hoped that Jerry doesn't shoot very straight![36] The highlight of the loading trials event came when two subalterns fell in and had to be fished out looking like drowned rats. We the spectators fell about with uncontrollable mirth and the colonel in charge danced up and down with rage. We were then given a long lecture on the fact that it might seem funny now but when we came to cross the Rhine and assault the east bank the smile would probably be wiped off our faces, et cetera ad nauseam. As one of our party remarked, it was better than going to the pictures. On 20 March we are told that the section has been allotted eight leave vacancies for the UK for April and Cliff Coles and I are to go on 18 April. The preparation for the Rhine Crossing is very thorough and there seems to be more fuss than before D-Day at Arromanches. Lots of bombers going over in waves. There is a continuous smokescreen at the river. The smoke candles are made by Brocks and Standard fireworks manufacturers. The smoke lies in a white mat over the whole area and is very pungent. Our throats become as dry as tinder. We move up to Appeldorn, some 800 metres from the river, where our guns find targets on the opposite bank. The

36 Rather obscure. Presumably Pete means that the simulated crossing was a shambles and its participants could suffer when making a real crossing.

medium regiments in our rear are using 222 airburst fuses. These are a barometric device and cause the shells to explode before touching the ground so as to cause havoc among troops not protected from above. The weather is clear at the medium guns' position but we are in a hailstorm and the 60 pounder shells are going off over our heads as the hailstones somehow trigger the 222 fuses. All and sundry dive under the vehicles for cover. We are in support of the 51st (Highland) Division and by the time we get through to their Div HQ about the shelling the hailstorm has stopped.

Alastair is to be in the first wave to assault but the 15th Scottish Div is not on our immediate sector. At 2100 the Black Watch and Argyll and Sutherland Highlanders cross the river against moderate opposition and are able to push out a small bridgehead. It is an amazing sight to witness a full airborne operation and now the smoke has gone we have a grandstand view of the whole spectacle. Parachute drops of men and material followed by glider-borne troops with light artillery and jeeps. The bridgehead is quite secure now and the engineers are pushing a Class 15 pontoon bridge across.[37] There is no immediate need for us to cross the river since we can still shell targets on the other side of the bridgehead from our present gun positions and tanks are of more importance. I hear that the Royal Scots have linked up with the Airborne. No news of Alastair. We cross at 0945 on 27 March just north of Rees and assemble at Speldrop. The following day the Regiment assemble closely at a location 5 km south-west of Isselburg near an autobahn where the Typhoons have a field day brewing up retreating Jerries. It seems that a breakout from the bridgehead is due at any time now as A Echelon come up with the 3-tonners bringing petrol for 100 miles and rations for six days. March 30th. Reveille at 0330 and off at 0500. We pull off the road at Anholt, where we receive a stonk of heavy shelling. RHQ troops take a few casualties, fortunately no one killed. The casualties are all occupants of soft-skinned vehicles. We move on to occupy a school between Anholt and Varsseveld.[38] The school has very recently been vacated by German troops. The sickly-sweet smell of the Wehrmacht is everywhere and some kraut has defecated enormously in the doorway as a welcome present for us. Great care is needed before entering any building or room for fear of booby traps, which are a favourite trick of the Hun. They don't even

37 A temporary floating bridge designed to support a load of up to 15 tons.

38 The Dutch–German border runs roughly east to west at this point. This move means the RHQ has moved back into the Netherlands.

leave a warning sign for their own people nowadays. In Normandy they used to leave a brush leaning against the wall of a house.

April 1st. On to Varsseveld proper and occupy an agricultural college of sorts, where we receive some sporadic shelling. Halford, with a couple of his linemen, walk around looking for billets in case we stay overnight. A movement is spotted in an upstairs window and we see a German steel helmet drop quickly out of sight. Jack sends his two chaps round to the back while he and I enter quietly through the front door. A gentle clumping sound comes from the floor of the upstairs front room. We bellow 'heraus' several times but there is no movement. Jack whispers 'I'll shift the buggers' and takes out a 36 grenade from his pouch.[39] Before he pulls the pin I suggest tying a length of field cable across the stairs a foot up from the newel post. This is done and we move outside under the front room window. Jack pulls out his grenade again but I make him unscrew the baseplug and take out the primer.[40] Having done that he hurls it through the windowpane of the bedroom. Instantly there is a rush of panic-stricken boots on the floor upstairs. They clatter down the stairs and on reaching the bottom all three fall in a heap at our feet, where we cover them with our stens. None of them is armed and they cower, quite terrified. Not yet out of their teens, they look pathetically vulnerable and foolishly I feel sorry for them but know quite well that they would shoot us instantly if they had a chance. A dreadful change comes over Halford and I see a side of his character that has never before appeared. He grinds his teeth horribly and menaces the prisoners with his sten and lets off a couple of rounds in the air. He makes them stand and lie flat alternately, growling like a dog all the time. I have to give him a direct order to pull himself together and calm down. Eventually we move off back to the RHQ area after detailing one of the linemen to collect Jack's grenade from the upstairs room. He also fetches two German rifles and a Schmeisser machine pistol.[41] There are other prisoners at the RHQ and ours join them where they stand in a desolate group. One of the gunner sentries upends his rifle and sticks it bayonet first in the turf as he turns his back to the group to relieve himself. One of the prisoners grabs the rifle and lunges at me as I am telling the Intelligence Officer

39 The Number 36 Mark 1 Grenade (Mills Bomb) was introduced at the end of the First World War and remained the standard British fragmentation grenade until 1972.

40 Disabling the grenade.

41 The Maschinenpistole 40.

the details of our captives' surrender. As I stagger back away from the lunge, I trip and he sticks the bayonet in my right calf. Halford just about cuts my assailant in half with a long burst from his sten. Again we see another side of Jack's make-up. More like the Halford at the funeral of the baby girl. He is now filled with remorse at the killing of the prisoner, who it transpires is a member of the SS bent on dying for the glory of the Reich. We do not grieve his demise.

We do not stay the night at Varsseveld but move on to a position just south of Lochem. It takes us all night to get there. The Hun is trying to get his stuff across a canal up ahead and we pull off the road to shell his retreat. Action on and off all day. Lots of prisoners coming back all day. The Dutch civilians are mad with excitement but are dreadfully short of food. At 0400 we move off at a wild pace towards the German border again and stop 3 km short of a big canal to put down a prolonged barrage on troops crossing. We hear that Hengelo has been taken. I receive letters from home on 3 April and learn that Alastair has been wounded in the head and has been evacuated to the UK. There is very little doing and no sign of an advance yet. Several of us heat water on the Hydra cooker and borrow a tin bath from a civvy house. It is a bit cold and scummy by the time my turn comes but I feel better afterwards. We heat another batch of water and wash our shirts and sock and drawers, cellular, short. Stand to at 0600 on the 6th and we move off at 1000 to Oldensaal. The civilians here are literally starving but we are unable to help since we have limited rations ourselves and these are 14-day manpacks. Cliff and I go looking for redstarts' nests in a beech wood, where we see some roe deer. Cliff has a rifle with him and we have visions of fresh meat but we cannot get close enough for a shot. Suddenly they dash away and we hear a shot from the other side of the clearing. It seems that someone else has the same idea as us! We talk to the civvies and one chap in particular who has been in a slave labour camp for months. He has TB very badly and tells us hardly credible stories of cruelties perpetrated by the Germans. At the time we think that he is line shooting but later we find that his experiences were very tame compared to some. On 9 April we leave at 0045 and push on back into the Reich through Nordhorn and laager in a beech forest 5 km short of Lingen. The weather is beautiful and we relax as much as possible in the sunshine. There is occasional shelling but nothing serious. We are protecting the northern flank of the advance and move about in fits and starts trying to keep out of the way of other units. Gradually we move forward through Haselunne and then on to 6 km north of Haselrake. Finally on 13 April we move up with Tac HQ and prepare to join 3rd Div at Bassum 75 miles up. On the 14th we have a lovely drive in glorious weather up to a location 20 km short of Bremen and stay at a farm near Bassum. On the 15th we arrive with 3rd Div and lay a line to their Div HQ. I visit Andy and the rest of F section. During our drive up to Bassum we are not shot at or bombed and we feel that the end is very near. Cliff and I are shattered to learn that our leave date has been put back. Bitter disappointment in one way and in another we feel that we would like to be in at the kill and not be on leave when the fighting actually stops. There are hundreds of civilians coming back from Bremen to get away from the bombing. We hear of several cases where German soldiers have robbed local householders of civilian clothing in order to desert as they know that the position is militarily quite hopeless. It is of no consequence to us but the SS have been given orders to shoot anyone who is even suspected of desertion.

At some time during this period of short sharp moves the RHQ pulled into a delightful little valley complete with small stream and shady trees. As soon as the decision to remain overnight was made, the trucks were camouflaged and the cooks set about providing a meal. Having little to do, Cliff and I walked up the valley with a view to looking at the feathered friends. There seemed to be an abundance of goldfinches, a species we had not encountered before on the mainland of Europe, probably because we had not been in the right place at the right time. Looking in his German dictionary, Cliff was fascinated to find that the German was 'distelfink' or thistlefinch. Higher up, say half a mile, the valley had been dammed and a millrace cut along one side below the small lake that had been formed. The mill itself was in disrepair and the millwheel had rotted away. A stone spillway allowed the surplus water to escape to the stream. In the stonework of the millrace end was a wooden gate fitted with a rack and pinion device for opening the gate to control the level of the lake. When we mounted the bank of the race we could see that the water was clear as crystal and full of brown trout up to a pound and a half in weight. At the same instant we both thought a good detonation would give the whole HQ a fish breakfast. While Cliff kept watch, I rushed back to the trucks and grabbed a couple of 69 grenades. These were made of bakelite and contained little or no metal beyond a steel ball. They were activated by unwrapping a tape which was wound round the middle of the cylindrical body. When thrown the tape unwound and initiated the delay of three seconds.[42] We figured that if we threw a grenade at

42 Because they were bakelite rather than metal, the 69 grenade had a smaller destructive radius than the Mills bomb, meaning the thrower did not have to be so concerned about defensive cover.

each end of the race the fish would rush away from the splash of the grenade entering the water and before the explosions took place. It was decided that at a nod from Cliff we would both throw together in the hope that the fish would swim to the middle. At the nod we both threw in unison. The detonation was surprisingly small, barely audible, but the eruption of water was quite spectacular. When we climbed up to look at our handiwork we could see that the wooden sluicegate had disappeared and the water was cascading down the valley in a tremendous flood. Not what we had expected. We made a long and very rapid detour right around the camp area, keeping out of sight in the trees until we entered the camp from the opposite end, 180 degrees from the dam end. The whole area of the camp was flooded to a depth of four inches and the troops were busy grabbing and clubbing trout and eels which were flapping about in the diminishing flood. Cliff and I feigned surprise at the sight of the deluge and demanded to know what was going on. There were several theories as to why the camp had suddenly been inundated, from a random bomb from aircraft to a German Volkssturm attack on our camp.[43] All miles from the truth! The only person who had any sort of clue was Jack Halford, who asked 'And where have you two buggers been for the past hour?'

April 22nd. We move to a farm which looks as though it had been a stud farm in the past. It is only 8 km from our last position but we have travelled 50 km to get here such is the congestion on the roads. The Adjutant is looking at a copy of the Daily Mirror of 16 April. The most appalling pictures of the inmates of a concentration camp at Bergen Belsen.[44] The victims are like corpses and their sticklike arms and legs are unbelievably thin. The skulls and shrunken eyes look dreadful and the bodies are clad in pathetic rags. The Adjutant tells his ack[45] to fetch the occupier of the farm. In a few moments there arrives a tall man of military appearance, about seventy years of age. He is accompanied by his daughter, a horsey looking woman of forty or thereabouts. The adjutant demands that they look at the pictures in the Mirror. Instantly the old boy dismisses it all as 'Britischer propaganda' and makes to walk away. The adjutant stops them and calls to me to

---

43 Volkssturm: Peoples' Storm; a mass levy of Germans not already in uniform in the last months of the war. Mainly Hitler Youth, the middle-aged and elderly, and those previously deemed unfit.

44 The camp was liberated by British and Canadian troops of the 11th Armoured Division on 15 April 1945.

45 Ack means assistant in 'gunnerspeak'.

fetch a Jeep. He makes them pile in the back and bids me drive at his direction. Consulting his map he guides me through Celle and byroads until we arrive at Belsen, a matter of 20 km. We halt a few yards from the Military Police at a double entrance gate and the Adjutant goes and talks earnestly to the MP. After a few minutes the Adjutant returns to the Jeep and bids me drive on through the gates. Half a mile down the road we come to another high fence topped with barbed wire and the usual trimmings for this type of establishment, observation towers and double wire fences. Another set of MPs who stop us. The Adjutant tells them that he wants to make the two Germans see what was going on under their noses. The MPs say that we are not going to like what we see. We drive on and an appalling stench assails our noses. I thought I had sampled a few smells in Normandy and the Falaise pocket. The all-pervading reek of death that seemed to penetrate the very clothes we wore. It wrapped itself around us and refused to leave for days afterwards. We drove on and were stopped again by an RAMC officer. Again the Adjutant said his piece about making our passengers see what was going on. He said that we might drive around for a few minutes but on no account were we to dismount from the Jeep. Again we drove on. We saw corpselike creatures that moved with slow motion gait like a film run at half speed. A detail of German soldiers loading bodies on to a truck under the supervision of a British serjeant. Further on outside a building surmounted by a chimneystack we saw a pile of corpses six feet high and twenty feet long. The building we were told was the crematorium. Further on in our drive we came across a pit bulldozed out of the ground in which were layers and layers of corpses all piled higgledy piggledy. The whole wretched place defied description and no words of mine are adequate to tell of the carnage in the revolting charnel houses that were lightly called 'accommodation blocks'. Row upon row of them covered many acres. The inmates had been quite callously starved systematically to death. I was so dumbfounded by the dreadful spectacle that I had not been paying any attention to our passengers in the back of the Jeep and it was not until I heard the woman retching over the side that I looked round and saw that she was vomiting her heart out. The old man was as white as a sheet and looked to be on the verge of a heart attack. The Adjutant looked pretty seedy as I must have done myself. He looked at me closely and said 'Are you all right, Serjeant Morris?' followed by 'I think we have seen enough. Let's go back.' The woman was still retching intermittently when we arrived back at the farm. There was a strict non-fraternising order in force, but the Adjutant went to his vehicle and brought a bottle of whisky and gave me and the two Germans a shot. As we drank the

Adjutant said to the old man 'Britischer propaganda.' He looked at us with the eyes of a thrashed dog and was unable to speak. As he got out of the Jeep and led his daughter to the house she was sobbing uncontrollably. As they entered their house the Lancasters and Stirlings were going over our heads to plaster Bremen again. Above the noise of the Merlins we could hear the air raid sirens in Bremen.[46] Cliff finds me to say that we are to proceed on leave tomorrow, the 23rd.

46 The Avro Lancaster and the Short Stirling were heavy bombers. The Lancaster was powered by Rolls-Royce Merlin engines, the Stirling by Bristol Hercules engines.

Chapter 8

VE DAY, DISPLACED PERSONS AND THE DIVE INN

The regiment cross the river Weser and its tributary the Aller on bridges that have not been blown, such is the collapse of German resistance. We travel about 60 km to cover a distance of 13 km from our previous location. Cliff and I get our kit together and go back with the EME (Electrical and Mechanical Engineer. Rank Captain. In command of LAD) to A2 Echelon where we stay overnight. Next morning we get to 205 CRC[1] and spend the afternoon walking through the woods to pass the time. The countryside is very beautiful in its springtime finery and it is most pleasant to wander along with only the responsibility of getting ourselves to 205 CRC before the truck leaves for Gennep.[2] On the morning of the 25th we left 205 CRC in a convoy of three-tonners on what was to be the most awful journey. It was far too hot to shut the back canvas of the truck and with it open the dust swirled in on the unfortunate passengers in choking clouds. Cliff and I climbed out on to the top of the canvas tilt and crawled to the front and held on to the front canopy rail. Here we were cool and fairly dust free. After a few kilometres we experienced severe cramp in our wrists from hanging on and developed the technique of holding first with one hand and then the other. We arrived at Gennep in the early evening and after having a meal we find a bedspace near some RASC boys who have a gallon jar of Quartermaster's rum. They said it had to be finished before getting to Calais. We did our best to help. We had another awful night after the effect of the rum wore off. The morning of the 26th was

1 Probably Corps Reception Centre.

2 In south-western Netherlands.

occupied after breakfast by noting what some of the men were taking home with them. Everything from large civilian radio sets to full-sized sewing machines, the new owners staggering along under the weight. The buzz from people returning from leave was that the Customs Officers turned their backs on imports to the UK and admitted almost anything. We read all the notices and regulations which were posted at strategic points in the camp. One of the most prominent stated that although the fraternisation ban had not been lifted, several of the permanent cadre of the camp had contracted syphilis from the local wenches and dire warnings were issued. Finally, the last sentence on the poster was, 'Take some loot home to your wife but not a dose of clap or worse!' Other notices advised us to be sensible about what we tried to take home. Large items were liable to be impounded since they might cause a hold-up. Dangerous substances or weapons would certainly be impounded. It would be better to surrender them now rather than incur the wrath of fellow travellers by causing a delay. Finally there was a list of times at which the military band would be playing for our entertainment. The train times were very flexible and were governed by the track conditions between here and Calais. We were told that it was still vital for military supplies to get up rather than for leave personnel to get down. At 1430 we board a train, at least that is what the RTO[3] called it, for Calais. The carriages had no glass in the windows and several of the compartments had large sections of roof missing. I do not know what we expected because the RAF had been using continental rail stock for target practice for years. For long sections of the journey the permanent way consisted of only one track and delays were inevitable to allow supply trains to come up. The road up from the Normandy supply points, known as 'Club Route Up', had been grossly overloaded for months and the surface had been hammered by the GMC six-wheelers of the US army transportation companies. The railway was a great relief for all concerned and the repair of the tracks was of great importance.

On our journey towards Calais sleep was virtually impossible, although Cliff and I lay down in the corridor and dozed for a couple of hours. We were unable to get comfortable since people walking up and down the corridor to the one toilet in the coach kept kicking us in vulnerable places with their ammos. At 2345 we halted at Lille for a cup of tea and a wad and finally arrived at Calais at 0400, dirty, tired, but very excited. Almost as soon as we boarded the ferry we could tell

---

3 In this context, Railway Transport Officer.

that outside the harbour the sea was pretty rough. The ship's captain came on the tannoy system and told us that by rights he should not put to sea. Did we want to take the chance? Because if we were game, he would take us. Instantly a huge cheer went up from every quarter of the ship. Half of those who cheered lost their enthusiasm as soon as the ship's bows were beyond the harbour wall. After all the seagoing Cliff and I had done in tiny boats we were confident that our sea legs were still valid. Alas we spent the entire crossing to Dover with our heads over the strategically placed ten gallon cans, spewing our hearts up. At Dover the walk from the ship to the assembly sheds dispelled any vestige of seasickness and we ate a good breakfast of bacon, beans and bread with lashings of tea before boarding a train for London. Our arrival in the capital ended the organised transport and we had to make our own arrangements from there onwards. Cliff headed off to King's Cross while I took the underground to Euston. An uneventful journey to Chester with a stop at Crewe from where I rang Rose at her billets. I was lucky enough to contact her at once and she was delighted to hear me and promised to meet me half an hour later at Chester.

Much water had passed since the last letter I had received from Rose or my mother. Alastair had taken a head wound after crossing the Rhine and was now in hospital in Leeds suffering from jaundice. My mother had sold our house and taken a flat in Liverpool Road in Chester. All our belongings were in storage so I couldn't get my shotguns. The car was not accessible and in general things looked pretty bloody awful. My sister was staying with my mother at Liverpool Road and we took a taxi there from the station. A meal was waiting. The whole family had not been together since 1940, so we had a great deal to talk over, like why the hell had my family home been sold without so much as telling me about thinking of parting with it. Not exactly acrimony but conversely not total harmony either. The next morning Rose and I took a train for Nannerch and Rose's home. My issue petrol coupons were burning a hole in my pocket so the first priority was to get the Austin Seven which had belonged to Bill Gurney, Rose's father, taxed and insured and generally fired up. Having borrowed a battery to start the engine, we drove it to a friendly insurance agent who gave us a cover note and it being Sunday dated it for the previous day. Taxing the thing could wait until Monday 30 April. To avoid taking too much out of the battery until it had received a fair charge from the dynamo, I started the engine with the handle. After a couple of days I was able to use the starter quite normally. Rose and her mother had received a buzz that Harry, Rose's younger brother, was due for some leave. He was a survivor of the sinking by the Japanese of HMS *Repulse* north of Singapore.[4] Getting the car serviceable for him killed two birds with one stone. On Tuesday 1 May we took my sister over to Leeds to visit Alastair and spent a couple of hours with him in the grounds of a very pleasant hospital. We were able to congratulate him on his recent promotion to major. Later in the afternoon we drove over to Burley-in-Wharfedale and surprised Cliff, who was serving behind the counter of his shop while his wife took a few hours off from running the business and household duties. We spent the rest of my leave pottering about between Chester and Rose's home, calling at the pubs we knew and drinking with those friends who were still about. It was devastating to have to drive past my old home without being able to go in and continue my life there. I think that during those few days I began to realise that nothing would ever be the same again and that the past few years had completed the transition from youth to premature middle age. Our generation had missed something intangible about growing up. We had been pitchforked into adulthood without the luxury of being allowed a mistake or two. Personally I considered myself lucky to have survived this far. Out of eight bosom friends, all good people whose friendship I cherished, only Eric Roberts and I remained. Eric was still in Burma with the 14th Army. While the Hun was all but beaten, there is many a slip 'twixt cup and lip. On leave I found it very difficult to sleep in a soft bed and on several occasions I found it necessary to wrap myself in an eiderdown and sleep on the floor in order to get any rest. The bed seemed to be full of women! People returning from leave had remarked on this before our turn came to go but I had disregarded their talk as nonsense. Also, the taste of civvy tea was putrid. I think that fresh milk was alien to my taste buds. The night prior to my departure was crowned by the two dear old ladies who kept the Rising Sun next door to Rose's house bringing me a going away present of 40 Players cigarettes – a great luxury for which I was most grateful.

On the afternoon of 7 May I met Cliff in London as arranged and we joined the huge returning leave draft in the Dover train. The throng of leave-expired troops were not quite as enthusiastic as they had been ten days earlier but since the fighting was almost at an end we were safe in

4 The battlecruiser *Repulse* and the battleship *Prince of Wales* were sunk in the South China Sea on 10 December 1941, two days after the attack on Pearl Harbor. (Hawaii is on the other side of the International Date Line.) Some 840 Royal Navy seamen died, 513 on *Repulse* – getting on for half the ship's company – and 327 on *Prince of Wales*. Harry Gurney, Pete's brother-in-law, was picked up from the sea.

the knowledge that being killed now was an outside chance. At a stop for refreshments on the morning of 8 May we heard that hostilities were at an end and that the Germans had unconditionally surrendered. It was VE Day! Later, at a transit camp, Cliff and I stood in a queue to get a cup of tea and a wad when at 2130 exactly the shutter of the canteen came down when we were a couple of feet from the counter. Talk about 'Canteen Open-Canteen Shut. Mind yer fingers Jack!' Not a drink in sight, not even a cup of pissy tea. When we got back to the Regiment we were told that everyone was drunk and had fired every cartridge in the Q-stores. The sky was lit up with coloured flares and star shells for as far as the eye could see. There had been no need to set a guard because no one had gone to bed. We joined the Regiment late on 9 May and were surprised to see the house occupied by the RHQ was a blaze of light. Harry Liley had liberated a 240 volt petrol / electric alternator set,[5] which he had towed behind his truck in readiness for when the fighting stopped. He just connected the output of the genny to the house fuses at any location we stopped at. The officers' mess was very impressed by the efficiency of the Signal Section. There followed a period of rest and rehabilitation for all ranks. There were a great number of specialist jobs that needed urgent attention. Jack Halford and his linemen were working flat out providing temporary line communication for the railways nearest to our location. My operators provided cover until the lines were through. For us there was very little R and R but the thought was nice.

The problem that was of paramount importance at this time was that of displaced persons. These were causing a tremendous problem to the Military Government and Army alike. Thousands upon thousands of people of all European and other nations were technically allies, in as much as they were opposed to Nazism and had been drafted into Germany as slave labour. As soon as the fighting stopped and the Wehrmacht had lost its potency, all these people had one fixed idea in mind – to get home to their families. To do this they needed to eat and looting of farm stock was carried out on a huge scale. The woods were full of wild-looking eastern Europeans cooking poultry and calves over open fires. The roads were full of these people on any form of transport that could be stolen. Since the Nazis had forbidden the use of any sort of radio equipment, the hordes of foreigners in Germany were totally ignorant of conditions in their homelands and

5 An electricity generator that uses a petrol engine to drive a rotor to produce an alternating current of electricity.

indeed the parts of Germany outside their immediate vicinity. They did not know that the Russians were hostile to anyone who had worked in Germany, since they could not prove conclusively that they had not collaborated with the Nazis. Summary execution was the norm for anyone who had not the necessary paperwork to show the Russians. We did not blame the Russians for this sort of justice, since the Germans had been dispatching Soviet citizens without any sort of compunction since 1941.

It was considered by the Military Government that the rivers were the best way of confining the DPs to small areas until the exact position could be explained to them in their own languages. While most of them were barely literate, some were scholars and linguists. These the MIL GOV endeavoured to recruit and feed and clothe in khaki in an effort to get them to take the lead in the fight to enlighten the other DPs. As a result of the river theory of DP control, it was decided to patrol as many stretches of river as possible by boat and to control the bridges which were still intact by Military Police and the newly recruited linguists. Since someone had learned that our section 'knew about boats' we were called upon to provide three crews for river patrol. I found myself with five of the operators dumped in a small place called Verden,[6] near a downed bridge on a tributary of the Weser called the Aller. I reported to a Major of the MIL GOV, who outlined our duties. When our boats arrived we were to patrol the river section allotted to us at irregular intervals and prevent anyone crossing the river from west to east. We were to turn back all attempts at crossing and arrest anyone who persisted or made any sort of affray. We were to draw fuel for the boats at the bridge near the Major's HQ and were to report to him once a day. Otherwise I was to use my own discretion. Rations would be drawn at the same time as fuel. In the afternoon two boats arrived on the back of GMC trucks driven by Americans. We offloaded our boat north of the downed bridge having previously fixed it with the Major to patrol the stretch northward to join the Weser proper. From there to Bremen the river was open and no bridges were down. The other boat was unable to get to our side of the bridge at Verden because not even the smallest rowboat could get under the wrecked bridge. The boats were quite splendid and had never been in the water before. We had to fill the engine sumps and fuel tanks from dry and even connect the dry charged battery. The electrolyte was provided in a glass container. The hulls were moulded

6 South-east of Bremen.

out of some sort of wood pulp in one piece. They had a Willys engine similar to that fitted in the Jeeps.[7] The steering tiller moved in a forward and back direction and not from side to side. I was agreeably surprised at the ten-knot speed.

When all was ready we put our kit aboard and shoved off up river to look for a suitable billet. There were a very few bridges but good roads up to the riverside, where there was usually a cafe on one bank and a rowboat ferry operated by the cafe proprietor. We went up for several miles looking at the various cafes and finally selected one where there were two daughters in the family. At least we thought they were daughters until we saw the proprietor and his wife and realised that the two girls were grandchildren of the old people. At first the old man was not at all pleased at our commandeering his cafe for our headquarters and billet but as the days went by we became a sort of magnet for the local people who came to gawp at our boat and our equipment. I found an ex-soldier who spoke fair English and explained to him at length what our duty was and what we intended to do about the DPs. I emphasised the bit about trying to stop the DPs looting the livestock and generally terrorising the German women and that our main job was to contain them on the west side of the river until they could be sent home on proper transport or at least fed by MIL GOV in the interim. The ex-soldier listened intelligently to what I had to say and then talked to the assembled people at great length. I had enough German to know what he was saying and that he was not spinning them any stories.

We could draw almost unlimited rations from the depot at Verden so the boys were able to flannel the old lady and the two girls into cooking our grub and doing a bit of washing for us. The occasional bar of Lifebuoy and a tin of bully worked wonders, bearing in mind that there was absolutely no soap available in Germany and it was very valuable currency for which many a fraulein submitted her virginity. Very soon my crew were saying 'Lend me your soap, Serj' in spite of the fact that the non-fraternisation order had not been lifted. We established our patrols of the river down the Weser to Bremen and were startled on one occasion by being flagged into the bank by a couple of German policemen, who indicated the river and said 'Achtung! Minen unter den Wasser.' They also showed us one that had broken loose from its anchor and was lodged in some reeds by the bank. L/Cpl Stan Lees fired about four rounds from the Bren and it blew up in a

7 Probably the Willys L134 engine, known as the 'Go Devil'.

cloud of mud and water with a tremendous explosion. We reported the mines to the Major and he alerted the Royal Navy at Bremen. It transpired that the mines were British and had been dropped in the river by our aircraft to stop the movement of shipping. So serious was the DP problem that the mines were cleared as far as Bremen in less than a week from our reporting them.

Anchored at the bank of the river were some huge barges. They were seagoing but had to be towed by a ship and were used for canal work with the occasional short sea trip. Two of them were flying Dutch flags and were therefore allies with whom we could fraternise. The boys also saw some very comely wenches sunning themselves on the hatch covers. They were huge craft some 200 feet in length and consisted of a very large hold taking up most of the length and very ample living quarters in the stern. The skipper invited us aboard and entertained us with schnapps which he had conserved for the day of victory. Up till now he had met no one with whom to celebrate. It seemed that the man and his family of wife and three daughters had been incarcerated in this stretch of river for almost a year unable to move because no ship was available to tow them up or down the river. There was no cargo in the hold and yet the hull was low in the water. When I asked about this the bargee said that over a period of months, with no fuel for the engine that drove the bilge pump, the ingress of water was so great that there was a danger of the living quarters becoming immersed. I sent one of the operators over the side to our boat and soon two four-gallon expendable cans were on their way to the bilge engine. Within a few minutes the outlet pipe to the pump was running full bore. When we called the next day with another couple of cans the barge was a good six feet higher out of the water and the bargee told us that the hold was almost dry. After this episode we could do no wrong with the family. We could have anything, except of course the daughters. The Dutch are queer like that! I deemed it prudent to report every incident to the Major at Verden and he applauded the donation of fuel to the Dutch bargee in the interests of good allied relations. Mr Phair, our section OC, called to see us and brought with him my spirits ration for the month of May. With this we were able to have a small party aboard the Dutch barge with an impromptu dance to the accordion music played by the barge skipper's wife. The girls were quite delighted to have some young fellows to entertain them. Any disappearance behind hatch covers or bollards brought the bargee out of his corner like a striking cobra.

There was a cafe-ferry a couple of miles downriver from our billet where the ferryman had been warned twice about taking passengers across the river in his boat. After we caught him with another load we took his boat in midstream and knocked a hole out of the planking and sank it with stones. Just after first light the following day he was there again in the same boat with another load of DPs. We never found out how he managed to retrieve the sunken boat from the middle of the Aller. This time we poured four gallons of petrol over it and burned it. Then we arrested him and took him up to Verden to have the Major's staff scare the daylights out of the old devil. Then he was made to walk home. We had to admire his tenacity. I told his wife that if he didn't curb his ardour I would take him out and shoot him. After all that he would still wave at us as we passed. The weather at this time was superb and we bathed and swam a great deal. Lees wrenched a door off a building and used it as a surf board behind the boat on our patrols, a practice that was frowned upon by the deskbound people at Verden. The Major was a splendid fellow and he told the moaners not to be jealous of our freedom because we had fought our way from Normandy while they had been pushing bits of paper around in England.

Anchored in midstream near a village called Bollen were several rather beautiful civvy yachts, all trim and sheeted down. We had boarded all of them in turn as part of our patrol duties and found them all to be in pristine condition, no doubt belonging to Nazi party officials. The best of them all was the 'Kondor', a fifty-footer with a full set of sails and a Mercedes diesel engine. Quite obviously she had been maintained right up to the cessation of hostilities. I would often stop off on her and browse around while the boys continued with the patrol. It was not difficult to daydream about sailing her through the Greek islands. One day I was standing on the well deck when an officer hailed me from the bank and asked to come aboard. I told him he would have to wait until our boat returned from patrol. Instead of waiting he stripped off down to his underpants and dived in and swam with a strong crawl to the Kondor, where I hauled him aboard. Since I was alone he asked me if I would help him get the yacht back to England. He said he'd been watching us patrolling the river but had not had the opportunity to speak to me on my own. Since he was almost naked I did not know his rank or unit. From the distance I felt sure that his shoulder flashes were those of 8th Armoured Brigade, the yellow mask of a fox. He quite obviously knew a thing or two about boats and was patently in the sailing league rather than engines. By the time our boat returned an hour later he was wearing my tunic to keep warm and was glad for us to take him ashore for his clothes. He said he would look me up at our billet later that evening to talk more about boats. He turned up in a jeep, alone except for a bottle of whisky, which we drank out of mugs. After a few minutes I was convinced that he was quite serious in his intention to take the Kondor to England. He was a major in the 17th/21st Lancers of our brigade and it seemed that he was due for his privilege leave in a week's time. He was annoyed that I had not long returned from mine, having assumed that I would jump at the chance of drowning myself in the North Sea. Would I help him to get the yacht ready for the trip? I told him that I would be delighted and that first I would need a twelve-volt battery of large capacity and about 100 gallons of diesel fuel. The following day he met us at Bollen with a three-tonner with a battery from a Sherman and two jerricans of fuel. We ferried these across to the Kondor and I sent the boys with the exception of Lees to get on with their patrolling up to Bremen. Lees and I poured in the fuel and connected the battery. After checking the lubricating oil in the sump and priming the fuel pump, we pressed the starter. The engine turned over fairly fast. So far so good. Locating the switches for the preheaters[8] was a bit of problem but eventually we were able to work out the sequence of events for starting. Allowing a full minute for the heaters was probably too long but better that than running the battery down with them too cold. When we pressed the starter again she coughed several times, threw out black smoke and finally burst into life. After running the engine for several minutes I gently tried the forward and reverse positions of the gearbox and found that all was working perfectly. With the dynamo charging nicely, we started the electric bilge pump and emptied her of all water. Next we tried the navigation light, masthead light and cabin lights, all perfect. The days that followed were occupied in changing the oil in the sump and completely filling the fuel tanks and stowing many jerricans of spare fuel in the bilges. When we had made everything ready for the crazy trip, the new skipper turned up with a couple of troopers and another officer who was in shirtsleeves so I could not see his rank. Lees and I showed the two troopers, who were mechanics, the method of starting the engine and where all the knobs were. I made the Major promise to write to me with the outcome of their trip and wished them luck. We towed the Kondor around to face downstream and they disappeared into the gathering gloom. They had decided to get through Bremen in the dark and then rest up the following day and

8 Used to warm the cabin and the engine, making starting the engine easier.

tackle Bremerhaven the following night. In spite of his promise to let me know of their progress, I never heard a word from the Major or any of his crew. They may have been stopped at any of the small towns along the journey to the sea or apprehended by the Royal Navy, or even sunk and drowned at sea. All we got was a great deal of fun in getting the boat ready for the trip.

After about a month of the river patrol the DPs seemed to get the message about unauthorised travel and the crossings became almost negligible. In one or two cases we had to fire a Bren over the heads of absconders to turn them back. Eventually we were recalled to our unit, which by this time had moved to Hanover. It was a fair trip to Hanover and the driver of the three-tonner which had come to collect the two boat crews, one George Ryder, was normally the driver of Harry Liley's workshop truck. He told us of peculiar happenings back at the regiment. All our equipment was being handed in to DADOS (Deputy Assistant Director of Ordnance Services) and the G1098[9] had to be checked and re-checked over and over. This was more, it was thought, to occupy the troops' time than from necessity. The fact remained that in a short time we would no longer be a viable fighting force. It was rather a sobering thought in view of the fact that we had spent so many years being taught how to kill. I had no intention of making the trip to Hanover in one day. In the event of any discussion on the subject we could always plead congestion on the roads or some such hold-up. In the evening George pulled up beside a small lake near a village. There was no sign of any other troops or vehicles, no sign of war damage or bombing, just the sound of a horse-drawn mowing machine in the distance and the rasp of a corncrake nearby. It was quite beautiful. As we prepared a meal from our dwindling rations, the sun set and in the afterglow someone suggested a swim in the lake. The water was surprisingly clear. The inevitable knot of inquisitive boys gathered to peer at us through the gloom. In spite of the non-frat order, we tossed them an occasional boiled sweet from the ration packs. The water was deliciously warm after the heat of the sun had been on it for several days and we all played about while the boys watched us from the high banks. As the moon rose the whole lake was flooded with a pale light. Several young girls had arrived on the scene and joined the spectators, whereupon the swimmers beckoned and shouted for them to join us. Without any ado they stripped off quite naked and leaped in off the bank. The sight of nubile young forms silhouetted against

9 The list of a unit's equipment.

the moonlight was not calculated to render the hairy-arsed signalmen in my charge easy to discipline. I climbed out and put on my trousers and yelled to attract their attention. I delivered a very brief speech. 'There still remains a non-frat order. However I do not have eyes in my arse and what I do not see I cannot report.' This was followed by shouts of glee and advice such as 'After you, Serj' and 'Get in the queue, Ryder.' All in all it was a memorable evening and no doubt the girls went home with lots of valuable currency in the shape of soap and cigarettes.

Hanover was a very sorry city. Viewed from a distance it looked to be intact with the buildings still standing erect. Most other bombed towns were flattened and the streets impassable with rubble. Here the damage had been done by firebombing and while the outer shells of the buildings still stood, everything inside the outer walls had just dropped and trapped thousands of the inhabitants in the cellars. The smell was appalling and likely to get worse as the heat of the summer increased. Our billets were located in a comparatively untouched suburb to the north of the devastation. Here the RSM had taken a private house for the Serjeants' Mess and was trying to establish some sort of peacetime atmosphere for us to live in. Anyone bringing his pistol beyond the front hall was duty bound to buy a round of drinks. It was hilarious to find that the first man to infringe the rule was the RSM himself. We had guest nights and invited the younger members of the Officers' Mess over for booze parties. Our section OC organised outings for the men and we would take them for picnics up to the Harz mountains.[10] We would take bags of rations and spend all day away from matters military. Such outings might have seemed rather juvenile to fighting men but our OC had been a schoolmaster for many years and knew that men are really small boys at heart. This sort of life was short-lived and soon all our stores had been disposed of and equipment collected by DADOS trucks. We knew that something big was afoot when I was instructed to parade the section and polish up their foot drill. All the old skills of barrack square-bashing returned and it was easy to pick out the men who had received proper drill instruction in their early training. At the end of it all General Brian Horrocks, Commander XXX Corps, arrived to take the salute as our guns and armour were paraded for the last

---

10 The most northerly highland range in Germany, marketed by the tourism industry as the land of fairy tales with steep-roofed houses, cobbled streets, dark forests and rushing streams, etc.

time, a very poignant moment for all concerned.[11] The whole of the Regiment lined the route in open order[12] as the vehicles drove past. We never found out where they were parked or which field they had been left to rot in. All the loving care and maintenance that had been bestowed on them came now to naught, they were just scrap metal. All very sad. It was not only guns and tanks that were thrown on the scrapheap. We were to learn that men and their feelings meant little to bureaucracy either.

The entire Signal Section left Hanover and was taken to Bruges in Belgium. Here was established a holding battalion in an old Belgian Army barracks. It was a deplorable place and very old-fashioned. It was probably designed to hold about a quarter of the number of troops that were now crammed in. The whole town was bursting at the seams with soldiers, predominantly Royal Signals who had been detached from their parent regiments and assembled at holding battalion for dispersal to other units or demobilisation. The morning after our arrival at Bruges there appeared on orders a very curt dictate to the effect that all ranks that were not war substantive (that is, had not been held for a period of two years) would be relinquished with immediate effect. Personnel holding such ranks would revert to their permanent war substantive rank. Our OC almost went beserk and stormed round to Battalion Office to object in the strongest terms. It was to no avail; he was told that it was a War Office decision and quite irrevocable. In my own case I was just two months off war substantive serjeant. This meant I would have to lose a rank down to Lance Serjeant and since there was no longer a L/Sjt rank I would have to come down to corporal.[13] It was a bitter pill to swallow. Loss of Serjeants' Mess privileges. Loss of pay. Loss of face before our own men. We had been

11 Horrocks had a remarkable life and career. He was twice a prisoner of war, captured by the Germans in the First World War, and then by the Red Army after he had been posted to Russia during the allied intervention in the Russian Civil War. After the Second World War he was Black Rod in the Palace of Westminster for fourteen years. Black Rod supervises the administration of the House of Lords; he, or she, is the one who bashes on the door of the Commons with the Black Rod to summon MPs to the House of Lords to hear the King's Speech. Next, Horrocks became a television presenter and writer and was a prominent contributor to the ITV series *The World at War*.

12 That is, with a larger space between men in the rank.

13 At this time the rank of Lance Serjeant was being abolished in the British Army, except in certain units such as the Foot Guards.

good enough to carry our stripes up the beach at Arromanches but not good enough to satisfy the pen-pushers who had never heard a shot fired in anger. It was very, very galling. All those affected just hated everyone and everything for days. I remember being told by Teddy Edwards to parade the men to march to dinner. I just told him to parade the bloody section himself and then drop dead! My dread was that people at home would have the impression that I had lost the stripe due to some misdemeanour.

Postings from the holding battalion were taking place every day and the section was becoming sadly depleted. Postings were willy nilly and it seemed that every effort was being made to split up friendships made over years. My posting came along with three other corporals, Meyer, Miles and another Morris. Meyer had come from an Engineers Signal Section and was a large South Walian from the Cardiff area. He spoke no Welsh. The other two, Miles and Morris W.J., had come from Line of Communication Signals and were probably Cypher Operators. They were too tight-lipped and close-fisted to say what their activities had been. Lofty Meyer and I did not ask them after the initial interest. While Miles and Morris W.J. were both splendid people, they were more interested in discussing church choral singing than going out to get pissed. Our new posting was to 1st Corps Signals at Cologne. The unit was located at a large Post Office building in Venloer Strasse, which as the name suggested ran towards Venlo in the Netherlands.[14] The city was in terrible condition and had been the scene of the most devastating firestorms in the whole conflict. Our billet was almost opposite the Post Office building and while it had very little roof left, our second floor flat was waterproof. We had the luxury of camp beds. The cadre was a mixture of American Signals Corps and Royal Signals. They operated a switching centre for the entire communications system coming into Germany from the west. We messed with the Americans, whose cook had been an employee of the Canadian Pacific Railway in the capacity of chef de cuisine on transcontinental trains. As long as he was stinko profundo he could cook like a dream. When sober he became a taciturn nightmare who couldn't boil an egg. By and large it was not a bad place to finish one's service and sit it out until demob and the four of us decided to make the best of our lot and not rock the boat too much. The Americans

---

14 Venloer Strasse is a major thoroughfare that runs from the centre of Cologne, within a stone's throw of the great cathedral and the Rhine, to Rommerskirchen in the outer north-west suburbs.

were in no way connected with us other than for messing and this was only for the convenience of both parties. The officer commanding the Royal Signals personnel was a Major Holden. He was a very kind and understanding officer who would bend over backwards to make our last few months in the service as comfortable as was in his power. At our original interview with him he told us that there was no real job for us as far as communications were concerned and that we had only been posted in as spare supernumerary bodies. Could we therefore help him by providing a canteen or club for the entertainment of the British and American troops at our headquarters? He could place at our disposal unlimited German labour and transport would be available for our personal use. Lofty and I thought that the whole idea reeked of promise but Morris W.J. and Miles asked to opt out on the grounds of not being much good at building things. When they left the office Major Holden remarked that he knew that he would have trouble with that pair as soon as he saw their hands.[15] He told us to take a Jeep and do a recce of the surrounding area for suitable materials for the job. In the meantime we were to recruit German labour to clear the site behind the billet, which at the moment was a sea of bomb rubble several feet deep.

Lofty and I boarded our Jeep and drove through the rubble-strewn streets to the MIL GOV HQ in the city. We put in a request for twelve workers for site clearance and were promptly issued with 25. I asked if anyone spoke English and several stepped forward. After a short conversation with each I chose one named Wilhelm Thiel, who had been an Oberfeldwebel[16] in the Luftwaffe until he had been transferred latterly to the infantry of the 92nd Panzer Lehr Division. This unit had fought opposite 8th Armoured Brigade on several occasions so Wilhelm and I had much to talk about. We appointed him foreman of the job and asked him to instruct the labourers to report to him at Venloer Strasse the following morning. In the meantime Lofty and I took him in the Jeep to show him the site and what needed to be done. When this had been done I inquired where he lived and was told that his 'dwelling' was at Bickendorf about five km further down Venloer Strasse. We offered to give him a ride home in the hope that he might show us a bit of the countryside. During the ride mention

15 One of Pete's mantras was 'Never trust an engineer with clean hands and a slide rule.'

16 Senior non-commissioned officer.

was made of the Koln Flughafen.[17] We made a slight detour and found the place a wreck after the RAF had been at it. There was, however, one wooden shed which had escaped serious damage. Part of the roof had been blown off but the general structure was sound and of good stout timber. Here it seemed was our canteen. The removal of it was only a matter of careful dismantling and transportation to the site. We decided to put some of our labour on to dismantling while the site was being cleared. We had fears of some other unit pinching it first and Thiel told us that the civvies were desperately short of fuel and were not above looting the best bits. It was still early afternoon when we dropped Thiel off at his dwelling, as he quaintly called his windowless cottage. He politely asked if he might present his wife and children and he brought out a very pretty girl and two lovely children. Why the hell had we been knocking the shit out of our two countries and killing each other when the recipients of the flak were great people like Wil Thiel and his family? It was beyond comprehension that a madman like Adolf Hitler had been allowed to get so far.

Promptly at 0730 next morning the German labour arrived and Wil Thiel set them to loading the open three-tonners provided for the job. The trucks were driven by Sapper Ginger Howes, a Royal Engineer who was attached to the HQ for rations and precious little else. He drove one truck to a bomb site, tipped and returned for the other truck while the first was being reloaded. In an incredibly short time the site was as clean as a whistle and swept clear ready for erection to start. The whole operation had taken only two days. When we had first surveyed the job we were reckoning in terms of weeks. On the morning of the third day we were able to start moving the material from the aerodrome into the cleared site. We had made a few rough preliminary drawings on scraps of paper and, having taken particular note of the method of construction of the original building, we had a team of bricklayers under Ginger Howes lay two courses of recovered bricks around the periphery of the new floor area. As soon as the brickwork was complete we were able to start erecting the timber sides and ends and finally the roof trusses. In order to keep the entire floor area clear of pillars to support the roof it was necessary to obtain a 40-foot rolled steel joist from a wrecked building in the street running parallel to Venloer Strasse. It was a huge thing and it took our entire labour force to dislodge it and carry it to our site. We built two square brick pillars outside each end of our building to support the ends of our RSJ. The

17 Cologne Airport.

underside of each roof truss was carried by the steelwork. When the place was complete the RSJ was disguised with matchboarding.[18] During the preliminary construction Will Thiel stood open mouthed at our audacity in doing such a project without sheaves of drawings and several architects. When the glass came for the windows I made a point of over-ordering so that we could replace the windows in our billet. At the same time I asked Lofty to call at Thiel's house to measure up his window frames. He was pathetically grateful.

As soon as the building was half-complete and the roof made waterproof, a temporary bar was installed and the chaps started to use it as a canteen. Raw Belgian beer and very low-alcohol German lager was available. The Belgian beer had a hangover in every bottle[19] but a good supply had to be always available to supply Brownie, the American CPR cook. The awful stuff was brought in from Brussels on the weekly supply truck. My spirits issue had been stopped on my reversion to the rank of corporal. It was possible to obtain fairly good schnapps for soap or cigarettes. Slowly the interior of the canteen took shape and a small stage was built and lighting and a public address system were installed. The place was reasonably comfortable by Christmastime. The Americans had a Bell and Howell[20] 16mm cinema projector and access to an extensive film library. Almost every night the canteen was turned into a picture house. We hired four waitresses and two stewards. The stewards were Herr Dolfuss and Fred Dehn. Herr Dolfuss had been a steward on the liner *Deutschland*[21] and spoke excellent English and French. Fred Dehn was a first class con man and we had to threaten to beat him up for attempting to fiddle the stock. The waitresses were Fraulein Hamacher, a bovine wench from Friesland who worked very hard and was screwed on a regular basis by Ginger Howes; Fraulein Fassbender, a tall gangling girl, full of fun but possessed of a long horselike face. She knew she was ugly but

---

18 Tongue and groove boarding.

19 An interesting topic, especially for those with a taste for Belgian beer, which can be almost as strong as wine. 'Raw' in this context means that the wort, that is the liquid produced after the mashing process, is not boiled, or only briefly. In theory this allows the beer to retain more of the flavours of the ingredients and it can also mean a higher alcohol content.

20 American manufacturer of cameras, lenses and movie machinery, founded in 1907.

21 A luxury liner launched in 1900 that for a time held the Blue Riband for the fastest Atlantic crossing.

didn't give a damn; Trudi Herlinger, a city girl with a sturdy frame and a blond tow head; and Frau Lill, who lived quite near our billet and nursed her very sick husband who had tuberculosis. Her ambition was to get him to a sister who lived in the Harz mountains. The difficulties of travel for civilians were almost insurmountable but by sheer chance I talked to a member of the MIL GOV who went to the Harz area every week in a large Humber staff car to collect weekly returns. By the good offices of Major Holden and our medical officer I got all the necessary paperwork and passes. It was fully three weeks before Frau Lill was able to contact her sister-in-law and get a reply that she was prepared to take her brother in. Finally all the arrangements dovetailed and off went the husband in the back of the Humber. All to no avail as the poor chap died six weeks later.

The talk at this time was mainly about demobilisation and demob numbers. A demob number was arrived at by a formula of age and length of service. I was 27 years old and had joined up in November 1939.[22] This combination gave a group number of 26. If a man was 40 years old and had done only two years' service he could still be in group 26. Some of the reservists had a combination of age and long service and could come up with a demob number of 4 or 5. Demobilisation would start with the lowest numbers and continue group by group until all were discharged. Group 26 was the largest of all and it was envisaged that it would take several weeks for all the people in it to be processed before 27 could be started. In any case it would be the spring of 1946 or possibly the summer before 26 group would be released. In the meantime life had to go on and we settled down to a round of activities connected with the running of the canteen. Lofty Meyer and I had the almost exclusive use of a Jeep and we made extensive forays into the countryside around the city. The bridge across the Rhine at Cologne was down in the river, thereby blocking the passage of shipping. We went to watch the engineers blowing the offending steelwork out of the way. The explosions were pretty spectacular. Shipping was still precluded from passage because of the temporary pontoon bridge the Royal Engineers had put across. A pretty good reason was needed to get permission to cross on the pontoon bridge. At the western end of the bridge stood Cologne cathedral. All the surrounding buildings were quite flat, bombed to rubble, and yet the cathedral had sustained only minor damage. Could it have been divine protection? Certainly

22 Pete's 27th birthday was 29 December 1945.

the night bombing of the RAF, looking for the bridge, could not have differentiated.

On one occasion we went looking for drinking glasses and entered the headquarters of the Cologne branch of the Nazi Party, the Hochhaus as it was called locally. The structure was pretty unsafe from the bombing but being young and stupid we both worked our way up the shattered stairs until we came to what had been the restaurant on the fourth floor. Here we came across a veritable goldmine of catering equipment, cutlery, glassware and crockery, all of the highest quality. We took samples to show Major Holden and returned to Venloer Strasse. Each item of our samples had a swastika engraved on it and the major did not think it would be a good idea to use it in our canteen. We did go back to the Hochhaus later and purloined some rather attractive gold-rimmed glasses, which I managed to send home by post. Five of them still survive today.[23]

Meyer and I got into the habit of frequenting a couple of cafes on Venloer Strasse where we were able to meet local people. Sometimes Wil Thiel and Frau Lill would accompany us. At first the locals were rather distant towards us but as time went by and our smattering of German improved they began to communicate. The British people had no conception of what bombing could be. The conditions in which these people were living were beyond belief. For five kilometres in any direction from the city there was not a whole roof and most of the inhabitants were living in holes in the rubble. Ill-clothed and fed on meagre rations, they had no immediate hope of regular work and the only lucky ones were those who managed to get employment from the MIL GOV. The coming winter was going to be dreadful for most of them with no alleviation from the grinding hardship. Our waitresses

---

23 It's not clear what building Pete is referring to. He might mean the EL-DE Haus, which the Nazis rented from a jeweller, Leopold Dahmen. The building took its name from the jeweller's initials. The Nazis used it as the Gestapo headquarters, so it was the scene of torture and murder. It doesn't quite square with Pete's account, because the EL-DE Haus was said to have been largely undamaged by the Allied bombing. Undamaged is a relative term, of course. The EL-DE Haus did have a fourth storey. There is no doubt about the story of the glasses. Five still survive, though one has a damaged stem. The EL-DE Haus is now the NS-Documentation Centre of the City of Cologne, a memorial to the victims of the Nazis and a research and teaching centre. The cell block in the basement is one of the best-preserved prisons of the Nazi era, its walls bearing nearly two thousand drawings and inscriptions by prisoners.

would look longingly at the army blankets which we used as padding on the canvas seats of our Jeep. Lofty noticed Trudi Herlinger and Frau Lill fingering the quality of the wool and whispering to each other. We wondered what was so bloody marvellous about smelly old blankets. We could lay our hands on hundreds. Since we both used the more convenient sleeping bags, our issue blankets were redundant. At the time we were standing on the balcony outside our room and we called them to come up. Not daring to disobey, they reluctantly came up, no doubt fearing rape or worse. We offered them a blanket each, with a choice of blue, brown or grey. Less than a week later they proudly showed us smart new coats, one in blue and the other in brown. Both were lined with parachute silk. We did not ask where the silk had come from. It could have been German. Later, Lofty told me that Trudi had knickers of the same material.

There was always a large amount of black marketeering being carried on in Germany at this time and MIL GOV were doing their best to eradicate all forms of this type of trading. Huge amounts of American stores were changing hands and being shipped to all parts of the British zone. The Provost Marshal for the XXX Corps district had issued orders that all vehicles moving at night were to be stopped and searched for contraband stores and equipment. The guard for our HQ was located below our billet and the sentries patrolled the street below. Two red lamps were placed one at each side of the road and at the approach of a vehicle the sentries were to wave a further red light to warn the driver of the vehicle to stop. Standing orders stated quite categorically that the sentries were to open fire on any vehicle that failed to stop. One night when Lofty was guard commander I was wakened by a burst of Sten gun fire and looked out to see a car reversing at high speed after having passed the checkpoint. It stopped near the guardroom and out stepped a senior officer shouting and raving and threatening to shoot the sentry who had opened fire. By now Lofty had come out of the guardroom with all the off-duty guard personnel. The officer was quite obviously very drunk and had commanded his driver to ignore the red lights and drive through towards the city. When the driver heard the bullets hitting the car he decided that it was time to stop. I shouted down to see if Lofty wanted any help and he yelled to me to ring for Major Holden. When I got back from the phone Lofty had a ring of sentries all pointing their Stens at the officer, who was still roaring and raving that he would shoot everyone in sight. This stalemate lasted until Major Holden arrived ten minutes later and managed to calm the idiot down. It transpired that the officer was a major from the Provost office who had been to a party and assumed that he could flout the regulations issued by his own department. Our CO took him back to the officers' mess to sleep off his drunkenness. The very scared driver spent the night in our guardroom. Lofty did not get a word of apology from the idiot, who could have been the death of one of the guard.

The black marketeers soon established where the regular checkpoints were located and worked out routes to avoid them. To counter this, roving patrols were organised and we would have to roam around the roads and halt any vehicles that ventured out. They very seldom stopped when challenged. We always opened fire on them as soon as we realised that the driver was accelerating instead of braking. Once when I was patrolling with an interpreter who was attached to our HQ we fired on a large Bussing-NAG lorry that was running on producer gas and therefore not very nippy.[24] It faltered and finally ran into a wall about a hundred metres further down the road. When we got up to it we found the cab empty but blood on the passenger seat. It was loaded with American PX stores and jerricans of petrol. I sent my companion back to ring the MP but not before we had loaded him up with coffee and cigarettes. While he was away I stashed a cache of goodies under the rubble of a nearby building. Lofty and I collected it the next morning with the Jeep. Money was quite valueless and for 100 Players cigarettes I had my teeth overhauled by the leading dentist in Cologne, Herr Doktor Heinrich Dohm.[25] Producer gas was a system employed extensively by the Germans when deprived of petrol for their heavy lorries. The gas was produced by roasting any available wood in a steel cylinder. The combustible gas driven off was piped to the induction manifold of the engine, where it was drawn into the engine cylinders in the usual manner. It was a very cumbersome system since the truck had to carry the gas producer, with its fire beneath in a grate. The fire had to be attended constantly and the wood had to be replenished through a gas-tight trapdoor. To maintain a fairly even pressure to the induction manifold a sort of balloon was inflated by the gas coming from the producer. It was a very inefficient system and produced only about fifty per cent of the power of an equivalent petrol engine.

---

24 Bussing was one of the oldest lorry manufacturers in Germany. Many thousands of Bussing-NAG lorries were made in the 1930s. Producer gas was produced by blowing steam through hot coal or coke – obsolete technology. The process gave a mixture of hydrogen, carbon monoxide and nitrogen. It was much less efficient than other gas fuels. Pete gives his own account of the wartime German version below.

25 Not verifiable.

I came across Brownie the CPR cook on several occasions during our sorties to the local cafes.[26] On one occasion in particular when Lofty was escorting a damsel home I encountered Brownie in an advanced state of alcoholic delight. He had no idea where he was and like a fool I offered to take him home to his room, where he was living with a widow. I knew the building but not the floor or which room he occupied. When we entered the foyer of the building Brownie seemed to recognise his surroundings and slurred 'Here we are. Come on. Let's have a drink.' He turned a doorknob and butted the door open with his backside and with a yell disappeared into a black maw. Wrong door! I struck a match and tried to see where he had gone. The idiot had dropped into the cellar from which the inhabitants of the building had taken the wooden stairs for fuel to cook with. Getting the only decent chef in the area out of the predicament was no mean problem. A low mumbling sound was emanating from the depths and repeated shouts of 'Are you all right, Brownie?' brought no response. I needed a light and a rope, neither of which was forthcoming from the knot of people who had gathered. I found that one of them was Brownie's widow and I told her to keep an eye on the situation while I ran all the way back to our billet. Just as I reached the guard room Lofty pulled up in the Jeep. I got a lamp, hand, electric and a length of rope from our toolshed and rushed back in the Jeep to see if Brownie was still alive. Lofty swung the Jeep into the entrance of the building so that the headlights lit up the hallway. He then lowered me down to where the victim was sleeping as soundly as a baby with his head cradled on one arm. He seemed to have sustained no injuries, so I looped the rope under his arms and shinned back up the rope to help Lofty haul him up into the hall. We carried him into the room of his widow, who undressed him and put him to bed, still fast asleep and probably unaware of the panic he had caused. Breakfast as usual next morning as though nothing had happened. With the inevitable glass in his hand, he watched his minions serve out the food. The old adage about drunks and lunatics being able to fall about without damage was in this case very true.[27]

---

26 When he mentions Brownie, Pete usually calls him the CPR cook – reminding us that he had been a cook on the Canadian Pacific Railway.

27 Worth a footnote because Pete mentions this again a little later. He seems to be creating an adage of his own, particularly in the case of what he calls 'lunatics'. It's no surprise that drinking heavily increases the chances of a fall, but it's a myth that a drunk person is less likely to

The 'Dive Inn', as our canteen had been christened, was nearing completion by Christmas 1945 and we were able to use it and its rather splendid facilities for the festivities. Quite a few of us were 'adopted' by German families, probably because of the food that the troops could get their hands on, food that was completely unavailable to the Germans. The American boys with us at Venloer Strasse could get unlimited supplies from their PX stores by submitting an order together with the cash. They were only too pleased to order stuff for us as well, so that we suffered no shortages in the food department. Alcoholic drinks were not available from the PX stores. We made do with the fiery Belgian bottled beer. Lofty and I spent part of Christmas day with the unfortunate Frau Lill, whose husband had recently died. She had not been able to get to his sister's neighbourhood for the funeral. I don't know if she had any children since she never spoke of any. Trudi was of the opinion that she had had a daughter who had been killed in the bombing. It seemed that she was now completely alone in the world. We did what we could to help.

By the new year of 1946 the Dive Inn was considered about ready to hold a proper party. On 31 December most of the cadre attended private parties so that nothing was organised formally and those who stayed in the HQ area got happily plastered on their own account. It was decided to hold a full-scale guest night on 7 January and Major Holden authorised the release of cash from the PMC funds.[28] This together with a large contribution from the Americans gave us something to work with. To avoid any gatecrashing, the party was to be by invitation only strictly on an RSVP basis. All the drinks were to be free and the ladies were to receive small gifts. These gifts were surprisingly easy to arrange. The American PX provided about fifty pairs of ladies stockings and the British side provided fifty bars of Lux toilet soap.[29] A buffet for a hundred people was child's play for Brownie and his staff. The arrangements for this type of function had been quite routine for Herr Dolfuss in his seagoing days and he was in his element issuing orders to his staff of waitresses. We hired a couple of extra bartenders just for the evening. A four-piece orchestra for the dancing was deemed adequate. There were so many out of work musicians in the Cologne area at the time that we could have had a

be hurt when falling. One study suggests that a drunk person is MORE likely to sustain a cranio-facial injury if they fall.

28 Probably, in this context, President of the Mess Committee.

29 A brand launched by Lever Brothers, later Unilever, in 1899.

symphony orchestra. On the afternoon of the 7th there was such a large load on the cable from the billet to the canteen that the insulation took fire and several of us had to set to and replace the cable with several lengths of 'quad' telephone cable all in parallel. It was just as well that the fault occurred when it did and not during the evening's fun. The evening was a colossal success and we the organisers were showered with praise. A couple of Brigadiers, Royal Sigs., who looked in briefly, remarked to Major Holden that 'it was a terrific morale booster.' The two ladies who accompanied the Brigadiers spoke only German and we noted that 'what was sauce for the goose ...' etc. In the absence of any British or American artistes, we hired a couple of German acts. The humour was lost on most of the English-speaking guests but those who spoke fluent German roared with laughter and it seemed that the late Adolf Hitler was the butt of most of the jokes. There was no set time for the party to end and gradually the guests drifted away until three o'clock saw Lofty and me in the Jeep taking the temporary staff home. On the return journey I was travelling far too fast and drove straight into an unfilled bomb crater. Everyone was thrown about but completely unhurt. Another example of drunks and lunatics getting away with accidents unscathed. In four-wheeled drive we just managed to extricate the Jeep after a great deal of pushing and shoving. We completed our journey at a much more sedate pace.

By mid-January 1946 the lower demob numbers were being eroded quite rapidly and our group 26 was due for release early in February. At a small party in the Dive Inn Lofty and I were presented with a small memento in the shape of a 'before and after' group of photographs taken during the construction. Some clown in company office had the wrong initials printed on the caption and my gift had Morris's initials W.J. instead of mine. Miles and Morris W.J. never lifted anything heavier than a pencil all the time they were at 3 Company 1st Corps Sigs. Still it was a very nice thought and was greatly appreciated by Lofty and myself. Life would have been very boring without the challenge of building the Dive Inn. Each member of Group 26 was called in to see Major Holden on the day before leaving for the UK. When my turn came he begged me to re-enlist for another year, saying that he himself was staying on. Rose and I had discussed this prospect at length and had both decided that it was time we started a family since she was turned 30 years of age[30] and she did not want to rear children in married quarters. She had only just been demobbed herself. When

30 Her thirtieth birthday was in November 1945.

Group 26 left 3 Company, Major Holden would be left with a corporal as senior NCO, all the serjeants and the CSM having gone. The Major offered to bump me up immediately to company serjeant major if I would stay on. I was sorely tempted but couldn't go back on my word to Rose.

On 4 February a group of us left for the UK. This time the journey was far more comfortable. The railways had improved, the trains were less crowded and the Channel was quite calm. Three of my companions on the journey were bound like myself for No. 7 MDU (Military Dispersal Unit) at Ashton-under-Lyne. We arrived there at lunchtime and had our documents stamped before being sent to No. 7 CCD to collect our issue civilian clothes. This was a very large building which seemed to have been an old cotton mill. Endless racks of clothing stretched from wall to wall. Suits of every colour and size. Boots and shoes of brown and black. Hats, caps, deerstalkers and bowlers. Overcoats and mackintoshes. Sports coats and pullovers. Within an hour I had kitted myself out with what I thought to be adequate. I had every reason to believe that Rose would laugh like hell at my choice. A dark suit, single-breasted. A mackintosh, belted. Black shoes. A green pork-pie hat. Socks. Tie. Shirts (two). I pushed the civvy gear into my half-empty kit bag, preferring to travel home in my comfortable old uniform. I had not worn civilian clothes for over five years and felt that I needed the guiding advice of my wife before attempting anything daring. Ninety minutes after leaving the Civilian Clothing Depot I was in Chester with forty-five minutes to wait for the train to Nannerch and Wern Mill, where we were to live temporarily with Rose's mother until we could find a place of our own. As I drank a pint of beer in the bar of the Queen's Hotel opposite the station, I looked back in my mind's eye over the past five years. I had been lucky enough to come out of it all. I counted the friends who had not made it:

James Anthony Meade
Harry Reid Stothard
Ronald Ford
Edward Booth
Samuel Booth, alive but using a wheelchair
Iorwerth Davies
Gilbert Wood.

Those names belonged to those with whom I drank and played from my home environment, and did not include those members of the sections I had served with in Europe who had lost their lives. Remembering the list of names on the tablet at the Memorial Institute at home in Caerwys, I thanked heaven that the slaughter had not been so appalling as in 1914–18. This time the civilians had taken a tremendous number of casualties as a result of bombing. Waking from my reverie, I had to run like the wind to catch my train. Mr Charlie Wilcox, the local taxi and garage proprietor, was just leaving his premises to have his evening pint at the Rising Sun and was able to give me a ride to Wern Mill, which was next door. Since my arrival was not expected, the excitement on both sides was intense. Officially I was still in the army until 23 April and from 6 February I was on 'release leave'. Rose and I had about £75 between us and considered ourselves well off.[31] After a few days spent in getting my old MC Magna[32] back on the road I started looking for a job. It was not very long before I found one. That however is another story.

---

31 Eight decades of inflation would make this about £4,000, but £75 in 1946 would have gone further than £4,000 in the 2020s, not least because there was far less to spend it on.

32 Probably the MC Magna L-type manufactured in 1933 and 1934. A stylish soft top sports car with running boards.

AFTERWORD

I was born in 1953, the youngest of Pete's three children, so I don't know anything about Pete's doings immediately after the war, or what sort of job he took in 1946. But the first decade or so after the war saw him involved in a couple of failed business ventures. I can remember quite hard times. These hard times were made much worse by the death of my mother, I believe from a stroke, early in 1958. This must have been a terrible blow to Pete, but he never spoke of it – at least, not to his children.

He recovered in both his professional and personal life. Once he began working for others, rather than in his own businesses, he started to do well. He invented, designed and built machinery for production lines and ended up making a decent living, though he tended to make money for others rather than for himself. He had spells working in Enfield and in the Irish Republic, but he was happiest in his home town. He didn't like charging people for the work he did, and this must have been part of his failure as a businessman. As the clock episode in his memoir makes clear, he just enjoyed fixing things. After fixing some mechanical or electrical problem at the local sawmill, he would be as likely to come home with a load of logs in his van as with any cash payment. The owner of the sawmill said to me just before his funeral "He did many a good turn, and never a bad turn."

Pete remarried, very happily, ten years after the death of my mother, thereby gaining three stepchildren about the same age as his own children. His second wife, Edith, ten years his junior, outlived him by twenty years; she died in her nineties in 2022. Pete is survived by his two daughters and me, two step-daughters, seven grandchildren, seven step-grandchildren, thirteen great-grandchildren and three step-great-grandchildren. My own children remember him well. My niece Flora had a special bond with him because they shared a birthday.

I like to think that you never really die while there's somebody alive who remembers you. And if you can get a memoir into print you can live on even longer.

MM
2026

INDEX

A

Aachen, Battle of 100 (fn)
Aberdeen 18 28 (fn)
Addinsell, Richard 120 (fn)
AFV (Armoured Fighting Vehicle) 80, 105
Air Observation Post (AOP) 64, 86
Airspeed Oxford 53 and fn
Aldis lamp 48
Altgaltraig 49
Aller river 130, 135, 138
Andrews, Andy (operator) 14, 29-32, 35, 37, 55, 126
  promoted to sergeant 120
Anholt 123
Anne of Cleves 117 (fn)
AP (armour piercing) ammunition 85
A-packs 121
Appeldoorn 122
"aquatic sports" 47
Ardennes 110
Ardisier 46
Army Lamp Signalling Daylight Mark III 48
ARMY UNITS

  BRITISH
    Armies:
    2nd Army 65
    14th Army 133
    Territorial Army 32 and fn, 37

    Corps:
    1st Corps Signals 143, 153
    30 (XXX) Corps 107, 109, 117, 141, 149
    Royal Army Medical Corps (RAMC) 128
    Royal Army Ordnance Corps 34
    Royal Army Service Corps (RASC) 48 and fn, 49, 63, 75, 93, 116, 118, 119, 130
    Royal Corps of Signals 57, 98 (fn), 103, 142-144, 153

    Divisions:
    1st Airborne Division 99 (fn), 101, 102 and fn
    3rd Division 32, 37, 69, 108, 120, 125-6
    11th Armoured Division 127 (fn)
    15th Scottish Division 115, 117, 123
    42nd Armoured Division 56
    43rd Wessex Division 107-109
    50th Northumbrian Division 66, 69, 76, 83
    51st Highland Division 123
    53rd Welsh Division 115, 119, 120
    Guards Armoured Division 99, 100, 109

    Brigades:
    7th Guards Brigade 31
    8th Armoured Brigade 55, 60, 66, 80, 83, 84 (fn), 85 (fn), 92, 109, 113, 138, 144
    231 Brigade 66 and fn, 69, 75 (fn), 76

Regiments:
4th/7th Dragoon Guards 60
7th Field Artillery Regiment 32, 34, 108
13th/18th Hussars 60, 66, 69, 80
17th/21st Lancers 60, 86, 139
33rd Field Artillery Regiment 32, 34
76th Field Artillery Regiment 32, 34, 56, 57
147th (Essex Yeomanry) Field Regiment 55-57, 69, 75 (fn), 98 (fn), 110
Argyll and Sutherland Highlanders 123
Black Watch 123
Duke of Cornwall's Light Infantry 108
Hampshire Regiment 45
Royal Engineers 95, 145, 147
Royal Scots 123
Royal Tank Regiment 60 (fn)
1st Battalion Royal Scots 115
2nd Battalion Essex Regiment 82, 83

Other formations:
3 Company 1st Corps of Signals 152, 154
3rd Divisional Signals 24, 28, 33, 38, 120
36 Squad 4, 18
413 battery 55, 76, 77
431 battery 55, 76
511 battery 55, 76
A Echelon 113 (fn), 120, 123
A2 Echelon 130
AGRA, Army Group Royal Artillery 57, 60, 65, 108, 115
B Echelon 106, 112, 113 and fn, 114, 121
F Echelon 112, 113 and fn, 117, 118
F Section Signals (of 3rd Div Signals) 33, 55, 126
OS 13 squad of Operators' Battalion 14, 18, 21, 24
Royal Engineers Field Company 100

AMERICAN
4th Armoured Division 110 and fn
10th Armoured Division 110
82nd Airborne Division 99 (fn), 100
84th Infantry Division 100 (fn) 107 and fn, 108 and fn
101st Airborne Division 99 (fn), 100 and fn 110 and fn
American Signals Corps 143
Railsplitters 100 and fn 107 (fn)
Screaming Eagles 100 (fn)

OTHER ALLIED
3rd Canadian Infantry Division 69
1st Polish Independent Parachute Brigade 99 (fn)

GERMAN
Army Group B 92 (fn)
5th Panzer Army 92 (fn)
7th Army 92 (fn)
9th SS Panzer Division 100, 102 and fn, 109
10th SS Panzer Division 108
92nd Panzer Division 144

Arnhem 99 and fn, 101, 102 and fn, 103, 106, 109
Arnhem: The Battle for the Bridges 102 (fn)
Arras 99
Arromanches 69, 77, 79, 122, 143
Ashton-under-Lyne 154
Atherfield Point 42
Austin pick-up 33
Austin Seven 132
Austin truck, 65

Avranches 91
AVRE (Armoured Vehicle Royal Engineers) 80
Avro Lancaster (bomber) 36 (fn), 129 and fn

B

B1 Morse qualification) 22, 24, 52
B2 (Morse qualification) 22
B3 (Morse qualification) 19, 22-24
Bailey Bridge 95 and fn, 100
Bailey, Sir Donald Coleman 95 (fn)
Banneville-la-Campagne War Cemetery 98 (fn)
Bastogne 110
Bassum 125-6
Bath 28
Battle of Britain 36
Battle of Normandy 73, 90 (fn), 92 (fn)
Bayeux 69, 79, 82, 83 and fn 95
Bayeux-Caumont road
BBC News bulletins 116
Beach Signals 50, 51, 74
Bedford 65
Beevor, Anthony 102 (fn)
Beek 114
Belgians 99, 112
Belgium 24, 92, 100 111 and fn, 115 (fn)
Bell and Howell 146 and fn
Bergen rucksack 47 and fn, 67, 68
Bergen Belsen 127-9
Berlin 57
Bickendorf 144
Birmingham 53 (fn)
Black Lion (pub near Caerwys) 14, 16
Black Rod 142 (fn)
Blair, Captain A.T. , medical officer 34, 85, 88, 97, 98
Blandford Forum 37
Blue Riband 146 (fn)
Bocage 83 and fn, 90
Boer War 28 (fn)
Bollen 138, 139
Bomber Squadron (77) 15
Booth, Edward 154
Booth, Samuel 154
Bourg Leopold 115 and fn
Bournemouth 42, 63
Boys Anti-tank Rifle 4
Bradley, General Omar 81 (fn), 100 and fn
Brandon 59-62
Bremen 126, 128, 135 (fn), 136, 137, 139
Bremerhaven 140
Bren Gun 4, 36, 64-66, 75, 78, 94, 101, 106, 136, 140
Bristol 27, 39 and fn
Bristol Channel 35
Bristol Hercules engines 129 (fn)
British Expeditionary Force 32 (fn)
Brno 4 (fn)
Brocks fireworks manufacturer 122
Brownie "the CPR cook" 143, 146, 151 and fn, 152
Bruce, Bob (operator) 85
Bruges 142
Bruno (St Bruno tobacco) 7
Brunssum 111 (fn)
Brussels 99
Brylcreem Boys 60 and fn
BSA 4 (fn)
BSA motorcycles 33, 116, 120
Burley-in-Wharfedale 55, 56, 110, 133
Burma 133
Bussing-NAG lorry 150 and fn

C

Caen 91, 95
Caerwys vii, 40 and fn, 155
Caerwys platoon of D Company of 3rd Flintshire Battalion of Home Guard 40 (fn)
Calais 130, 131
Caledonian Canal 45
Calvados (department) 82, 95, 98 (fn)
Calvados (brandy, spirit) 95, 96
Cambuslang 55, 58
Camels (cigarettes) 52

Canada vii
Canadian Pacific Railway 143, 151 (fn)
Capstick, Bombardier (MO's orderly) 113
Cardiff 143
Caumont 90, 91 and fn
Canadians 65
Celle 128
Central Ordnance Depot 36
Chappell (recruit) 7
Cheeky Charlie (call sign) 86
Cherbourg 63 (fn) 91
Chester 14, 15, 40, 132, 133, 154
Chesterfields (cigarettes) 52
Chief Signals Officer 32
chore horse 114, 115
Class 15 pontoon bridge 123
Club Route Up 131
Cognac 96
Colchester 56, 59
Coles, Corporal Cliff (leading operator) 55, 56, 62, 79, 81, 87, 88, 110, 115, 117, 120, 122, 125, 126, 128, 130-134
Colt .45 Automatic 16, 71 and fn, 77, 104
Cologne 143 and fn, 147, 148 and fn, 152
Cologne Cathedral 143 (fn), 147, 150
Commer truck 65
Commons 142 (fn)
Commonwealth War Graves Commission 83 (fn), 84 98 (fn)
Cook (recruit, operator) 14, 29, 35
Cornwall 65
counter-battery firing 108
Coventry 39
CRA (Commander, Royal Artillery) 115 and fn
Craven A (cigarettes) 23
Creed Morse training machine 18, 19
Crewe 10, 15, 132
Culloden, battle of 46 (fn)
Customs Officers 131

D
D5 field telephone 84, 87
D-Day vii, ix, 63 (fn) 66 (fn) 73, 91 (fn)
DADOS 140, 141
Dahmen, Leopold 148 (fn)
Daily Mirror 127
Daimler scout cars 83
Dangerous Moonlight 120 (fn)
Davies Iorwerth 154
Decimilisation of the UK currency 4 (fn), 7 (fn)
Dehn, Fred 146
Delicate, Serjeant Bill 36, 37, 39
demobilisation numbers 147
Denbighshire 1 (fn)
Deutschland 146 and fn
Devon 63 (fn), 64, 65, 90
Dewlish 37, 40-42
Dewlish House 37, 38, 41
Dick, Signalman Bill (operator) 58, 64, 66-70 73, 74, 76-78
Dinant 109
Displaced persons (DPs) 130, 134-8, 140
Dive Inn 130, 152, 153
Dohm, Herr Doktor Heinrich 150
Dolfuss, Herr 146, 152
Domiat 66 (fn)
Dorset 37
Dover 132, 133
Dundee 32, 55
Dunkirk 24 32 (fn), 34
Duplex Drive "swimming" tanks 46 and fn, 60, 66, 75 and fn, 80, 81 and fn
Dutch East Indies 105

E
E-boats 63 and fn
East Lancs Regiment 26, 27
Eden, Anthony, Secretary of State for War 27 (fn)
Edgeworth Flake tobacco 52
Edinburgh 15

Edwards, Serjeant Teddy 61, 62, 88, 93, 96, 97, 103, 104, 110, 113, 115, 122, 143
Egypt 61, 66 (fn)
88mm shell 75, 78, 112
Eindhoven 100, 115
Eisenhower, General Dwight 63 (fn) 81 (fn) 109 (fn)
El Alamein 109, 116
EL-DE Haus 148 (fn)
Elgin 18
Elst 101, 103
EME (Electrical and Mechanical Engineer) 130
English, "Sam", Second Lieutenant, OC F Section Signals 42
English, Sam (footballer) 42 and fn
Enfield 4 (fn), 156
Epsom College 61, 82
Essex 56, 59
Euston 132
Exercise Tiger 63 (fn)

F

Falaise 91, 92
Falaise Pocket 92 (fn), 128
Fassbender 146
Fawley 67
FBO (Forward Bombardment Officer) 82, 85, 86
First World War, 1914-18 War 28 (fn), 45, 71, 142 (fn), 155
Flintshire vii, 1, 40 (fn)
Ford 30 cwt trucks 33
Ford Jeep 53
Ford, Ronald 154
Forgotten Dead, The 63 (fn)
Fort George 45, 46 and fn, 68
Fosker, Signalman 96
14-day manpacks 125
France 24, 27, 30 32 (fn) 35, 92
Fraser, Charlie (operator) 38
Free French 65
French 75 mm guns 34
Frome 28
Frome hospital, 30
Fuhrer 57, 112
Fuller, Algernon 19 (fn)
Fullerphone 19 and fn, 20

G

G1098 (list of equipment) 35 and fn, 62, 140
Gavin, General James 102 (fn)
Geilenkirchen 107 and fn 108 and fn
Geldern 121
Gennep 130 and fn
George II 46 (fn)
Geverik 103, 105, 106, 113
Gestapo 105, 148 (fn)
gin palace (wireless vehicle and mobile signal office) 33
Glasgow 51, 53, 55
Glastonbury 32, 35
Gloucester 26
GMC truck 52 and fn, 135
GMC six-wheelers 131
Goch 115, 119-122
Gold Flake (cigarettes) 23
Gold Beach 66 (fn) 69, 70, 91 (fn)
Gracie Fields (paddle steamer) 32 and fn
Grave 100
Greenfield 15
Groesbeek 116
Group E (Eddy) Morse qualification, 19, 21, 22, 37
Guinness 22
Gunfire 14 and fn 110
Gurney, Bill 132
Gurney, Harry 132, 133 (fn)
Gurney, Rose viii, 132, 133, 153-5

H

Halford, Corporal Jack (head of line section) 55, 70, 83-86, 88, 89, 93, 96, 98, 101, 110-112, 119, 121, 127, 134
and the dead baby girl 119-120
a dreadful change comes over Halford 124
filled with remorse 125
Halkyn 23

Halstead 56
Hamacher, Fraulein 146
Hanover 140-142
Harmel, General 108
Harrington (recruit) 4, 14, 25, 26, 29
Harris, Robert (novelist) ix
Hartley, Signalman Bobby 97, 98 and fn
Harz mountains 141 and fn, 147
Haselrake 125
Haselunne 125
Hau 119
Hawaii 133 (fn)
Hawker Aircraft 90 (fn)
Hawkins (recruit) 3, 14, haemophiliac, admonished for nettles incident 29-32
HE (high explosive) 77, 85
Heckmondwike 87 and fn, 110
hedgehogs 74
Hengelo 125
Henry VIII 117 (fn)
Herlinger, Trudi 147, 149, 152
Heutz, Anna 105
Heutz family 103-105, 113
Hitler, Adolf 99 (fn), 145, 153
Hitler Youth 127 (fn)
Hobart, General Sir Percy 80 and fn
Hobart's funnies 80 and fn, 81 and fn
Hochhaus 148
Hodgkinson (Signalman) 39
Holden, Major (CO in Cologne) 144, 147-9, 152-4
Holland 100, 103, 105, 106, 113, 114
Holyhead 10
Holywell 14, 15
Home Guard 40 and fn
Honey tank 119 and fn
Horrocks, General Brian 107, 141, 142 and fn
House of Lords 142 (fn)
Hoven 108
Howes, Ginger (sapper) 145, 146
Humber Snipe 43
Humber staff car 147
Humber wireless pick-ups 33
Hurricane (fighter aircraft) 35, 36 (fn)
Hydra burners 106, 107 and fn, 125

I

Impulse magneto 118 and fn
Inchmarnock 48, 64
Instagram vii
Inverness 45, 56
Irish Mail 10
Irish Republic 156
Isinglass 111 and fn
Isle of Bute 47
Isle of Wight 42
Isselburg 123
Item sector 69

J

Jacobite threat 46 (fn)
Jankers 42 and fn
Japanese 105, 132
Jeep 52 and fn, 53, 54, 61, 103, 106, 114, 128, 136, 139, 144, 147, 150, 151, 153
Jerusalem crossroads 83 and fn
Jig sector 66 (fn), 69
Johnson, Dan (recruit) 10-14, 22, 24, 25
Jowett petrol engine 114
JU 252 118, 119 (fn)
JU 287 119 (fn)
Juno Beach 69

K

Kevelaer 121
King Edward cigars 52
King's Cross 132
King's Regulations 58
King sector 69
King's Speech 142 (fn)
Kleve 115, 117 and fn, 118, 119
Knackebrot 101 and fn
Koln Flughafen 145 and fn
Kondor yacht 138, 139
Kranenburg 117
Kyles of Bute 48, 49, 64

L

Lancing College 36, 82
Landing craft mechanised (LCM) 47-50, 64, 66, 67, 73-75
Landing craft tank (LCT) 47, 48, 50, 63, 64, 66, 74
Landing Ship Infantry (LSI) 63 and fn
Largiemore 50
Larkhill 64
Layton, Turner 16 and fn
Lee Enfield (rifle) 8 and fn
Lees, Lance-Corporal Stan (operator) 58, 64, 66-70, 73 ,74, 76-78, 136, 138, 139
Leeds 87 (fn), 132, 133
Leica 3C 117 and fn
Le Pont Roc 86, 88
Lever Bros 152 (fn)
Liege 109
Light Aid Detachment (LAD) 34, 43, 56, 94, 113, 115, 118, 121
Liley, Corporal Harry (electrician) 55, 62, 87, 110, 114, 115, 117, 118, 122, 134
Lill, Frau 147-9, 152
Lille 99, 131
Limburg 103, 105, 115 (fn)
Lingen 125
Liverpool Road 132
Loch Fyne 50
Loch Striven 49
Lochem 125
London 16, 18, 29, 132, 133
Long Tom (American field gun) 116 and fn
Luftwaffe 39 (fn) 110, 144
Luger pistol 71, 77
Luger, Georg 71 (fn)
Luttwitz, General Heinrich von 110 (fn)
Lux soap 152 and fn
Lymington 42
Lysander (aircraft) 64

M

M-14 International half-track 65 and fn, 114, 117, 118 and fn, 122
M-14-1 121 and fn
Maas 100
Maastricht 115 (fn)
Maas-Waal Canal
MacIntyre, Captain Alastair (Pete's brother-in-law) 115, 117, 123, 125, 132
Maconochie's stew 28 (fn), 79
Materborn 117
MC Magna 155 and fn
McNair, General Lesley 107 and fn
Meade, Tony (Pete's close friend) 14-16, 40, 154
Squadron Leader 53
death, 54 and fn
Meillerwagen 113 (fn)
Mercedes diesel engine 138
Merlin engines 36 and fn, 129 and fn
Messerschmidt-109 65 and fn
Messerschmidt-262 119 (fn)
Meyer, Corporal Lofty 143, 144, 146-53
Middle East campaign 61
Milborne St Andrew 37
Miles, Corporal 143, 144, 153
Military Government 134-6, 144, 147-9
Military Police 128, 135, 150
Milligan, Spike 120 (fn)
Mills bomb 53 and fn, 54, 126 (fn)
Mills, William 53 (fn)
"moaning minnies`" 84 and fn
Moir, Jock (signal section serjeant) 55, 57, 58, 61
Moll 115 and fn
Mongolia 92 (fn)
Montgomery, General, then Field Marshal Bernard 91 and fn, 95 (fn), 99 (fn), 107, 109
Moray Firth 45
Moorveld 114
Morphew, drill serjeant 2-7, 14, 18

Morris, Douglas Ogilvie (Pete's father) 1, 14, 15, 24, 40 (fn)
 death and funeral, 39, 40
Morris, Pete
 joins Royal Signals 1
 issued with kit 4
 begins squad drill 6
 cleans rifle 8-9
 on picquet duty in ice storm 9-14
 abhors Army guardrooms 11-12
 on leave at Christmas 1939 14-17
 21st birthday 16
 Morse code instructor and acting Lance Corporal 18-20
 commands squad for first time 21
 passes B3 and gets pay rise 22
 B2 qualification ratified, posted to 3rd Div Signals 24
 arrives in Frome to await permanent posting 28
 interviewed about nettles incident 31
 posted to 76th Field Artillery Regiment 32
 finds discipline in new unit sloppy 33
 finds unit pathetically short of equipment after Dunkirk 34
 moves to weston-super-Mare, then Worthing, suffers sunburn 35-36
 notes better training and discipline among militiamen compared to Territorials 37
 moves to Dorset 37
 promoted to Lance Corporal 38
 death and funeral of father 39, 40
 steals bottle of wine 41
 moves to Shorwell, mends clock, rewarded with five pounds 42-45
 moves to Scotland, begins training in "aquatic sports" 45-48
 fails to return to base on time after engine trouble at sea, is reprimanded 48-50
 falls into loch in full kit 51
 sees American troops for first time 52
 last meeting with and death of close friend Tony Meade 53, 54
 promoted to serjeant, posted to 147th Field Regiment 56-58
 teaches new section the Signals anthem 57
 dislikes paraphernalia and regiment bullshit of new regiment 56-7, 59, 61-2
 joins efforts to toughen new section 62
 practising assault landings 63-66
 on board HMS *Nith* before D-Day 66, 69-72
 on D-Day 73-82
 at Jerusalem crossroads and Point 103; "frightening and unlucky" 83-86
 and the Falaise Pocket 92
 and the Battle of Arnhem 99-103
 in cold winter of 1944/5 106-107
 admiration for Montgomery and distaste for Patton 109
 finds cache of food and gives it to local people 111-112
 scrounges engine and solves battery charging problem 117-8, 121
 "the most moving recital I have ever heard" 120
 witnesses the horrors of Bergen Belsen 127-9
 home leave and VE Day 130-134
 and displaced persons 134-40
 helps major to take yacht 138-40
 loses rank of Serjeant 142
 building the Dive Inn 144-153
 demobilisation and trip home 154-5

Morris, Corporal W.J. 143, 144, 153
Morse Code 18-20, 22, 24, 38, 48, 51
Mosquito (aircraft) 36 (fn)
Muir of Ord 56-58
Mulberry harbours 91 and fn

N

NAAFI (Navy, Army and Air Force Institute) 3, 17, 19, 21
Nairn 45
Namur 109
Nannerch 132, 154
Nazi(s) 15, 75 (fn), 105, 130 (fn), 134, 135, 138, 148 and fn
Netherlands 111 (fn) 123 (fn) 130 (fn) 143
Newark-on-Trent 55, 110
Newfoundland HMS 66 (fn)
Nijmegen 100, 101, 115
Nith HMS 66 and fn, 67, 69, 71, 73, 74, 76, 77
No. 7 Civilian Clothing Depot 154
No. 7 Military Dispersal Unit 154
Noordhorn 125
Norfolk 59
Norman petrol engine 114
Normandy 69, 73, 82, 86, 92 (fn), 95, 100 (fn) 107 (fn), 124, 128, 131
North Sea 139
Northumberland 43
Norton motorcycle 33
NS Documentation Centre of the City of Cologne 148 (fn)

O

OP (observation post) 64, 78, 82, 97
Oberfeldwebel 144 and fn
Oerlikon 71 and fn
Officer Cadet Training Unit 42
Okehampton 64
Oldensaal 125
Omaha Beach 46 (fn), 69, 80, 81 and fn, 91 (fn) 107 (fn)
Ontario vii
Operation Clipper 108 (fn)
Operation Market Garden 99 (fn) 102 (fn)
Operation Veritable 115 (fn)
Ostlegionen 92 (fn)
Otley Grammar School 79
Otterburn Artillery Practice Camp 43, 45

P

Palace of Westminster 142 (fn)
Palmer, Serjeant Pip 77
Panzer 4 (fn)
Paris 92 (fn)
Park Drive (cigarettes) 23
Patton, General George 91, 109 and fn, 110 (fn)
Peebles, Serjeant Freddie 32, 36, 37
Peruvian Navy 66 (fn)
Pfaff sewing machine 121
Phair, Lieutenant Max, OC signal section ("the OC") 55, 59, 61, 82 and fn, 83, 86, 87, 93, 97, 98, 101, 103, 104, 113, 114, 117, 118, 137, 141, 142
Phayre, Lieutenant Colonel Robert Arthur (CO of 147th Field Regiment, "the CO") 56, 61, 66, 67, 69-71, 73-79, 95, 96
phoney war 15
PIAT bomb 90, 91
plastic 52
Players (cigarettes) 23, 68, 133, 150
PMC 152 and fn
PMG certificate (Morse Code qualification issued by the Postmaster General) 19, 20
"Point 103" 84, 85 and fn, 86
Poisson, Claude 86
Poles 65
Pollokshields 51, 52
Pompey 71
pom-pom 71 and fn
Port-en-Bessin 69
Prestatyn 1, 24-26, 38
Prestatyn Training Centre, 30

Price, Dr Alfred (RAF historian) 90 (fn)
Prince Albert tobacco 52
Prince of Wales, HMS 133 (fn)
Producer gas 150 and fn
Provost Marshal 149
Pugsley, Driver and Batman 62, 113
PX (American store) 52 and fn, 150, 152

Q
Quad, Field Artillery tractor 36 and fn
Queen's Head (pub in Greenfield) 15
Queen's Hotel Chester 154

R
R boats 50, 51, 74
RAF 15, 60 and fn, 64, 74, 90 (fn), 94, 107, 113, 145, 148
Railway Inn (pub in Prestatyn) 22
Rangers FC 42 (fn)
RAP (Regimental Aid Post) 85, 120
Ratcliffe, serjeant in charge of OS13 19-22, 24
Rawsthorne, serjeant in charge of Light Aid Detachment 56
Reardon, drill serjeant 2, 4-8
Red Army 142 (fn)
Red Funnel Line 32 (fn)
Red Label Bentley 44 and fn
Rees 123
Reichswald 114, 115, 117
Repulse, HMS 132, 133 (fn)
Rhine 99 (fn), 100 (fn), 109, 110, 114, 122, 132 143 (fn), 147
Rising Sun (pub near Caerwys) 133, 155
Roberts, Eric 133
Robinson (despatch rider) 112, 116,117
Rommerskirchen 143 (fn)
Roscoe, Mrs, the Reluctant Dragon, landlady of the Black Lion 16
Rothesay 47-49
Royal Navy 66, 82, 137, 140
Royal Signals trades 26
RTO 131 and fn
"run-in" shoots 47, 48, 74
Russia 92 (fn), 142 (fn)
Russian(s) 92, 121, 135, 148 (fn)
Russian Civil War 142 (fn)
Ryde 71
Ryder, George (driver) 140, 141

S
Saeffelen 113, 115 (fn)
Saint Lo 107 (fn)
Sam Browne belt 2
Schimmert 112
Schmeisser machine pistol 124 and fn
scrip 69
Scripps V8 48, 75
Sealand 54
Sealand Flight Training School 40 and fn
Second Signals Training Centre 1, 4
Second World War 116 (fn) 142 (fn)
Seelow Heights 116 (fn)
Seine river 94, 95
Self-inflicted wound (SIW) 31, 36
self-propelled (SP) gun 77, 86, 90, 100, 118, 119
Sennybridge 64
Shepton Mallet glasshouse 42
Sherman tank 59, 60, 63 (fn) 83, 93, 107, 108, 139
s'Hertogenbosch 115
Shoesmith, Lieutenant Colonel 61
Short Stirling bomber 129 and fn
Shorwell 42, 43
Shrewsbury 26, 40
Sicily 109 and fn
Siegfried Line 100 (fn), 107, 108 (fn)
Simmonds Nut Brown Ale 6
Singapore 133
Sittard 111 (fn), 113
60 pounder field gun 116 and fn, 123
69 grenade 126 and fn

Slapton Sands 63 (fn)
Smith, Second Lieutenant, OC F Section Signals 33, 42
Smith, Corporal 'Smudger', assistant to Serjeant Ratcliffe 19-21
Smith, Signalman 45
Smith, Driver 94, 95, 106
Solent 70
Somerset 65
Southampton 66
South Wales 61, 64
Soviet Army 116 (fn)
Spandau MG 42 gun, "Hitler's buzzsaw" 77 and fn
Speldrop 123
Spencer, Staff Serjeant Ron 108
Spitfire (fighter aircraft) 35 36 (fn) 65 (fn), 118
Spurling, Bombardier (MO's orderly)
SS 125, 126
St Pierre 85 (fn)
Standard fireworks manufacturer 122
Stanier, Brigadier Sir Alexander (commander of 231 Brigade on D-Day, "the brigadier") 66 and fn, 67-69, 74-78, 93
Star (cigarettes) 23
Sten gun 67, 68, 71, 120, 124, 149
Stevens (recruit, operator) 29, 30, 32, 35, 37, 55
Stirling 32, 37
Stothard, Harry Reid 154
Stuart, Atholl (operator) 38
Suez Crisis 66 (fn)
Suffolk 59
Susteren 111 (fn), 112
Switzerland 71
Sword Beach 46 (fn)

T

Temple Meads Station 27, 39
Thackeray, lineman 78
Thiel, Wilhelm 144-6, 148
Third Reich 105
36 Grenade 53 and fn, 54, 124 and fn
38 Enfield pistol 67 and fn
Thompson sub-machine gun 67, 104
Three Nuns tobacco 6,14
Tiger Moth 118
Tiger panzerwagen 90, 107
Treaty of Versailles 71
Trebeek 111 and fn, 112
Turkestan 92 (fn)
205 CRC 130 and fn
20mm anti-aircraft guns 121 and fn
25 pounder guns 34, 74
Typhoon (aircraft) 90 and fn, 91, 93, 119, 123

U

Unilever 152 (fn)
Utah Beach 69
USAAF 107, 108

V

V1 113
V2 rocket 113 and fn
Vale of Clwyd 15
Varsseveld 123-125
VE Day 130, 134
Venlo 143
Venloer Strasse 143 and fn, 144, 145, 148, 152
Verden 135-7
Vickers 71 (fn)
Vire 91
Volkssturm 127 and fn

W

Waal 100
Waddy, Major John 102 (fn)
Warminster 39
Ward, Serjeant 'Tashy' 30, 31
War Office 142
Warsaw Concerto 120 and fn
Weasel (all-terrain vevicle) 114 and fn
Weeze 121
Wehrmacht 110, 123, 134

Wern Mill 154, 155
Weser river 130, 135, 136
Western Front 116 (fn)
Weston-super-Mare 35
Westwall 108
Whate, Corporal Eric (leading operator) 55, 62, 96, 117
Whitby 42
White Swan (pub near Frome) 28, 29
Wilcox, Charlie 155
William Younger's Best Scotch Ale p 14
Willys engine 136 and fn
Willys-Overland (motor manufacturer) 53
Wilson, Trained Soldier 2-4

Wireless Sets
18 wireless set (manpack) 47 and fn, 67, 68, 102
19 wireless set 65, 97
38 wireless set 68, 103
58 wireless set 68, 103

Wood, Gilbert 154
Woodbines (cigarettes) 23
World at War (ITV Series) 142 (fn)
Worthing 36
WRENs 49 and fn
WVS 39, 58 and fn

X
Y
Yarmouth 42
Young, Serjeant Andy 32, 38
Z
Zurich 71 (fn)